Writing Realistic Fiction
Symbolism, Syntax, and Truth

M. Colleen Cruz

LUCY CALKINS, SERIES EDITOR

Photography by Peter Cunningham

HEINEMANN ◆ PORTSMOUTH, NH

This unit within the information writing progression

GRADE 6

In *Personal Narrative*, students write true stories, learning strategies to generate meaningful story ideas, manage pace, elaborate on important scenes, and deepen insights.

THIS UNIT

GRADE 7

In *Writing Realistic Fiction*, students write engaging short fiction by creating action-filled plots and believable characters and by crafting nuanced, memorable scenes.

GRADE 8

In *Investigative Journalism*, students learn to use sharp observations of life to write news and investigative articles about meaningful topics, crafting vivid narratives and elaborating multiple perspectives.

This unit within the grade 7 progression

THIS UNIT

UNIT 1

In *Writing Realistic Fiction*, students write engaging short fiction by creating action-filled plots and believable characters and by crafting nuanced, memorable scenes.

UNIT 2

In *Writing About Reading*, students intensify their engagement with reading by writing innovative, reflective companion books that explain, develop, and extend ideas about books they love.

UNIT 3

In *The Art of Argument*, students learn to write essays that build convincing, nuanced arguments, balancing evidence and analysis to persuade readers to shift their beliefs or take action.

This book is dedicated to my seventh-grade English teacher, Susan Wuerer, who took the time to call my house to tell me I was a writer. You affected me more than you'll ever know.

—*Colleen*

firsthand
HEINEMANN

DEDICATED TO TEACHERS™

*first*hand
An imprint of Heinemann
361 Hanover Street
Portsmouth, NH 03801–3912
www.heinemann.com

Offices and agents throughout the world

The author and publisher wish to thank those who have generously given permission to reprint borrowed material:

Excerpt from "Thirteen and a Half" by Rachel Vail. Text copyright © 2002 by Rachel Vail. Reprinted by permission of Writers House LLC, acting as agent for the author.

Cataloging-in-Publication data is on file with the Library of Congress.

ISBN-13: 978-0-325-05946-4

Production: Elizabeth Valway, David Stirling, and Abigail Heim
Cover and interior designs: Jenny Jensen Greenleaf
Series photographs by Peter Cunningham and Nadine Baldasare
Composition: Publishers' Design and Production Services, Inc.
Manufacturing: Steve Bernier

Printed in the United States of America on acid-free paper
18 17 16 15 14 EB 1 2 3 4 5

Acknowledgments

THIS BOOK WAS A LABOR of love that has been more than a decade in the making. It started many years ago in leadership groups and classrooms with teachers who were looking for a simpler way to take advantage of students' passion for reading and writing realistic fiction well. In a way, this is a third incarnation of the realistic fiction unit of study that came out a decade ago, co-written with Lucy Calkins. The core of this current unit comes from that first unit Lucy and I hammered out with the help of countless educators. The work in this book feels very much like a continuation of a journey.

There are countless people to thank for their help along the way. First and foremost, I am deeply grateful to Lucy Calkins. She is one of the most intellectually generous people I have ever had the pleasure to learn from. I am awed by her staunch belief in student' and adult agency. It is not possible to adequately thank Lucy for all she has done for the study of fiction at the Project, and in turn, her gracious support of me, my work as a staff developer, and this book. I would also like to thank Mary Ehrenworth who has been instrumental in my learning about middle-school instruction. I owe a debt of thanks to the entire TCRWP middle-school team past and present, particularly Audra Kirshbaum Robb and Emily Strang-Campbell. I am also very grateful for Maggie Beattie Roberts' unfailing support in not only the middle-school work, but also in the role of story and spirit in the writing process. I owe an additional debt of thanks to Kate Roberts, friend and colleague extraordinaire who helps me in ways big and small every day. During this process, it was she who offered the simplest, and best solutions for the difficulties that could sometimes seem insurmountable. And of course, the numerous other TCRWP colleagues past and present who have piloted concepts, suggested mentor texts, given feedback, or simply offered incredible cheerleading and a shoulder to lean on: Brooke Gellar, Kathleen Tolan, Amanda Hartman, Rob Ross, Grace Chough, Janet Steinberg, and Beth Neville.

I am extremely grateful to all the teachers and other adults who helped bring this book to the finish line. I would especially like to thank the original piloting teams at P.S. 321 and M.S. 88 from years ago. I would also like to thank the folks across the country who piloted the unit in its various versions including Sophie Bell, Joseph Entin, and Naomi Lontz of the San Ramon School District and the Tarkington School in Chicago, Illinois. I am incredibly thankful for the huge contributions made during the final piloting phase by PS/IS 499, their principal Helene Jacob, and especially teacher John Strohschein and his seventh-grade classes. This book is much stronger because they welcomed me into their classes and gave invaluable input.

There have been additional colleagues, helpers, editors, and magical beings who have helped along the way. Many, many thanks for the incredible assistance and contributions from Julia Mooney, Tracy Wells, Karen Kawaguchi, Jenny Bender, Abby Heim, Elizabeth Valway, Shannon Thorner, Dave Stirling, and as always, Kate Montgomery.

And of course, a huge thank you to my family for allowing me to slip out often and for large chunks of time to write. I am humbled by the amount of slack my partner Nadine took up with two young children, one of them an infant. I am also grateful to the boys for pulling me away from my desk when it was most needed with a firm, "Work is closed, Mommy."

The class described in this unit is a composite class, with students and partnerships of students gathered from several classes in many different contexts across years. The unit was written this way to bring you both a wider array of amazing, quirky, adolescents and also to help show the predictable and unpredictable reactions and responses the teaching in this unit has created across the country and world.

—Colleen

Contents

BEND I Creating and Developing Meaningful Stories and Characters

In this session, you'll teach students that fiction writers get ideas for writing stories by paying close attention to the small moments in their lives.

In this session, you'll teach students that writers get ideas for stories by imagining stories they wish existed in the world—stories that uncover and explore truths about their own particular circumstances, longings, and struggles.

In this session, you'll teach students that fiction writers test out their ideas for characters by writing everyday scenes to see how the characters might move, think, and act.

In this session, you could teach students that writers can develop characters by exploring their characters' motivations and struggles and also by creating scenes that show these things.

In this session, you'll teach students that writers sketch out possible plotlines for stories, often using tools such as story arcs, timelines, lists, or mentor texts that can help ensure their stories are built with traditional story structure in mind.

BEND II Drafting and Revising with an Eye toward Meaning

In this session, you'll teach students that crafting scenes is, in a sense, about making the two-dimensional plans of the writer into a three-dimensional experience for the reader.

Bend III Meticulous Revision and Precise Edits with Audience in Mind

Welcome to the Unit

SEVENTH GRADE is uniquely positioned in a student's middle school experience. Middle school is no longer new, ingrained as students are in the culture of middle school. Yet, they are not quite the mature, one-foot-in-high-school adolescents they will be next year. They are no longer the newbies, not yet the veterans.

Seventh graders are the middle children of middle school.

Of course, as anyone who has been a middle child can tell you, the best way to combat the feeling of "not specialness" is to stand out in some way. One way to do this is to start the year with a statement unit—that is, a unit that will launch the year in a way that declares to your students, "Welcome to seventh grade. You are going to accomplish a lot this year. It will be different from any other year—because *you* are different."

There are few genres that students are more excited to write than fiction. Adolescents, as entrenched as they are in discovering and forming their identities and personal truths, often find fiction a particularly attractive outlet for that development. From the safe haven of imagined and created characters and plots, students can explore true-life issues, people, and ideas that would feel riskier if students were to write another genre without the veil of fiction to hide behind.

The work in this unit stands on the shoulders of decades of work on teaching students to write narratives. It builds upon thousands of educators' best work fine-tuning narrative structure, craft, and significance in fiction writing. Versions of this unit have been taught in countless classrooms from elementary through high school. This unit, then, picks up where those units left off, by tailoring it to match the unique interests and needs of seventh graders, while also keeping in mind the Common Core State Standards for English Language Arts, as well as other community narrative writing standards. If you

have taught a version of one of the Teachers College Reading and Writing Project's realistic fiction units in the past, you will hear echoes of that work throughout this version. You will also, likely, depending on your students' backgrounds, see evidence of the increased emphasis on writing in the younger grades, as the students coming into your classroom each year enter with more writing skills. Our hope is that this unit will allow you to build upon the strong foundations of the students who have those experiences, as well as offer enough support and scaffolding for those who do not.

OVERVIEW OF THE UNIT

The first part of this unit, or first bend, begins with teaching students a few ways to see the world as fiction writers see it. That is, students learn how to see the fictional possibilities in their true lives, from moments that happened to them to values they hold dear. We then move them quickly into concurrently developing characters for their story ideas while also beginning to practice the fine art of scene creation. This is done through a "boot camp" where students are taken through a guided practice session in order to experiment with the elements of scene writing while exploring their main characters. This boot camp work is designed to give students either a crash course in scene writing or a rigorous refresher. This scene writing work is placed so early in the unit because scenes are the bedrock of fiction writing, and little else can truly be created without an understanding of how they are meant to go.

Students will learn other character-developing techniques such as exploring characters' motivations and obstacles, their quirks and passions, their internal and external lives. This will all be in service to their quest of creating realistic characters who will be the perfect vehicles for the meanings they want their stories to convey. After spending a little more time developing their characters, students will move on to shaping their stories, putting into practice their years of experience as writers and readers of narratives. I encourage you to resist the urge to teach a formula for writing a story, insisting instead that students consider the arc of a story and the natural journey it takes the reader on. They will be reminded to use a story arc (or any other planning tool they prefer) as a means of not only preparing to draft, but also as a sort of front-end revision. Students will see the efficiency of planning, planning again, and planning one more time, so as to save many steps (and pages!) later.

In the second bend in the unit, students move quickly into drafting and revising, the reason being that our seventh graders already know so much about narrative writing that they can pull it all forward with them as they begin. There is no reason for them to wait until later in the process to do their best writing now! That, and the reality is, many professional fiction writers often mix their drafting into their revision and vice versa. Why wait to revise when you know the way you want it to go in the first place? Just a few years ago Toni Morrison, when asked about her revision process, replied that since she had been writing for decades she should know more about how to get a piece in good shape before it ever hits the page. In this vein of focusing on revision from the beginning, you will notice that time and again this unit calls on students to consider what they know from their reading lives and to bring it into their own repertoire of moves as writers. For example, we show students the connection between the evidence they are forever citing when backing up an idea from literature they have read and the evidence they can use as writers to ensure that they are showing and not telling while in the midst of a scene.

The third bend in this unit moves into preparing these pieces for audiences through deep revision work and editing. The depth is possible because most of the cosmetic revision work was included in the second bend. Since the stories will be long, even with the streamlined planning structure, much of these revisions will be focused on the meaning and messages behind students' stories. By focusing on where the heart beats in the story, our hope is that students will not get lost in the pyrotechnics and razzle-dazzle of fiction, but rather look to crafting and developing in ways that help push the meaning into the spotlight.

One of the ways the unit aims to support that effort is by focusing on work students have likely only previously experienced as readers. Students will be sitting on the other side of the desk as they work at developing imagery, sprinkling in symbols, and exploring the role of other literary devices, such as foreshadowing, in their writing work.

Students are also led to rethink the evolution of their stories. Oftentimes they approach fiction without a clue as to how to draw the story to a close, short of a mystical deus ex machina style ending where everything is magically fixed in the end. You will instead show students that they can create endings that are worthy of their beginnings—and of their aspirations. You will show them how often the best endings in stories were before their eyes all along, and only need a deft hand to mold them into a shape that will best fit their stories. This is something that completely aligns with the Common Core Standards' emphasis on narrative endings.

Throughout the whole of the unit, you will see a clear emphasis on the glamour of grammar. Time and again ideas such as comma usage, sentence types, syntax, and the reduction of redundancy will be posited not as *right* ways of doing things (which, as we well know, is unlikely to tempt an adolescent to our side). Rather, we will entice students by showing the power and importance of conventions and usage, such as their effect on clarity, rhythm, and even meaning. These concepts are sprinkled throughout the unit so as not to inadvertently teach students that we only concern ourselves with grammar when we are done with a piece, but rather it is something we check on frequently and wear on ourselves constantly, like a watch.

You will likely have noticed that in contrast to the other units in this series, this book only calls for students to publish one short fiction story. This decision was made for a variety of reasons, not the least of which that students tend to write very long fiction pieces, no matter how we might try to curb them. In this way, working over a few scenes, which are really mini-stories, students do get the repeated practice and transference we are after in the other units. Additionally, as part of the unique work of fiction, the process of plot and character creation makes it challenging to develop multiple story ideas within one six-week time frame. However, if you feel as if your students could benefit from additional work in fiction writing, I encourage you to either consider having your students try their hands at a genre fiction unit that aligns with your reading work, such as historical or fantasy fiction. Or, perhaps better still, spend a week teaching your students how to launch their own independent fiction reading projects that they can carry on with during the rest of the year. For more information on that option, see my book *Independent Writing* (Heinemann 2004).

ASSESSMENT

Before teaching this unit, we suggest you take a little time to establish a baseline understanding of your students' skills as narrative writers by setting them up to do a narrative writing task. In *Writing Pathways: Performance Assessments and Learning Progressions, Grades 6–8*, we describe the instruments—learning progressions, rubrics, checklists, and a set of student-authored exemplar texts—that will help you to see where, in the trajectory of writing development, each of your students lies. This initial assessment will help you and your students track their progress over the course of this unit and the year, and can also serve as a valuable source of information to inform your own teaching.

You may be tempted to assess your students by giving them a fiction on-demand writing task rather than a personal narrative one. But, you might consider this: most students are apt to produce writing that accurately reflects their narrative writing skills when the onus of coming up with a fictional character, a bit of challenge or trouble that character faces, and how he or she handles that trouble, is lifted. In other words, it's far easier to recall a true-life story on the spot and then use the allotted class period to write a one-scene story that is focused, includes detail, introduces setting, weaves together action and dialogue, and so on. If you want a measure of your students' skills in and understanding of the narrative genre, then we suggest you use the Learning Progression for Narrative Writing that you'll find in *Writing Pathways*. After all, the basic qualities of writing that make a strong narrative are the same ones that make a strong piece of fiction.

For this initial assessment to provide accurate baseline data on your writers' narrative skills, be careful not to scaffold your students' work. Don't panic if their work is not where you would hope it would be during that initial assessment! Try to focus on the facts that your students will grow and the more poorly they perform now, the more dramatic their progress may be later. You'll want to simply remind students of the basic qualities you'd expect in a piece of narrative writing, then step back and leave them to their own devices. We recommend that you give students this prompt to start them off:

"I'm really eager to understand what you can do as writers of narratives, of stories, so today will you please write the best personal narrative, the best true story, that you can write? Make this be the story of one time in your life. You might focus on just a scene or two. You'll have only forty-five minutes to write this true story, so you'll need to plan, draft, revise, and edit in one sitting. Write in a way that allows you to show off all you know about narrative writing. In your writing, make sure you:

- Write a beginning for your story
- Use transition words to tell what happened in order
- Elaborate to help readers picture your story
- Show what your story is really about
- Write an ending for your story."

Some of you may worry that welcoming adolescents to the start of a new year by telling them you are going to evaluate them might turn them off. Don't let that stop you from getting to know your students as quickly as possible. Instead, tell students you want to get to know them right away. Or, that you want to get as much of their writing up on the walls as soon as possible so that everyone can see that this is a classroom that writes. Or let them know that this bit of writing will help you know how to be the best teacher you can be for them—and it will help them study their own growth in writing across the year. This is a particularly important message for buildings that emphasize the growth mind-set.

Whatever you decide, you will want to administer the actual assessment task—and then respond to it—in a way that is consistent across your department. We recommend that you and your colleagues meet as a team to decide on conditions so that these are the same and you can then compare the students' results not just in your classes, but across the entire grade.

We suggest that when you read the prompt and additional suggestions, students are sitting at their seats with enough paper on hand. If it's possible to do so, we suggest you copy each student's piece of writing and have them tape it to the inside on their writer's notebook. The piece can then serve as a reminder of their starting point as writers in their seventh grade year. As the year progresses, students can periodically review that piece, making sure that they are doing work that is increasingly more developed and stronger than this start-of-the-year writing. Certainly, as students collect narrative entries in the days ahead, you'll suggest they look back frequently at their on-demand piece.

Of course, the immediate goal of this initial assessment in narrative writing is to understand where the bulk of your class falls in regard to the Learning Progression for Narrative Writing, letting that information inform the upcoming units of study. Read through each student's draft, comparing it to the exemplar texts (bear in mind no one piece will perfectly match the learning progressions), and then read the specific descriptors to determine your student's strengths and needs. The descriptors will be particularly useful as you suggest specific steps each writer can take to improve his or her writing. If a writer's on-demand narrative is grade 7, you and that student writer can look at the descriptors of say, character development for grade 7 and note whether the writing adheres to those. If so, tell that student—or the whole class, if this is broadly applicable—"You used to develop the people in your stories by . . . ," and read the descriptors from the prior grade, "but now you develop them this way," and read the grade 7 descriptor. Then offer a pointer from the grade 8 descriptor for how to improve. You can even say, "Let me show you an example," and then cite a section of the grade 8 exemplar text.

One final word. This baseline assessment is not assessing you. It is assessing the background your students have when they enter your classroom. But when this unit ends, you'll repeat this assessment exactly, and when you collect the student writing and look between the first on demand and the second, the progress that you see will allow for an assessment not only of your students but also of your teaching, and of this curriculum too. Remember, always, that the goal of any writing instruction is not to produce strong writing. It is to produce strong writers. It is essential that we teach in ways that lift the level not only of today's pieces of writing, but of any piece of writing that a writer does on any given day. We're confident that if you view this baseline data through the lens of wanting to improve your writers and your teaching, you'll be able to say, as the year progresses, "Look at your progress!" And this will describe both the student's progress and yours.

GETTING READY

Because this is the first unit of the year, the chances are pretty good that you are up to your eyeballs in things that need to get done right now. If this is your first year teaching a writing workshop, or you are new to working with the Reading and Writing Project, you might want to first read or skim *A Guide to the Common Core Writing Workshop*. This book goes into detail about the ins and out of workshop structure, room environment suggestions, and tips for workshop management. Depending on your background, some of the suggestions for classroom set up (such as meeting areas, teaching charts, writing supply options, and students sitting in clusters) might be new to you and worth spending some time looking through when you have a quiet moment. Often these structures can help the whole writing workshop run much more smoothly.

I also know from being in the teaching trenches that getting ready for this particular unit, likely your first writing unit of the year, can become just one more thing to add to your list as you prepare for the school year. You will likely want to scan this section quickly for the must-dos and then move on from there, knowing that you can take another stab at this unit next year. If, however, you have more time, perhaps because you are reading this in the spring before the school year starts, or else during your summer vacation, then by all means, take a leisurely way through this unit and in preparing for your year in writing workshop.

Try not to simply focus on the contents of this book, but rather, immerse yourself in the genre of realistic fiction. Seek out recommendations for short stories and picture books that your students or other adolescents have loved. I have provided a list of suggested mentor texts on the CD-ROM. Take time to make friends with your local librarian or independent bookstore owner. Ask them to tell you what the latest, greatest examples of short realistic fiction for seventh graders are. Another great source are periodicals and literary magazines. Look for clear, realistic plotlines, a few central characters, and good writing. Study your stack of stories to see what they have in common, what you admire, and what you think you might want to teach.

Next, you will want to dig through the piles to locate your favorite story to use as a class mentor text. It is vital you choose a text you will want to read again and again. I chose Rachel Vail's short story "Thirteen and a Half." It has been one of my favorite examples of realistic fiction for adolescents for years. It has a deceiving sense of simplicity that is layered over a rather deep story of growing up, relationships with peers, and understanding our place in the world. It is told in understandable yet beautiful language that is well crafted and laugh-out-loud funny. I know, however, that it is focused on a female main character, and might not be relatable to all your students. If you feel that it is a mismatch with your students, then by all means choose a touchstone text that you and your students will learn the most from.

Finally, and I realize this is stretching it a bit, you and your students would all be well served if you were able to carve out some time to work on your own fiction story to use as a demonstration text. This will give you not only time to hone your own fiction writing skills but also create a powerful teaching tool you and your students will turn to again and again throughout the unit. Try out a few teaching points from the beginning of the unit. Or, better still, gather some colleagues to write together—perhaps even cowrite a demonstration text. When writing, you might find it easier to choose a character and plot your students can relate to and be engaged by—the best ones feature characters whom are seventh graders whose struggles are of the typically adolescent sort. Take five minutes now to write, knowing that even five stolen minutes every few days will add up over time and make a huge difference in your teaching.

Creating and Developing Meaningful Stories and Characters

Imagining Stories from Everyday Moments

IN THIS SESSION, you'll teach students that fiction writers get ideas for writing stories by paying close attention to the small moments in their lives.

GETTING READY

✔ Entries from your own writer's notebook that you can use to demonstrate thinking about potential stories, and a pen (see Teaching and Share)

✔ Before this session, find a premade chart from a sixth-grade classroom, or create your own with strategies you know your students learned in sixth grade titled "Strategies for Generating Personal Narrative Topics" (see Active Engagement and Mid-Workshop Teaching).

✔ Have one copy of a Grade 6 Narrative Writing Checklist to project for the class and enough additional copies to provide one to each student (see Share).

✔ Students' writer's notebooks

COMMON CORE STATE STANDARDS: W.7.3.a,b; W.7.5, W.7.10, RL.7.3, SL.7.1, L.7.1, L.7.2, L.7.3

IF YOUR STUDENTS ARE LIKE MOST STUDENTS, they will be thrilled to kick off their seventh-grade year with this unit! Though fiction is one of the more challenging genres to write well, it is also one of the most beloved. Students—even middle-schoolers—are eager to imagine, to create make-believe characters and storylines, and to enjoy the freedom to write whatever they want versus the facts as they actually occurred.

The trick, of course, is teaching students to make believe without making a mess on the page. For anyone who has tried teaching fiction—or has shied away from teaching fiction—you are probably all too familiar with the stories that go on and on—and on—without any real purpose or clarity.

Keep in mind that when done well, one of the beauties of teaching fiction is that it allows you to "market" lessons on the qualities of good writing. First, you grab students' attention with the announcement that they'll be writing fiction. Then, with kids fully engaged, you teach them how to write with focus, meaning, and detail. With the right structure and scaffolds, which this unit provides, your students will produce pieces full of craft and significance—ones that entice readers.

"The trick is teaching students to make believe without making a mess on the page."

Today's session launches the unit with instruction in how to generate ideas for fictional stories. Building on what they know from writing personal narrative in past years, you will teach students to look to their own lives for moments worth fictionalizing. You will also challenge them, from Day One, to reflect on how well they craft those moments, so students can embark on this unit with not only a love for story, but also a clear path toward success.

Imagining Stories from Everyday Moments

CONNECTION

Tell students that you already know a lot about them as writers, and remind them that they already know a lot about writing.

"Writers, I spent last night looking over the quick on-demands you wrote yesterday. They made me both excited and terrified. Excited, because you already know so much about writing from all your years as writers. You know a ton about how to craft a tight personal narrative. But I also know from talking to your other teachers and to you that you also know a lot about other kinds of writing, too, like how to write sophisticated information pieces and literary essays thick with evidence."

I leaned forward and made eye contact with each one of my newly minted seventh-graders scattered across chairs, benches, and patches of floor in our meeting area. "But you can also see how that might terrify a writing teacher, can't you? Because you already know so much about writing, I have to bring my A-game to teach you something you *don't* already know! I decided that the best way to do that would be for us to jump into realistic fiction. This way, you can bring all your hard-won writing skills out right away, and I can teach you some new, high-level ones."

❖ Name the teaching point.

"This is an important day in your lives as writers. You're about to start gathering and sifting through ideas for stories. Here's the most important thing I can teach you: just as it works for almost every other type of writing, writers get ideas for fiction by paying close attention to the small moments in their own lives."

TEACHING

Share how you came to realize that fiction writers get their ideas from real life, drawing on a couple of published authors' inspirations.

"Let me tell you a secret. When I was in seventh grade, I decided I wanted to write fiction. The school I went to didn't have a regular writing workshop, so my notion of how fiction writers worked came from my imagination. I thought fiction writers just looked up at the clouds and *imagined* make-believe stories about exciting adventures and heart-breaking dramas.

Because today's session launches your writing workshop for the year, your goal for the day expands far beyond your teaching point. Yes, you want to teach students how to gather ideas for fiction, but above all, you want to rally their excitement for writing—which includes fostering a sense of community, the notion that you are all (yourself included) writers together, embarking on a journey of exploration and learning. And of course, you want to lay the groundwork for a productive workshop, which means imparting, whether explicitly or implicitly, the rituals and routines that will carry you through the year. Many of your students will come to you with years of experience with writing workshop, but others will need to learn quickly what the various roles are during a minilesson, independent writing, conferences, and small groups.

Sharing stories of myself as a writer, whether they are from past or present, is a critical means of engaging students and developing a community of writers. The more I share my real-life writing struggles and successes, the more likely kids are to share their own writing stories—which soon enough will also make them more apt to see themselves as writers. Sharing stories of my writing life supports more specific aims, as well. For example, when I tell an "I-used-to-but-now-I-realize" story as I do here, it is typically to encourage students who identify with my old way of thinking to embrace new thinking.

"But as I grew up and matured as a writer, I learned the truth about how fiction writers get their story ideas. I realized that fiction writers often get story ideas from observing not the clouds, but real life. Did you know that S. E. Hinton got the idea to write the *Outsiders* when she was fifteen years old, and one of her friends got called a 'greaser' and beaten up while walking home from school? S. E. Hinton was so angry about what happened to her friend that she went home and started to write a story inspired by that incident. And did you know that John Green got the idea for *The Fault in Our Stars* from a friend of his who was sick? I bet he wrote an entry about one of the times he spent with her, and then later, sitting at his desk, he reread his notebook, recalled that moment, and thought, 'There's a story here!'

"Of course, when I say that writers get ideas for writing by paying attention to their own lives, I don't mean that writers just record exactly what happened and call the text fiction. When S. E. Hinton raced home after hearing the news about her friend to start pounding out her story, she didn't record everything that happened. Her friend wasn't named Pony Boy, and there wasn't really a fire."

Convey to students the power of imagination: it allows a writer to see story ideas in the grit of everyday life.

"Fiction writers do, however, pay close attention to their lives. They cup their hands around tiny true particles of their lives, and they wait. Sometimes, while they wait, the idea for a story grows. And here is my biggest tip of all. The imagination that *really* matters to fiction writers is this. Fiction writers—like S. E. Hinton, John Green, any fiction writer that you know—can find significant stories in the most ordinary, maybe even boring moments from their notebooks. And you, as budding fiction writers, can do this, too. You can write a Small Moment story from your lives—or anything else you have seen or done—and you can say, 'Wait a minute. This is giving me an idea for a fiction story. Maybe I could write a fiction story about . . .'"

Tell students what to watch for as you demonstrate writing the start of a Small Moment story from your life that could be a seed for a fiction story.

"Let me see what I can do here. I am going to think about a small moment from my life, remembering some of the strategies I learned in the past for getting Small Moment stories, some of the strategies you learned in sixth grade or maybe even elementary school. Like, one of my favorite strategies is to write about times where I was feeling strong emotions. And I think that's a particularly good strategy here because I know that strong emotions can make for great fiction stories too." I opened my notebook, uncapped my pen, and prepared to write, clearly indicating that I was thinking through what I was going to write, that it wasn't coming to me easily.

"One time I remember that I had some really strong emotions was when I was in seventh grade, and I was walking up to Ms. Wuerer's classroom, and all the kids standing outside started singing a song about what a goodie-goodie I was. I was so embarrassed. I'm going to try to write that story now, as a Small Moment story, telling it bit by bit, but also remembering, in the back of my mind, that I'm on the lookout for ideas for possible fiction stories." I started writing quickly and read aloud as I wrote.

"There she is," I heard someone whisper as I stepped up to the crowd gathered around Ms. Wuerer's door, waiting for the bell to ring. I pulled my backpack up on my shoulder. Then, all of the sudden I heard this soft singing under a few kids' breath, "Goodie-two shoes . . ." My mouth dried up.

There are many ways to develop cohesion or unity within a minilesson. In this one, I thread references to imagination, friends, S. E. Hinton, John Green, and The Outsiders *throughout. This helps to make the minilesson clear to students.*

You have probably prepared this story before class, and you've already written it into your notebook. Here, you can jot down some words as you demonstrate this process for your students.

Pause to convey additional story ideas you got from this one life story. Share these with students as you jot them in your notebook, under the story beginning.

"Oh, writers, I'm going to stop right there! As I was writing down that story, I realized I don't even need to finish writing it down, because I started to get some possible fiction story ideas from my real-life story. I started thinking I could write a whole fiction story just about a girl who likes to play by the rules, even though other kids make fun of her for it. Or maybe I could write a story about a kid who changes who she really is so that people will stop making fun of her. But that's not the message I want to convey! So maybe I'm just going to draw a line under my first entry here and jot down a couple of little story blurbs, just my thoughts for possible story ideas." I wrote down my ideas in my notebook:

Notice how the ideas I record in my notebook are more fleshed out than a single phrase or sentence. Rather than simply writing, "a girl who always likes to do the right thing" or "I could write about a girl who is teased," I am already beginning to imagine how each story might unfold, from a character's wants and desires, to the obstacles she might face, to pinnacle moments that could spur change.

- I could write a story about a girl who always likes to do the right thing, even though she knows some people think she's a little strange because of it. But, it does make it hard for her to make friends and she gets really lonely. Maybe one day something happens, and she just loses it.
- Maybe there's a story about a kid who gets picked on every day for being different. Sometimes it's name-calling, sometimes it's worse. He's afraid to go online because he knows that's the place he gets it the worst. Perhaps his teacher starts a unit that's going to need a lot of online time, so he decides he needs to change something.

Debrief. Reiterate the steps you took so that students will be able to replicate them.

I put down my pen to indicate that I was moving out of writer mode back into teacher mode. "Writers, did you notice how first, I thought back to all my personal narratives from my past and remembered one of the strategies that works best for me, so that I could begin collecting small moments in my notebook? Did you see how I started writing a Small Moment story, and then, as I got some ideas for possible fiction stories, I jotted those down?"

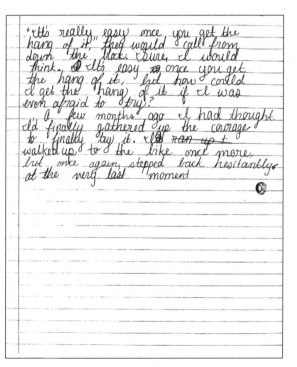

FIG. 1–1   Annabelle writes a personal narrative entry to help generate fiction ideas.

ACTIVE ENGAGEMENT

Set students up to recall shared-class Small Moment stories that could lead to possible fiction ideas. Refer students to their sixth-grade "Strategies for Generating Personal Narrative Topics" chart in case they get stuck.

"Let's think of a small moment you've had together as Class 702 since the first day of school. Luckily it hasn't been long, so it should be really easy for you to think of a moment. If you're having a hard time thinking of one, look back at your old sixth-grade 'Strategies for Generating Personal Narrative Topics' chart for help." Some students stared at the ceiling, some referred to the chart, and some whispered to each other.

Strategies for Generating Personal Narrative Topics

- Think of a person who matters to you, list Small Moment stories, choose one, and write the whole story.
- Think of first times or last times you did something, list Small Moment stories you could tell about each, choose one, and write the whole story.
- Think of moments that really mattered because you realized or learned something, list those moments, choose one, and write the whole story.

Ask partners to story-tell their Small Moment stories to each other, as well as any fiction story ideas these generate.

Once I felt like a fair number of students had an idea, I continued. "Now can you share your Small Moment story with your partner, making sure to tell it like a small moment with dialogue, action, and thinking? If, as you're telling your partner your story, you get an idea for a possible fiction story that could be built off of it, go ahead and share that new idea with your partner, too."

LINK

Repeat the teaching point, celebrating how fiction writers find story ideas in the moments of their lives.

"Writers, I have always known that fiction writers need imagination to write. But I used to think that most fiction writers found ideas by looking up into the clouds and imagining stories. What you have shown me today is that fiction writers *do* have imaginations. They look into everyday moments of their lives—into moments as ordinary as observing a friend's troubles or a kid playing basketball—and they see possibilities.

"Today and whenever you want to write fiction, you might gather small, true moments from your lives, or read your notebook once it's tattered and filled with them. Look at these real moments from your lives with a fiction writer's eyes. It's easy to just bury the story about something that happened to you, or trouble that happened to a friend, thinking, 'That's not important.' Don't do that. Have the imagination to say, 'Wait. There might be a story here.' And when you get a story idea, mark it with a sticky note, and then write a new entry based on your original entry, putting the idea it sparks onto your page."

If you have a handful of students who are new to your school or to writing workshop and have never before seen a chart like this, do not fret. Even without the chart, what you are asking of them—to remember something that has happened since school began—is within their reach. Referencing the chart sends two important expectations: first, that they draw from everything they have learned before to help them as writers, and second, that they rely on available resources for guidance, rather than turning to you day in and day out for step-by-step direction.

I typically revisit the teaching point several times throughout a minilesson, including in the link, where I want to remind students before they go off to write to add the day's teaching to their writer's toolkit. Often, I also revisit tiny details from the beginning of my minilesson—like I do here when I reference the friend's trouble. Like the many authors who craft a circular opening and closing, I connect the beginning with the end to pop out an important idea—in this case, that great fiction ideas reside in tiny, surprising details from our lives.

Especially because this is the first minilesson of the year, I want students to be inspired. I want them to believe, as I do, that there is something majestic about finding significance in the small moments of our lives and developing these meaningful moments into stories. I also want to spell out very concrete, doable strategies they can use today, so they can, especially at the start of the year, return to their seats and feel successful as writers.

Using Your Imagination to See Promise and Power in Students' Work

IN TODAY'S MINILESSON, I have helped students see that writers need the imagination to look into everyday moments and see possibilities. I have urged adolescent writers to resist flicking away the little bits of life and to instead get used to saying, "Wait. There may be a story here."

Of course, this advice is valuable for students, but it is even more important for *teachers*. Your students will bring you entries and story ideas. You need the imagination to look at what they bring you and to see that these entries hold the potential to become something amazing. Even if you can't quite see what the writer values in his entry, it is important to remember that almost any topic can become a spectacular piece of writing. The secret to finding something of value in all writing is to slow down, to listen to what the writer is saying, and to be moved by the details of the subject. Teachers, therefore, would be wise to be pushovers. "What a topic!" you might say. "This is going to be a brilliant story! You definitely need to write the details, because this is amazing stuff."

You may find as you move around your classroom, or from your initial on-demand assessment, that there are students who are struggling to come up with Small Moment story ideas or are simply struggling with the focus and control of a Small Moment story. If so, you will likely want to gather those students together into small groups and perhaps, using the sixth-grade *Personal Narrative* unit as a guide, teach these students a few strategies that will help move them along.

MID-WORKSHOP TEACHING   Tap Settings as Another Possible Place for Fiction Story Ideas

I stood in the middle of the classroom and raised my hand, the signal to students to give me their attention.

"Writers, I hate to bother you—especially when so many of you are on fire coming up with tons of ideas for possible fiction stories. I've noticed that so many of them are not just great ideas, but they're also written well—as if they are the blurb that shows up on the back of a book! But I know some of you are running out of ideas, or you will run out of ideas soon, and I just wanted to throw another possible strategy your way. One that you tried a version of last year when you were in sixth grade working on personal narratives.

"Often fiction writers, just like personal narrative writers, will turn to settings, or places, that can hold a lot of stories. Since you're writing realistic fiction stories, almost any real place will do. The principal's office, a backyard, a grandmother's kitchen, a fast-food restaurant. Each of these places is distinct and can launch a writer's mind into a million different possibilities of stories that could take place there."

Strategies for Generating Personal Narrative Topics

- Think of a person who matters to you, list Small Moment stories, choose one, and write the whole story.
- Think of first times or last times you did something, list Small Moment stories you could tell about each, choose one, and write the whole story.
- Think of moments that really mattered because you realized or learned something, list those moments, choose one, and write the whole story.
- **Think about a place that matters, use pictures, a map, or quick notes to jot about the small moments that occurred there, choose one, and write the whole story.**

Using the Narrative Checklist to Set Goals to Improve Writing

Congratulate students on filling up their notebooks with Small Moment stories that lead to fiction ideas.

Once the students had all gathered back in the meeting area, I began. "I am so in awe of you today, writers! I knew our plans for today were ambitious—to remember what we learned about narrative before we came to seventh grade and to come up with possible ideas for fiction stories to boot. But look at you! Your notebooks are already overflowing with Small Moment stories and fiction ideas. I see that some of you have four, five, six pages filled already. Incredible."

Tell students that they are going to revisit the work they were able to do in sixth grade to see how they have changed (or not changed) and use that knowledge to improve their writing.

"I thought because you have really shown yourselves as having remembered quite a bit from years past, that it might make some sense to look back at what the expectations were for narrative writing in sixth grade, to see how many of those things you remembered to do in your notebook entries today."

I projected a copy of the Grade 6 Narrative Writing Checklist. "Some of you might remember using this, or a chart like this, last year or in years past. You'll notice right away that it has three main categories to think about: structure, development, and language conventions. Underneath each of those categories you'll see different things that strong writers do when writing a narrative. You'll also notice that the chart has three different ways for you to describe how you're doing with each category: 'Yes!' (I definitely am doing this), 'Starting To' (I do this sometimes), and 'Not Yet' (I haven't done this in my writing).

"As I pass out a copy of this to each of you, would you flip through your notebooks and star not one, but two or three small moments that you think represent the kind of work you typically do as a writer? By looking across more than one entry, you can get a better sense of what you do, not just once or twice, but consistently. In other words, you can get a sense of not simply how good (or not good) a single scene might be, but of how much you know (or have yet to learn) as a writer."

Invite students to help you assess your writing first, so you can teach them how to use the checklist effectively.

After passing out the checklists, I said, "Since this is your first time working with the checklist this year, we're only going to focus on a couple of parts today—elaboration and craft. Take a moment to read and discuss those two parts with your partner. Then look up, so we can use the checklist to assess a couple of my entries together." I projected my entries to show the students.

> "There she is," I heard someone whisper as I stepped up to the crowd gathered around Ms. Wuerer's door, waiting for the bell to ring. I pulled my backpack up on my shoulder. Then, all of the sudden I heard this soft singing under a few kids' breath, "Goodie-two shoes . . ." My mouth dried up.
>
> * * * *
>
> Mike looked at me. I looked at him. We both looked at the broken vase. My face burned. I knew mom was going to kill us. She had warned us not to wrestle in the living room. Mike bent down and started to pick up the pieces.

After several seconds I reconvened the group. "I'm going to read aloud two of my entries, and as I do, look for places where I *do* do things on the checklist." After reading my entries, I said, "One thing I realize is how hard it is to check for everything at once—my brain can't focus on all the items at the same time, meaning I need to reread, probably several times, moving back and forth between my writing and the checklist.

"I do notice a couple of things I do, though. Do you?" Students nodded and I said, underlining several parts of my entries, "Like here, in both these entries, I develop the actions of my character. And even though I don't use any dialogue in the second entry, I of course use it a lot in the other, and I feel like I'm pretty good at it. I just didn't have a real purpose for dialogue, at least not yet, in the second entry. Now I feel like I need to reread the checklist and my writing again to see what else I do and don't do. Let's all do that now quickly, but this time, talk with your partner about something I *don't* do—either not at all or not consistently enough."

I gave students another minute to assess my writing with a partner while I circulated, gathering their observations and saying things like, "Don't just look at the one entry. Look for patterns." And "Look back and forth between each item

Narrative Writing Checklist

	Grade 6	NOT YET	STARTING TO	YES!
	Structure			
Overall	I wrote a story that has tension, resolution, realistic characters, and also conveys an idea, lesson, or theme.	☐	☐	☐
Lead	I wrote a beginning that not only set the plot/story in motion, but also hinted at the larger meaning the story would convey. It introduced the problem, set the stage for the lesson that would be learned, or showed how the character relates to the setting in a way that matters in the story.	☐	☐	☐
Transitions	I not only used transitional phrases and clauses to signal complicated changes in time, I also used them to alert my reader to changes in the setting, tone, mood, point of view, or the time in the story (such as *suddenly, unlike before, if only she had known*).	☐	☐	☐
Ending	I wrote an ending that connected to what the story is really about. I gave the reader a sense of closure by showing a new realization or insight, or a change in the character/narrator. I might have shown this through dialogue, action, inner thinking, or small actions the character takes.	☐	☐	☐
Organization	I used paragraphs purposefully, perhaps to show time and setting changes, new parts of the story, or to create suspense for readers. I created a logical, clear sequence of events.	☐	☐	☐
	Development			
Elaboration	I developed realistic characters, and developed the details, action, dialogue, and internal thinking that contribute to the deeper meaning of the story.	☐	☐	☐
Craft or Language	I developed some relationship between characters to show *why* they act and speak as they do. I told the internal, as well as the external story.	☐	☐	☐
	I wove together precise descriptions, figurative language, and some symbolism to help readers picture the setting and actions, and to bring forth meaning.	☐	☐	☐
	I used language that fit my story's meaning and context (for example, different characters use different kinds of language).	☐	☐	☐
	Conventions			
Spelling	I used resources to be sure the words in my writing are spelled correctly.	☐	☐	☐
Punctuation and Sentence Structure	I used punctuation such as dashes, parentheses, colons, and semicolons to help me include extra detail and explanation in some of my sentences.	☐	☐	☐
	I used commas and quotation marks or italics or other ways to make clear when characters are speaking.	☐	☐	☐

on the checklist, and try to point to places where I do that thing. If you only point once, or not at all, I could probably make the technique a goal.

"Okay, writers, eyes back up here. Several of you talked about how I don't really develop the inner thinking or the setting in either entry. You also talked about how it's hard to tell some of the other items—like whether I develop my characters' complexities—since both of these moments are so short. That's an important observation, though. It's a reminder to me to work toward doing those other things, which might come naturally when I write longer."

Set students up to assess their own Small Moment entries.

"Take a couple of minutes now and start to assess your own writing." As the students looked over their pieces alongside the checklist, I circulated, nodding to writers who were being particularly honest, gently nudging students who were perhaps being less so. I also encouraged students to chat with their partners if there were any particular things they weren't sure about. Then I brought them back together.

"Writers, I can hear so many of you becoming more and more proud as you look through this checklist. There are so many things you have already done, or were planning to do. And maybe just a few you needed to refresh your memories about. Sometime in the next week or so, I'll introduce the seventh-grade Narrative Writing Checklist. Until that time, you'll want to work toward making sure most of your writing is matching up with what you learned in sixth grade."

SESSION 1 HOMEWORK

GENERATING IDEAS FOR FICTION STORIES

"Carl Hiassen has said that one of the ways he gets ideas for fiction is to read through newspapers to get inspired. He looks for interesting and quirky stories that really happened and then imagines how he might change them. Tonight, for homework, I'd like you to push yourself to get as many possible ideas for fiction stories as possible and jot them down in your notebooks. You could use one of the strategies we talked about today. You might read a newspaper or blog for some current events to inspire you, or you might even invent your own strategy."

Imagining Stories You Wish Existed in the World

TODAY YOU WILL CONVEY AN IMPORTANT MESSAGE to your students. Whereas yesterday you told them that fiction writers often spin stories out of the ordinary moments of their lives, today you announce that fiction writers also create stories they *wish existed in the world*—ones that reflect the sorts of characters and situations and hopes and struggles that are near and dear to them. This is, of course, simply another way of telling students that writers often draw from their own experience to create fiction. What's important about today's teaching is the implied lesson that fiction is not just fun but meaningful—that fiction allows writers to give voice to their most personal hopes and struggles, and to give *themselves* a place in the world of books. This notion is particularly important for adolescents, because they often feel as if no one understands them or their experiences. Fiction gives them an opportunity to create a world that reflects their perceived reality.

Meanwhile, you will accomplish another important task on this day. Because students will be asking themselves not "What elaborate story about the most unlikely scenario can I write?" but "What do I, Jerome, wish I could read about? What story don't I see on the shelf that would really mean something to *me*?" you ensure that your students' stories, while lively and imaginative, will also be grounded in reality. The end result is that students will write not about a person who saves the world from a terrorist attack or about someone who goes on a mission to Mars, but about a kid who lives on a farm in Kentucky who secretly fears animals, or a girl who uses a wheelchair who also dreams about entering the Roller Derby. That is, kids will tap into their own precise real-life hopes and struggles and experiences to write stories, and in so doing, will give their stories the specificity and honesty that the very best stories have.

Throughout the day, you will want to tuck in tips about how to turn an image or a scrap of an idea into a story, how to put ordinary details onto the page so that they convey significance, and how to be ready to record anything that strikes one's attention—a detail that feels significant, a flashing moment, an observation, a thought, anything.

IN THIS SESSION, you'll teach students that writers get ideas for stories by imagining stories they wish existed in the world—stories that uncover and explore truths about their own particular circumstances, longings, and struggles.

GETTING READY

✔ Your writer's notebook and your own idea for a story that you wish existed (see Teaching).

✔ Use chart paper to make a chart titled "How to Find Ideas for Fiction" (see Link and Mid-Workshop Teaching).

✔ Bring your own writer's notebook with you to use during conferring (see Conferring and Small-Group Work).

COMMON CORE STATE STANDARDS: W.7.3, W.7.4, W.7.10, RL.7.3, SL.7.1, SL7.6, L.7.1, L.7.2, L.7.3

Imagining Stories You Wish Existed in the World

CONNECTION

Explain that in life, when things that we seek aren't there, we need to create them. The same is true with stories.

"As you all know, you don't live in a perfect world. And you all know me well enough to know that I am a big believer in people being problem solvers in their own lives. So if you don't have friends, you should work to make them. If you are unhappy with the privileges that your parents give you (or don't), you should have conversations with them to convince them to see things the way you see them. It's also true when it comes to reading. If you don't see the books you want to read—that reflect your families, your friends, your interests, your lives—you should write them. Believe it or not, sometimes fiction stories, whose facts you can manipulate to make things seem more believable, feel closer to the truth than true stories from your lives."

Always, I want the writing that I ask students to do to be purposeful. I don't want them to write for me, their teacher, I want them to write for themselves. I want them to write because writing matters in the world, and more than anything, I want it to matter to them. Here, I use my connection to frame today's teaching point in a way that I hope will serve this larger, more meaningful goal. I tell them how thinking up story ideas to craft into fiction is, in fact, about empowerment.

Name the teaching point.

"Today I want to teach you that writers collect ideas for stories not only by discovering tiny details that could blossom into whole stories, but also by thinking about the stories *they believe should exist*. Sometimes they get ideas for stories by thinking, 'How can I write a story for people like me so I can see myself in books?'"

TEACHING

Point out that readers hope to find themselves in the pages of books.

"Often times, when you are looking through the library shelves for a book, you are looking to find yourselves in a story. I may find myself wanting a book about someone like me who is afraid of her parents getting divorced, or a book about a kid who is usually the last one picked for sports because she's not any good at them, or a kid whose mother said, 'You need to be grateful for everything you have because not everyone is as lucky as you are,' exactly when the kid was feeling his lowest.

"Maybe one of you searches library shelves for a kid who lives with his aunt, or a kid who likes to draw anime and dreams of having an anime blog. If you long to find yourself in a book, and no book seems to tell the story that you

Purposeful details are a characteristic of any good writing, because they bring meaning to a piece. Similarly, I often use specific details in my lessons to serve a purpose. Here, I hope to paint a picture of young people who long to find themselves in a story, with the hope that the details will inspire students to reflect on their own longings—and hence, inspire them to generate meaningful fiction ideas.

want told, then you might decide it is important to put your truth onto the page in your own story. The author Thomas Berger once said, 'Why do writers write? Because it isn't there.'"

Demonstrate how to create a story idea from your desire to see books you'd like to read but that don't exist—in this case, books about people like you.

"Let me show you how I use this strategy to come up with a story idea," I said. "The first thing I do is to think about the books I want to read. I always wish there were more books about people like me who are half Mexican—kids whose fathers are Mexican and whose mothers aren't. *And* who are maybe wanting to be more popular than they are. So in my notebook I'll write down my story idea. I don't just write the big outline of my story—girl with Mexican dad and American mom. I want to put the stuff about a Mexican father together with true little details, like the part about myself being afraid of the dark and wanting a night-light. Those had been separate items on my list—the girl who is half Mexican, the girl who wants to be more popular—but in a story plan, I often combine things that were once separate. Watch."

Then I wrote:

> A girl who is half Mexican lives with both her parents but she thinks her father works too much. She wishes her father were around more because when he's around she feels less lonely. But his job keeps him far away and the girl tries to put on a brave face so her parents don't worry about her.

Debrief. Point out that you came up with a story idea you wish existed in the world, one that features a character who has desires and difficulties, as all memorable characters do.

"Do you see, writers, that when writing my story idea, I didn't just say, 'I wish there were books on kids who are half Mexican'? I actually jotted a few sentences about how such a story might go. And specifically, I thought about what the character might want and what she might struggle for. Characters in all stories have big longings.

"Here's an idea you should hold onto: when you are collecting ideas for stories in your writer's notebook, you get ideas not only from rereading old entries, but from thinking about books *you wish existed* in the world."

ACTIVE ENGAGEMENT

Set students up to try turning a wish for a certain kind of book into a story idea.

"So let's try it. Maybe you think to yourself, 'I wish there were books about kids who aren't that good at sports.' Remember that to make that wish into a story idea, you need to invent some details. You can do so by asking questions of your story idea. Why isn't the kid in the story good at sports? Which sports? What has happened lately that shows these struggles?

Of course, this is a unit on fiction, but the message you want to get across to students is that by pushing the truth *on the page, they can develop ideas for fictional stories. Truth can indeed lead to fiction. Donald Murray once taught that we should write the Truth with a capital T, but not necessarily the exactly true story. "Change things around so that you convey the Truth of your experience," he said.*

Before embarking on any unit of study, I identify the qualities of good writing that I especially want to teach, not only so I know what lessons to plan, but so I can refer to and implicitly model those qualities as often as possible—like I do here when I tuck in the fact that characters in all stories have wants and struggles. You'll find these qualities woven throughout this unit, in teaching points and story examples. One important understanding I want students to leave with is that stories are not made of magical happy endings. Rather, they are made of tensions—the kind that build when a character longs for something that she cannot easily attain.

"I can see some of you sports experts shaking your head like you can't imagine this. But this is fiction! Even if this character doesn't resemble you, try putting yourself into the kid's head. Later, you'll have a chance to think about stories with characters that resemble ones you wish existed in the world—ones more like you. This is just a quick exercise to get you warmed up!"

Ask students to turn and talk about the character traits and the struggles the character in the exemplar story might encounter.

"Tell your partner how you could turn this into a story idea. Remember, think about the character, his or her character traits, and the character's very particular struggle. Think about what the character wants, and about what he or she does."

As students talked, I circled the room, listening in to their ideas and taking note of their ease or challenges with this step in the process. I coached in as needed.

After a few minutes, I shared a few kids' story ideas aloud, pointing out how the same seed idea had led to such a variety of story ideas.

Debrief. Share a couple of kids' story ideas aloud, and review the steps your students just followed.

"Looks like I got a roomful of imaginative writers! You took the same simple seed idea for a character who doesn't like sports, and you came up with such different story ideas. Carmen imagined a clumsy girl who's always tripping over her feet. She decided that the girl, whom she named Claudine, particularly struggles at team sports—and that she's always picked last in PE class. Lately, all her friends are trying out for JV teams and she's feeling kind of bad about herself because she's just not athletic. She feels left out. And Peter came up with the idea to write about a boy named Ted who dreams of being a professional basketball player. Ted's got two older brothers and a dad who all played college basketball—but Ted's much shorter and just not inclined toward the sport. To make matters worse, his best friend has recently shown interest in—and a knack for—basketball!

"These are just two of your ideas, and each one has such promise for making a good story.

"Let's recap what we did so that as you go off today to think of stories you really did wish existed in the world, you can use this same strategy.

"First, you thought, 'I wish a story about—in this case, it was a kid who's no good at sports—existed in the world.' Then you thought, 'Why does he struggle with this thing? What exactly does he struggle with? And what's been happening lately that shows this struggle?'"

My main goal here is to help students come up with story ideas, but I also take the opportunity to tuck a subordinate tip into my teaching. First, I tell kids that writers embellish their ideas with details. Then I go further and ask a sequence of questions that will help them do this. The sequence is important; the questions, asked in this order, scaffold students to think deeply and do some good work. The questions channel a writer to think about the character's traits and related struggles, and then the questions move writers to consider how these struggles play out in an event.

Because you just gave a hypothetical starting point, this is just an exercise. You don't expect students to write about the character from the day's minilesson, but instead to invent their own characters. There will probably be a few students, however, who decide that the story idea you have given them could become their very own idea, and that's okay.

LINK

Remind students of their growing repertoire of strategies for finding fiction ideas, and then send them off to continue collecting ideas.

"So, writers, you played a bit with my idea of wishing there were more stories about kids who aren't good at sports, and then you imagined a character in such a book. You might find it helpful to think not just about who you are in the world, and how you wished you saw that identity represented. You might also consider thinking of some of the issues that matter most to you that you also think should be written into a story that other adolescents might want to read.

"When you are living your life as a fiction writer, you know you won't write about the character *I* created. You'll invent your own characters. For now, you'll continue collecting story ideas. You can use any of the strategies we've learned, or others that you invent, to do this. Let's start listing these strategies in a chart," I said, gesturing to the list I had started on chart paper.

How to Find Ideas for Fiction

- Pay attention to the small moments in your life that could be fictionalized.
- Consider places where stories could take place, and then imagine those stories.
- Read about current events in newspapers, blogs, magazines, etc. Allow yourself to be inspired by true events that could be fictionalized.
- Ask, "What stories do I wish existed in the world?" Let this question lead you to invent a character with traits, struggles, actions.

In the early sessions of any unit, we'll offer students a repertoire of strategies for gathering entries that pertain to the work, and genre, of that unit. Notice, however, that when we send students back to their seats, the message is not, "Now do what I just taught you." Rather, the message is, "Add what I just taught to your repertoire of knowledge, and draw from there whenever that makes sense for you." You'll see that this message will appear time and time again in the link section of the minilessons. After today's lesson, for example, I want students to continue to gather fiction ideas—but whether they do that by thinking of stories they wish existed or by some other strategy is up to them.

Using an Exemplar Text to Respond to Predictable Problems

AS YOU CONFER AND LEAD SMALL GROUPS, you may find that many students have come up with lengthy lists of undeveloped story ideas. Perhaps students are not sure whether they are expected to write actual stories in their notebooks or whether you are asking for lists of story ideas—and actually, you are hoping for something in between. You'll want to teach kids to stay a little longer with each idea, fleshing it out a bit. You might carry with you the first story idea you wrote in your notebook. For example, I had started with this:

Girl wants to be more popular

Then I revised my initial vague idea to say a bit more.

The girl wants to be more popular. She knows that's dumb. That popularity isn't the most important thing in the world. But, she often gets lonely and only has a few friends she can talk to. She has a birthday party coming up and her mom wants her to have a party, but she knows that if she invited only her friends there would just be three people there.

MID-WORKSHOP TEACHING   **Sharing Struggles with Characters**

"Writers, can I stop you for just a quick minute? I want to teach you one more strategy for collecting ideas for fictional stories: You can write stories in which the character wrestles with issues that are important to you. You can get yourself launched in that work by just quickly brainstorming a few issues that matter to you, then choosing one to write at the top of an empty page in your notebook. You could then spin a bunch of story ideas off that one issue. For example, if you think honesty is an important issue, you could write that at the top of the page, and then think of as many stories as possible that could stem from honesty. Maybe one about a character who lies and gets caught. Maybe another about a parent who always insists on honesty, except one time the kid . . ."

I added the new strategy to the chart so that students would have a reminder of it past today.

How to Find Ideas for Fiction

- Pay attention to the small moments in your life that could be fictionalized.
- Consider places where stories could take place, and then imagine those stories.
- Read about current events in newspapers, blogs, magazines, etc. Allow yourself to be inspired by true events that could be fictionalized.
- Ask, "What stories do I wish existed in the world?" Let this question lead you to invent a character with traits, struggles, actions.
- **Think about an issue that is important to you, and create a character who struggles with that issue.**

16

I will probably want to carry both versions with me as I make my way through the classroom. When conferring, it helps to carry your own exemplar text around with you so that if you decide to use the teaching method of demonstration, or the "explain and show an example" method, you'll have the materials to do so. But don't let the fact that you have materials under your arm propel you into using them. As always, begin your conferences by asking, "What are you working on as a writer?" and by trying to understand what the writer has already done and is trying to do.

It will help if, before this unit begins, you and your colleagues try to predict the conferences you'll probably need to conduct early in this unit. As I mentioned earlier, you can expect that you'll often need to help students say more when they write about their story ideas. You may also:

◆ Suggest to students that they postpone closure, so they have a chance to explore a wider range of story ideas. Some students will generate a story idea and immediately start writing that story from start to finish. Teach them that writers force themselves to imagine more possibilities before making a commitment to one story idea. And once a student does settle on a particular story idea, the student needs to spend a lot of time rehearsing before she begins a draft. I think of this unit on fiction as a unit also on rehearsal and revision.

◆ Remind students that they know a lot about how stories generally "go," and specifically, remind them that story ideas usually originate from a character who has motivations and faces a predicament. If a student imagines a story in which an unnamed guy lives through ten daredevil activities, you'll want to explicitly teach the importance of developing a very particular character. You'll also want to show that a character's traits and motivations lead that character to encounter struggles, and in this way a story hangs together.

◆ Guide your seventh-graders to use the specific details of their own lives to grow story ideas. It is inevitable that some will want to write over-romanticized adult stories, and you'll want to channel them toward dramas they know from the inside. Remind students that if they think about it, there's probably plenty of drama in their own lives, and that personal drama can be mined for story ideas.

◆ Anticipate that students will imagine their stories as containing a multitude of events. Teach them that they are writing short stories, and this generally means they'll be writing two or perhaps three Small Moment stories.

It is helpful to plan for and anticipate conferences, but if you find yourself giving mostly preplanned, almost canned conferences, then you probably need to listen more intently and to expect students to surprise you, to take you to new places. It's helpful to expect that when you confer with kids, they will stir up new ideas in you. As you draw a chair alongside a student and ask, "What are you working on as a writer?" expect that the kid's response will be instructive to you.

Sharing Story Ideas, Then Choosing One to Develop and Writing Long about It

Engage students in a symphony share, during which they share just one story idea.

"Writers, you have done some fantastic work over the past couple of days coming up with a variety of possible ideas for your short realistic fiction stories. Bravo! I know from walking around and talking with you that you have pages and pages of story ideas at this point, each one more compelling than the last.

"I want to give you a chance to share your ideas, quickly, before writing time is over. When I point to you, give a short synopsis of just one of your story ideas. Maybe this will be the one you choose to develop for publication. Tell us the name of your character, what his or her struggle or longing is, and the circumstances he or she is in that swings the story into action. Here's the rule, everyone—as you listen, no commenting. I don't want to hear suggestions of how to make the story more juicy or the struggle even harder. This is just a chance to share and hear all the story ideas buzzing around the room. As the week goes on, you'll have lots of chances to advise one another.

"Okay, let's start!" I pointed to Samee, who shared his idea about two lifelong friends who end up having a huge fight that tears them apart, and then to Penelope, who shared her idea about a group of friends that starts to unravel when a new girl joins in. I pointed to each student until the whole class had a chance to share.

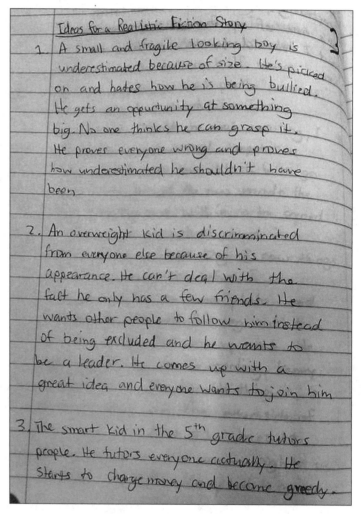

FIG. 2–1   Samee generates ideas for fiction stories based on stories he wished already existed.

CHOOSING A MEANINGFUL STORY IDEA

"Tonight for homework, I want you to think a bit about which story idea you like the best. Which one do you think you want to take all the way to publication? Which of these stories feels the most meaningful to you? Or you might even consider, which one does the world need you to write? You might even decide to write a bit about why *this* story idea. Don't write the story itself, just something along the lines of, 'I think this is an important story for me to write because . . .' Then explain what the story idea does for you and what you imagine it would do for your readers. You might think about what you're really trying to say to the world and how fiction writing, where you can disguise the characters and other pesky facts, can help push you to a deeper truth. Then push yourself to write long about your thought process. Sometimes, figuring out the meaning behind the story before even beginning to draft can lead to more powerful work in fiction."

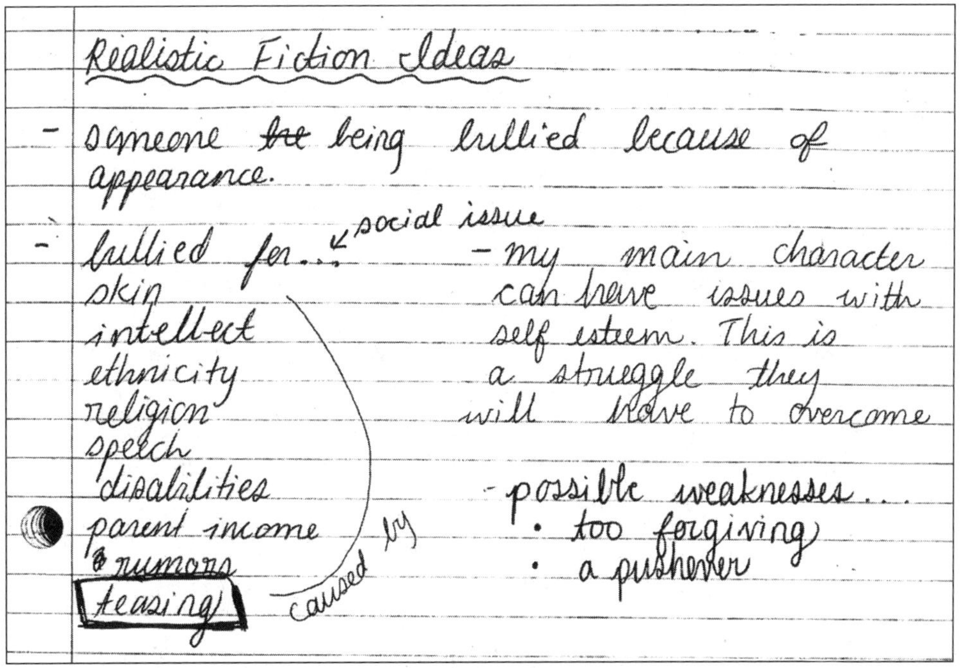

FIG. 2–2 Annabelle thinks of a social issue that matters to her and used it to think of possible fiction ideas.

Developing Believable Characters through Scene Boot Camp

IN THIS SESSION, you'll teach students that fiction writers test out their ideas for characters by writing everyday scenes to see how the characters might move, think, and act.

GETTING READY

✔ Bring your own writer's notebook with a character and storyline that you will use to model throughout the unit (see Teaching and Active Engagement)

✔ Students' writer's notebooks and pens (see Teaching and Active Engagement)

✔ "Scenes" chart (see Teaching and Active Engagement)

✔ "How to Write Compelling Fiction" anchor chart (see Link)

T ODAY IS A CRITICAL DAY. It is one of those sessions that hits a lot of key points that will propel students' work forward for the rest of the unit. In this session, students will try their hand at a character development strategy that is probably as old as the novel. I first learned it from my writing teacher, the best-selling novelist Jennifer Belle. She taught me that one of the best ways to get to know a character is not to write pages and pages of notes, but rather to just try the character out in an everyday scene. As the writer develops the scene, it is almost as if she is being introduced to the character—how he moves, speaks, thinks, and most importantly, what he wants.

For many students, the idea of writing a scene can often be more daunting than getting to know one's character. Whether this is because they have not written narrative in a long time, or they do not have a lot of writing workshop experience, this session is designed to support those students who might still have the smell of summer vacation on their skin. You will do this by taking students through a rapid-paced guided practice session that we call "boot camp"—one in which the teaching and active engagement are combined, so you can move back and forth between modeling something and coaching students as they try the work themselves. This is a quick, down-and-dirty way to give students a lot of experience and support when tackling something that would otherwise be very challenging. Today's session is not designed as a typical minilesson. It will certainly take longer than ten minutes.

"For many students, the idea of writing a scene can often be more daunting than getting to know one's character."

Of course, if your students have a ton of scene-writing experience, or you know from your on-demand assessments that they have a very high level of mastery of scene writing, you might opt to skip the boot camp method of instruction suggested in this session and instead simply teach it as a more typical demonstration minilesson.

COMMON CORE STATE STANDARDS: W.7.3.b,d; W.7.4, W.7.9.a, W.7.10, RL.7.3, SL.7.1, L.7.1, L.7.2, L.7.3, L.7.6

20

Developing Believable Characters through Scene Boot Camp

CONNECTION

Congratulate writers on how much thought they have given to choosing story ideas, and tell them that they are ready to take these out for a "test-drive."

"Yesterday for homework I asked you to choose your story idea. I could tell from the talk this morning that that was still happening as you started to get settled in, that some of you are still torn: 'Did I pick the right idea? Maybe I should have picked the other one.' Believe it or not, I think it's great that you are still very much thinking about your decision. It tells me that your story ideas really matter to you, which means they will really matter to your readers. It also tells me that you are ready to take your stories—your characters, to be more exact—out for a test-drive."

❖ **Name the teaching point.**

"Today I want to teach you that, just as people take a car for a test-drive before buying it, writers take their characters from a possible story out for a test scene. They place their characters in everyday scenes, outside of the storylines, and then see how their characters move, think, and act."

TEACHING AND ACTIVE ENGAGEMENT

Tell a story about writing advice someone gave you about how you can get to know your main characters by writing about them in everyday scenes.

"A few years ago, I was working on a book, a fiction story, and I was just at the beginning. I wasn't exactly sure how my story would go or what my character was really like. But then my writing teacher made a suggestion. She said I should take out my notebook, set aside the story I was thinking about, and just place my main character in an everyday scene. You know, like washing dishes, or getting up in the morning, or having dinner. Something the character does almost every day, as a way to get to know who the character really is, what the character thought about, wanted. So I tried it. I actually tried just getting my character ready for bed. But as I wrote the scene, something really interesting started to happen—not only did I get to know the character better, but it almost felt like the character was coming to life, almost as if she was writing the story."

◆ COACHING

It is true that students' story ideas matter very much to them, just as famous fiction writers' story ideas matter enormously to them. The characters and storylines may be fictional, but the writers behind them are putting bits of themselves and their lives—and certainly their imaginations—onto the page. The chance to test-drive their characters is not just a fun writing exercise, but is a way for students to grow more knowledgeable of—and confident in— their creations.

Your chance of engaging students and drawing them in to the work of the day increases exponentially when you link the work you are teaching them to do with anecdotes about yourself. Your seventh-graders will be excited to try something that you, too, have done, and this particular exercise also offers a really fun, concrete way to get to know the characters they are creating.

Review what a scene is composed of.

"Right now, we're going to try this as a class, using my story idea. I think for this to really work as a strategy for understanding character, though, we can't write in summary. We need to write in scene. So let's quickly look over this chart that mentions some of the things I know many of you learned in years past about what makes a scene."

Scenes

- Are small moments or mini-stories
- Include a clear setting that is woven throughout the moment
- Have characters who are thinking, talking, acting, or perhaps doing all of those things
- Contain a character motivation and obstacle of some sort

Explain the procedure for scene boot camp.

"What we're going to do is a scene boot camp. I'm going to lead you through a writing exercise where you write fast and furiously, getting as much writing down as possible, while you also practice your scene writing skills. I'll give you a little tip, then I will model it with my own writing. Then you will give it a go. Then it will come back to me, and I'll model something different, and then, finally, it will be your turn to try."

"Here's the thing about this, though. Not everything I teach you will be something you will be able to do or will work for your scene right now. That's okay. Just keep working on the last thing you were working on and then catch up with me on the next move."

Demonstrate how to come up with traits for a character whose story you plan to write.

"First, I need to think about the character and story idea I chose: the girl who knows it's silly to feel this way, but she wants to be popular—mainly because she has a birthday party coming up and wants people to come to it. Now, I have to think a bit about who she is as a person and jot a few notes."

I picked up my pen and jotted as I talked, making it very clear these were notes by writing in abbreviations and phrases. "I know her parents are old-fashioned, so they would give her sort of a traditional name, like . . ." I made a point to pause, to show that I was really considering the options. "I'll call her Esmerelda, which is a beautiful name, but not exactly the cute little name people sometimes associate with popular people. And I also know that she is actually very friendly, but because she's a bit strange, sometimes when she tries to be friendly, it just comes off as almost annoying." I jotted the following list:

- Parents are old-fashioned
- Name: Esmerelda
- Strange
- Wants friends and is friendly
- Tries too hard and comes off weird

This is important to emphasize. What you are offering students today is just one way to get to know a character better. This doesn't mean that the exact steps you follow during the demonstration will be the exact steps that each kid in the class follows. Instead, you present this strategy—and others on other days—so that students have a growing repertoire of strategies that they can draw on as needed, anytime they write fiction.

Give students a chance to try this first step.

"Now, writers, go ahead and try this right now with your story idea. If you're not completely committed to your idea, just pick the one you think you are most likely to go with. Think a bit about that main character, then jot your thoughts really quickly in your notebook." As students got to work, I moved around the meeting area, looking over shoulders and giving gentle nudges when needed.

Lead students through the next step of placing a character in an everyday scene and writing the start of it.

When it looked like most students had at least gotten started, I said, "Now that most of you have an idea about your character, let's try them on for size. Let's try them in an everyday scene. The goal here is to think of possible scenes that will give us a stronger understanding of what kind of person this character is. The more ordinary the moment, the more our character can be himself or herself. So, I think I'm going to start with Esmerelda having lunch at school. While that doesn't directly link to the party, it should give me some insights into what she's like socially. I'm going to start this scene by jumping into the moment, so I'm not tempted to summarize." I wrote quickly, and then read aloud:

> Esmerelda walked into the lunch room, holding her lunch bag in her hands. Even though everyone else in the school, it felt like, bought school lunch, Esmerelda was a picky eater.

The goal here is that students do this work quickly, not perfectly, so the encouragement to just pick the idea they are most likely to go with (even if they aren't yet committed to one) is wise. This guided practice will move quickly, and kids need to be on the same page with you, ready to follow each step.

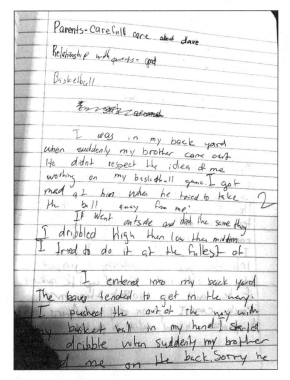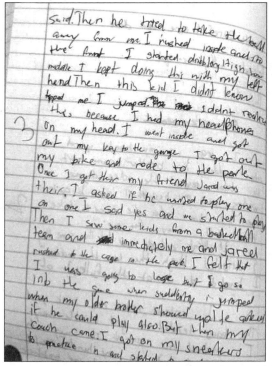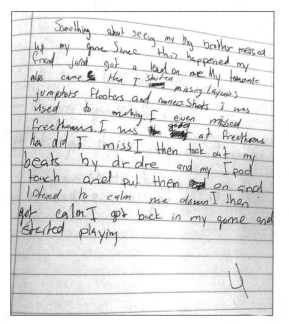

FIG. 3–1   Immersed in scene boot camp, Ryan pushes his pen across pages.

Debrief. Share what you are learning about your character and about writing from this process, and try writing the scene another way—in first person.

I stopped myself. "You know what? As I'm writing this little bit of a setup, I'm learning something about Esmerelda—that she's a picky eater. That she's different even when it comes to lunch. *But I'm also learning something about my writing.* I wrote in third person, but I'm wondering if the scene might flow better—if I might be able to get into the character better—if I wrote in first person. In realistic fiction, you can do either. I'm going to draw a line under my third-person try and then start my first person try right below it."

> I stood in the doorway of the lunchroom, half hiding behind the vending machines, clutching my lunchbag. There were a few kids who also brought their lunch from home, but almost everybody else bought from the cafeteria. I waited for Tilly to come through the kitchen doors. Then waved to her as she headed to our table, the one closest to the janitor's closet.

"Oh, I like that better. I think I'm going to stick with first person for a while. At least in this scene."

Debrief. Reiterate the steps you just followed, and set up students to do the same with their own stories.

I looked over my writing for a bit and then turned back to the class. "Did you see how I developed the setting a bit more and started to work in a little bit of information about Esmerelda as I wrote? I tried to show what she was feeling—that she was a little nervous—by having her hide behind the vending machine and wait until she saw her friend before she headed to her table. Can you try some scene writing? Can you just jump into your everyday scene, right in the action, being very aware of the setting, and also trying to show the character's feelings?"

Circulate as students work, offering tips and prompts about how to give characters movement.

The students opened up their notebooks and started writing. Again I circulated as they wrote, giving nods and thumbs up to students who were getting into it, and quick reminders to folks who were not writing or were slowing down. After a few minutes, I brought the class back together.

"Nice work. I saw that some of you already have written a page in just a few minutes, and as I read over your shoulders, it's pretty clear that for many of you, your characters are really springing to life. Now I think you're ready for more. Whenever you write scenes, you want to make sure your characters are doing things. These can be small things, like folding a piece of paper, or big things, like getting into an argument. Your characters might be talking or thinking. But it's important that you *show* them doing something, that you don't just *tell* about it. If you're getting stuck on something for your character to do, ask yourself, 'What does my character want? What's his (or her) motivation?'"

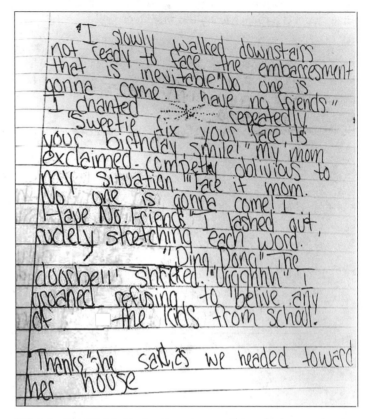

FIG. 3–2   Yasmin tries to incorporate everything she knows about scene writing during scene boot camp.

The "realization" that first person works best for your story is, of course, intentional. Here you convey a stylistic choice that fiction writers must all make—and in the process, you offer a tucked tip about voice while in the midst of discovering something, too, about your character, and about revision on the go.

This is an important coaching tip for students. So many novice fiction writers (and seasoned ones, too!) struggle to make their characters active. Yet active characters seem more alive and fully realized and are key to engaging fiction. You may find yourself offering your writers this tip again and again.

This time, as the students bent their heads to their task, rather than just quietly whispering or nudging a student here or there, I called out a few reminders, or prompts, to keep them on track as they wrote. I chose what to say based on what I was reading over students' shoulders.

"Remember to include what the character is feeling. But don't tell us. Think of small actions that can show us."

"It helps to include some dialogue."

"Describe what the character wants in this scene and what obstacles are getting in his or her way."

Interrupt students to announce that as they continue working, you will call out tips about ways to add depth to their characters and scenes, some of which they should try.

After students had been writing for a few minutes, I interrupted them again. "Writers, you are crafting some fantastic scenes. I can tell by how fast your pens are going down the page and the looks on many of your faces that you are really getting to know your characters, and you are coming up with great scenes while you're at it. You'll continue to write, but this time, while you're writing I'm going to call out some things, some tips and reminders that can help you explore your character more deeply, as well as make a stronger scene. If what I'm saying is something that will lift the level of your writing, please try it. If it just doesn't work for where you are at the moment, then let it go, maybe jot it in the margin, but try at some point during the next few minutes to try out a couple of things I suggest."

The students nodded and returned to their work. As they wrote, I peeked over their shoulders, looking to see how their scenes were shaping up. Occasionally I would call out a prompt, such as:

"Show the setting. Where is the character right now? What little detail of the setting can you mention?"

"Describe what the character is thinking right now."

"Make sure someone says something in this scene."

"Show your character's actions. They can be big or small. Stepping into a room full of strangers. Kicking a soccer ball. Taking a sip of soda."

"Have your character make a decision. It can be big or small, just make sure your character is being active in the movement of the scene."

When most students had more than a page of writing, I pulled them all back. "Congratulations, writers. Looking over your shoulders I see that you've gotten started on some strong scenes, and you're getting a sense of who your characters are."

Notice, again, the emphasis on choosing from a list of possible tips based on what students determine their writing needs to be. This conveys the important message that writing is not a "one-size-fits-all" process, and it builds independence and agency in your seventh-grade writers.

LINK

Remind students of the many ways to develop a character, and introduce an anchor chart on how to write compelling fiction.

"Writers, as you know, there are lots of different ways to develop characters. You can try writing characters in scenes, you can create graphic organizers to explore their personalities, you can spend some time just writing long about them and their relationships to secondary characters.

"I've begun a chart to describe the work you've learned to do so far to write compelling fiction—including developing characters. We'll add to this throughout the unit. And of course, you may come up with other things that we can include, so let me know if you do."

How to Write Compelling Fiction

- Brainstorm a great story idea (small moments, places, events, issues, struggles, stories you wish existed in the world).
- Make your characters come alive.
  - Generate traits.
  - Reveal wants and challenges.
  - Consider character's attitude toward self.
  - Explore character's relationships with others.
  - Describe character's movements, facial expressions, tics, style, quirks, etc.
- Test-drive your characters in scenes.
  - Make sure character does things, big or small.
  - Show feelings.
  - Include dialogue.
  - Develop the setting.
  - Try different points of view (first and third person).

Remind students of their options for working today.

"I'm assuming a lot of you will be ready to work on your characters today. However, if you find that you are not ready, that maybe you haven't yet landed on the perfect story idea yet, you can always use today to finish up that work before you move on to character development."

Helping Students Figure Out Ways to Develop Characters

IN YOUR WORK IN INDIVIDUAL CONFERENCES or with small groups, you may see that many students start by just listing phrases to describe a character, in spite of what you have just taught. Perhaps this will surprise you, but this happens more often than not. When conferring with students, help them realize that their lists can be more specific and more elaborated. Pay attention to places where a writer provides a bit more detail, and celebrate this. You might also want to direct students toward fancier lists—or perhaps even graphic organizers. Many of your students might have tried developing their characters using a T-chart back when they were in elementary school. They can use this tool again now, dividing the T-chart into internal and external characteristics as a way to make sure not all the character development is cosmetic.

As you confer, you will also probably notice that many of the characters your students create seem like stereotypes, something like, "Esmerelda is shy but wants to fit in." This is natural. It would be tempting to teach students to think critically about the work they've done developing characters by putting their characters on trial: "Is your character a stereotype? Is your character simplistic?" I don't recommend this. For now, it is very important for students to connect with their characters, and therefore you are wise to avoid treating the character or the character development work too critically. If a character seems generic, stereotypical, or underdeveloped, instead of saying so, simply help the writer outgrow this surface-level character development.

Here's an example. If a student is writing about a character's internal qualities in a generic way, I can often help the student open up those generic terms by probing a bit and asking the right questions. If the character is "good at cheerleading," then I can point out that people can be good at cheerleading in different ways. "What is your character's *specific* way of being good at cheerleading?" I can even press further and ask, "What is going on inside the character that makes her so good at cheerleading?" Once the writer has answered these questions and goes on to create some revealing details about this dimension of the character's life, I might ask, "How does that connect to other things the character does?" It also helps to ask, "What's the downside of this?" The character who is always practicing cheers may not know when to relax, or maybe the character is struggling with the competitive aspects of cheerleading.

In a conference, after I've asked these questions, I will pull back and talk about the importance of asking (as well as answering) questions such as these. That is, I will pause in a conference and say, "Notice, for a moment, the questions I've asked you about your character, because these are questions that you, as a writer, need to be able to ask yourself and each other." It helps to chart these questions. My goal, of course, is

(continues)

MID-WORKSHOP TEACHING
Developing the Character's Self-View

"Writers, it's wonderful to see you writing so furiously, but please look up for a minute. As you work on creating the insides of your characters, it's important to remember one really important thing: You need to think about how your characters feel about themselves. As real people, you know that how you feel about yourself is really important—to your sense of well-being, how you react to problems, how others perceive you. It only makes sense, then, that your characters would think something about themselves too. Does your character like herself? Does your character think he is funny? If your character is weird, does she know she's weird? Is your character weighed down by self-doubt? Or does he think he is the best thing since sliced bread?

"One thing you might consider doing is spending some time brainstorming, maybe in a quick list or paragraph, about your character's attitude toward him or herself and your character's attitude toward others—toward the secondary characters in the story."

for the young writer to learn that another time, she can ask these same questions while writing. Partners can also ask these questions about each other's characters.

Sometimes I run into a character that seems wooden, lifeless. In that case, I often find the student has been trying to make up the character out of thin air. I try to guide the student to lend his own life experience to the character. A young writer can do this even if the character is in many ways very different from himself, especially by exploring deeper internal states and feelings, rather than surface activities or reactions to events.

Occasionally when I confer, I find that the writer feels as if she has hit a dead end with a character. I let the student know that sometimes problems with a character's development can be early warning signals that the story idea itself doesn't fit the writer or that the story idea has problems that need to be addressed. As a result, then, I may encourage the writer to rethink the entire story idea.

This may also present an early opportunity for the student to make a connection to her reading work, especially if she has been studying characters in reading workshop. Guide the student to open up her independent reading book, and have her point to some of the places where she learned about the characters. What did the author include? What did the author leave out? Why does the student think the author made those decisions? By guiding the student to look back at her reading, you not only include the student in the company of authors, but you also make clear and explicit connections between what the student is learning as a reader and applying that to her own writing. This is something the Common Core Standards explicitly calls students to do (CCSS W.7.9.a).

Finally, I always keep in mind that secondary characters need to be developed too! Everything that the writer has done with the main character needs to be done with the secondary characters as well.

Seeing through the Eyes of a Character

Compliment students on their hard work, and share an example of a student who has developed a strong character based in reality.

"I just wanted to compliment you on doing some impressive work today. The characters you are creating for your stories are becoming increasingly developed, and more importantly, increasingly believable. So many of you are using what you know about your friends and family members to help create these three-dimensional characters that are realistic, yet we know are fictional. Jada, for example, is basing her character on a neighbor who lives in her building, who has big troubles in her life. Jada has always sort of wondered what her life was like behind the doors of her apartment, and in writing the realistic fiction story, she is crafting a realistic character based on the persona of her neighbor."

Make a connection between the character work students are doing in reading and writing workshop.

"Many of you know from reading workshop, that one of the best ways to understand the characters in the books you read is to 'walk in the shoes of the character.' You try to imagine what the character is feeling, thinking, even the things he or she might be seeing or doing that aren't described in the story. This is exactly the type of work you should do when you are writing characters."

Ask students to share with their neighbor their process for fleshing out a realistic character.

"Right now, quickly share your process for doing this—and maybe a detail or two about the character you are developing—with the person sitting next to you."

SESSION 3 HOMEWORK

SEEING THE WORLD THROUGH YOUR CHARACTER'S EYES

"Tonight for homework I'd like you to try to see the world through the eyes of your character as a way to get to know him or her even better. Think to yourself, 'What would my character be thinking in this situation? What would he or she be doing?' Then take a few minutes before you go to bed tonight to jot those thoughts down. Maybe you'll even start dreaming your character's dreams as you drift off to sleep."

Giving Characters Struggles and Motivations that Mirror Real Life

ear Teachers,

Today, rather than including a minilesson, I offer a letter with suggestions and ideas for additional ways to help your students develop believable characters, thereby creating sturdier and more believable stories. This session should be personalized to meet the needs of your students. You should feel free to opt in or out of any of the suggestions in this letter, knowing that the most important thing is to help students put the finishing touches on their characters and story ideas, so they will be in a good place to begin plotting the actual structure of their stories in the next session. We include these letters throughout these units of study, with the hopes that doing so will give you a welcome opportunity to begin writing your own minilessons, tailoring them to the students in your classroom.

Up until today, you have likely seen your students moving toward fiction writing with varying degrees of facility and interest. This variety is not only due to the fact that students enter a new year at a range of writing levels—and with a range of writing preferences. It is also due to students' affinity (or lack of affinity) for fiction, or simply due to the fact that they are still warming up to you at the beginning of the year. That said, there is no reason to worry if, while reading over your students' work, you see a wide range of quality and skills. Today is a great opportunity to accelerate students' growth no matter where their narrative skills lie.

It is incredibly common for young writers, or for that matter amateur adult writers, to struggle with creating a character who is culpable in the trouble that exists in the plot. This could be because in the act of creating a character, the writer gets so attached she can't imagine the character possibly doing anything wrong. Or it may be that the character is, in fact, a fictionalized version of the author, so having the character make poor choices may feel like a reflection on the writer. There are, of course, oodles of other reasons a writer opts for a character who doesn't do much and to whom nothing much happens—or alternatively, a perfect character that bad things happen *to*. She broke her leg on the way

COMMON CORE STATE STANDARDS: W.7.3, W.7.5, RL.7.3, SL.7.1, L.7.1, L.7.2, L.7.3, L.7.6

to the skateboard tournament because there was a rock in the road. He got in trouble because a bully picked on him. All of this passivity leads to very dull and often unrealistic stories, indeed.

Clearly, one of the most dramatic ways to develop characters—and concurrently improve a dull plot—is to make characters more active. A great way for young writers to do this is to explore their characters' motivations or desires, as well as the obstacles that get in the way of what their characters want most. Ideally, the intersections between motivation and obstacle will result in a conflict that propels both the plot and the development of the character.

To prepare for this work, you will want to gather a few mentor texts whose characters have struggles and desires that you will showcase. These can be texts that the students know from reading workshop or from read-alouds, or texts that you have studied together to prepare for this unit. You might spend some time during a class meeting or during reading time talking about how these texts have characters who have motivations, as well as obstacles that get in the way of them achieving their hearts' desires. If it is too early in the year to rely on a short stack of texts that your students all know, you can always consider tapping their knowledge of pop culture, such as current hit movies, television shows, or even popular music videos. Some teachers even show short clips of these "texts" so that students who are unfamiliar with them can have at least a thumbnail sketch of how they go.

MINILESSON

The minilesson could go a variety of ways. If your students came to you with lots of writing and reading workshop experience, you could use today's session to remind them of what they already know about how characters work. You could even set up an inquiry of sorts in which they look through the texts they've read recently and list some of the motivations and obstacles that drive the characters in these stories. Students can then mentor themselves using those motivations and obstacles, looking to see what sorts of ideas they can develop that fit with the characters they've created.

If, on the other hand, your students have less experience, you might need to teach an explicit lesson in which you return to your demonstration text and explore your character's motivations, as well as the obstacles that might get in that character's way. You will want to point out that since they are writing short stories, the ideal motivations and obstacles are ones that can be addressed in a relatively short number of pages. Wanting to be a doctor, for example, for the confines of a short story focused on the life of a seventh-grader, will likely not have the sort of satisfying arc that they are hoping for. They can, however, explore one slice, one smaller desire connected to that larger desire, such as wanting to become president of the science club or applying to be a junior hospital volunteer. You will then want to show them how to craft manageable and realistic obstacles that might get in the way of the character's path to achieving his desire.

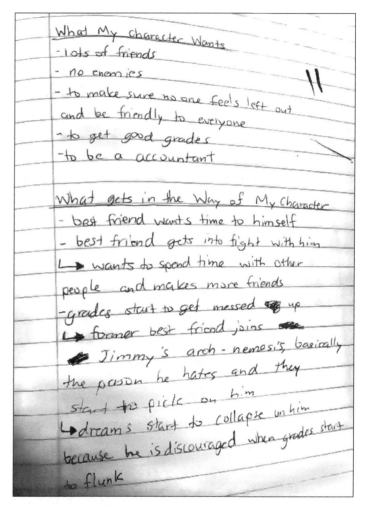

FIG. 4-1   Samee explores his character's motivations and obstacles.

Encourage students to continue to explore these things in a variety of ways. Quick jots and short conversations with partners are great ways to begin. Students might also try exploring the motivations and obstacles in short scenes in their notebooks.

It is important that no matter what your students' experience level with writing fiction, you highlight the value of both motivations and obstacles of not just the external, but also the internal variety. In other words, if the character wants to win the skateboard tournament, the trophy might be one thing the skater

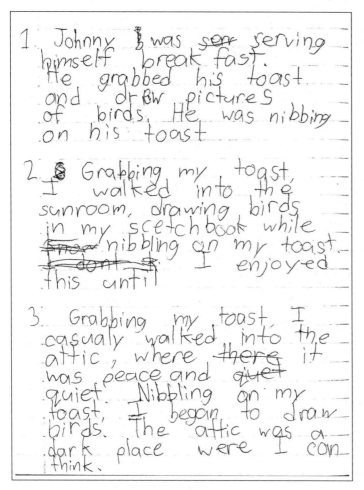

1. Johnny I was serr serving himself break fast. He grabbed his toast and drew pictures of birds. He was nibbing on his toast

2. I Grabbing my toast, I walked into the sunroom, drawing birds in my scetchbook while ~~then~~ nibbling on my toast. ~~dont I.~~ I enjoyed this until

3. Grabbing my toast, I casualy walked into the attic, where ~~there~~ it was peace and ~~quiet~~ quiet. Nibbling on my toast, I began to draw birds. The attic was a dark place were I can think.

4. Grabbing my toast hapily, I ~~grabed~~ casualy walked into the attic, I where it was peacful and quiet. Nibbling on my toast, I began to draw birds. The attic was a dark place where I can think I enjoyed the sense of independece, I then chose to right poetry, my other peason. ~~It was all nice until~~ I enjoyed writing about ~~be~~ birds too. Bird represent independence. They are ~~so~~ strong. Unlike me. I thaught, "I wish I was a ~~b~~ bird."

FIG. 4–2 Perspective, voice, and inner thoughts are highlighted as Gabriel experiments with character.

focuses on, but meanwhile, he might also be focusing on pleasing his dad or feeling more confident in other areas. The obstacle can be another, bigger, older skater or a particularly challenging trick. But it can also be overcoming his lack of confidence. Seventh-graders are ready to examine and balance the intersection of the internal and external, and because they are so often turning inward in their own adolescent lives, they are well positioned to explore those segments of character development.

CONFERRING AND SMALL-GROUP WORK

Many of your students might find this rehearsal work confusing. All of this scene writing and character exploration can sometimes feel and sound like the writer is drafting in her notebook. You might decide to pull aside students who appear to be writing fully fleshed-out drafts in their notebooks to explain the value of a lot of rehearsal before drafting. You might also point out that anything that seems like a gem in their notebook can be transferred later to a draft if it feels like it belongs there.

Alternatively, you might find that some students are champing at the bit to get drafting already and are wondering if they will ever get a chance to do the "real" work of writing. For these students it might help to have them work together and workshop their characters with other writers. That is, teach those students a protocol for giving and receiving feedback. For example, you could teach them to start the conversation with a specific compliment. Then move on to one specific suggestion or tip, possibly based on something they have learned in class, from the class charts or mentor texts. From there, they might want to leave room for questions or discussion between the writer and the reader.

MID-WORKSHOP TEACHING

An apocryphal tale about the importance of getting to know your characters well, often told in college-level writing programs, goes like this: once a writer was several hundred pages into his novel. He was drafting one of the last scenes of his book when he placed his main character at a cocktail party. A tray of food was being passed around, and the writer realized he had no idea what hors d'oeuvre the character would pick. Suddenly, the writer realized that if he doesn't know that, he hadn't yet done the work of developing that character, and if he continued to write, he would have holes in his story. He decided to stop writing that version of his novel and start over from scratch, throwing away hundreds of pages in the process.

You might want to share that story, or another, about the importance of dedicating time and energy to getting to know one's characters with great specificity and intimacy. Meanwhile, point out the importance of developing not just the main character, but *all* of the characters that will appear in a story. Encourage students to introduce their characters to partners, imagine their characters in scenarios that won't appear in the story, even mock-interview their characters to ensure that they know them as well as they know themselves.

SHARE

Make sure students understand that today is the last official day to develop characters. During the share, then, you may want to suggest to your writers that they take whatever steps they need to finish fleshing out their characters. Some may want to make a character list in their notebooks and then review each character's descriptions, words, and actions throughout the story itself, making sure there is enough detail to bring the cast to life. Others might instead engage in character introductions with a partner, after which the listening partner can share any insights, asking questions to clarify things about the characters or offering little tips of ways to bring out the characters even more. Here, though, you'll want to caution students not to get so carried away by their own fiction-writing imaginations (which are growing livelier by the day!) that they end up taking over the creative process of a classmate's character development. If students are still unsatisfied with their characters, they will want to set some writing time aside tonight to fix any issues they see. You might also want to have students read or reread a class mentor text if they haven't already done so. Tomorrow that mentor text will be used as part of the work around plotting.

Enjoy!
Colleen

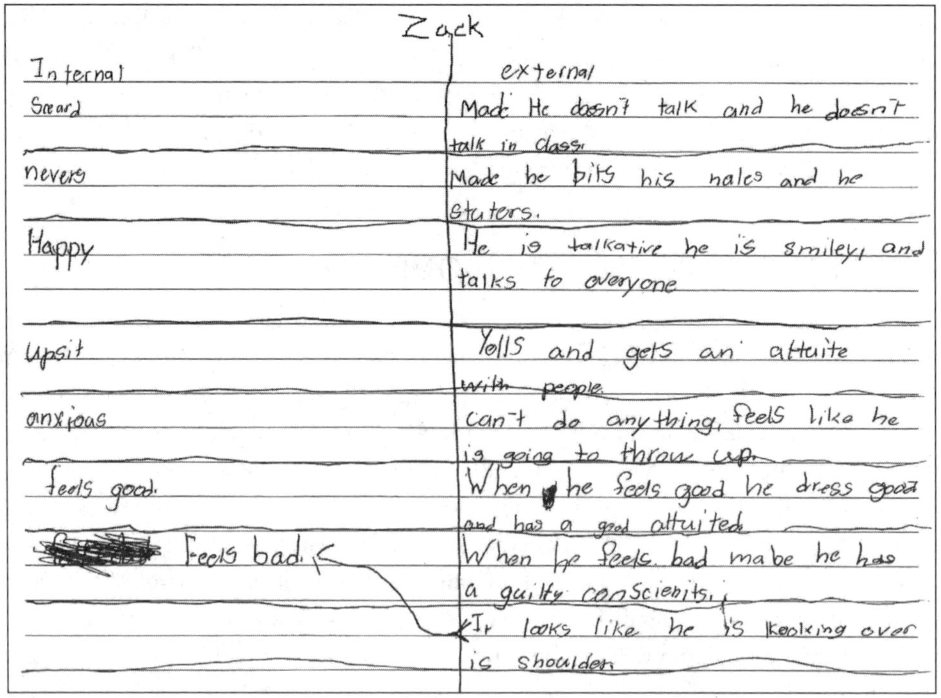

Zack

Internal	external
Scard	Mad: He doesn't talk and he doesn't talk in class.
nevers	Made he bits his nales and he stuters.
Happy	He is talkative he is smiley, and talks to everyone
Upsit	Yells and gets an attuite with people.
anxioas	Can't do anything, feels like he is going to throw up.
feels good.	When he feels good he dress good and has a good attuited.
Feels bad	When he feels bad mabe he has a guilty conscienits. It looks like he is looking over is shoulder.

FIG. 4–3 Using a T-chart helps Taylor expand on internal and external aspects of his main character.

Session 5

Plotting with Tools

Story Arcs, Timelines, Lists, Mentor Texts

BECAUSE AS READERS we typically see just an author's finished product, it is easy to imagine that when writers sit down to work, they think up a story and then, poof! Out it comes! When students generate "on and on stories," it is often because they believed they were doing exactly what professional writers do: they thought up a story, sat down to write it, and then, poof! Unfortunately, as we know, that's not how professional writers, or any successful writers of fiction, work. So we shouldn't be surprised when our students work in this way and out comes a meandering string of somewhat meaningless, disconnected events.

In this session, you will remind students of what they know from past years—that writers *plan* stories before they tackle the blank page. You will remind students—and emphasize—that most stories follow a predictable pattern, one in which a character wants something and faces increasingly challenging obstacles as he works to attain those wants. Tensions rise and fall as characters move along this trajectory, which is what keeps readers turning the page, eager to find out what will happen next. A character faces an obstacle and readers hold their breath, wondering, "However will she respond to *this* hurdle?" A character overcomes a challenge, and readers breathe a sigh of relief.

Before you send the class off to write, you will give them the option of drawing from the many planning tools at their disposal—from timelines to story mountains to lists. Meanwhile, you will teach them that regardless of the tool that best fits them as writers, they need to be guided by how stories go. Rather than planning a sequence of equally weighted events, they need to ask themselves, "How will my character reach for her desire? What obstacles will she face—and how will those obstacles get more challenging as my story progresses? When and how might my character overcome those obstacles—or else experience a shift in perspective that yields new clarity?"

Similarly, students need to ask themselves, "Is this event, this scene, central to my character's course of wants and struggles and success?" Tell students that more is not better. It is better to have just two or three well-developed, purposeful scenes than a clutter of events, especially since the more numerous the events, the more likely students will

IN THIS SESSION, you'll teach students that writers sketch out possible plotlines for stories, often using tools such as story arcs, timelines, lists, or mentor texts that can help ensure their stories are built with traditional story structure in mind.

GETTING READY

✔ Link to two predictable story arcs created by writer Kurt Vonnegut (see Teaching) 💿

✔ Copies of the mentor text, "Thirteen and a Half" (or another mentor text you have selected for the class). Your students should have read this text prior to today's session. (see Teaching) 💿

✔ "Story Arc" chart for the mentor text, "Thirteen and a Half," enlarged on chart paper (see Teaching)

✔ Chart paper and markers, for developing a story arc of the shared class story (see Active Engagement) 💿

✔ Revised anchor chart, "How to Write Compelling Fiction" (see Link) 💿

✔ Enlarged copies of the Grade 6 and 7 Narrative Writing Checklists as well as individual copies for students (see Share) 💿

✔ Students' writers notebooks and pens (see Share)

✔ Index cards (see Homework)

COMMON CORE STATE STANDARDS: W.7.3, W.7.5, RL.7.2, RL.7.3, RL.7.10, SL.7.1, SL.7.2, L.7.1, L.7.2, L.7.3

resort to summarizing rather than elaborating. Being thoughtful about each and every scene students plan to include will allow them to craft stories that are focused, meaningful, and engaging for their readers.

This session emphasizes that because writers use planning tools to envision the big picture, they often generate *multiple* plans before settling on the one they will implement. Similarly, writers often use planning tools to aid with revision—to *re-envision* how else a story might unfold. Remind students, then,

---

"Remind students that writers plan stories before they tackle the blank page."

---

that planning tools should take a central place in their writing toolkits, so they can draw on them for different purposes as they move through the writing process and a unit of study.

Finally, some students might balk at the idea of creating their own planning tools, instead preferring the comfort of a teacher-made and provided worksheet. Help those students to understand that your goal is for them to learn to write with independence. When they write in the future, they won't have a freshly photocopied worksheet. Instead, they should embrace the notion that they can create their tools in exactly the ways that best fit their purposes.

Plotting with Tools

Story Arcs, Timelines, Lists, Mentor Texts

CONNECTION

Remind students that once fiction writers have brought their characters to life, they use an understanding of the characters' wants and struggles to develop a possible plotline.

"Students, you may remember a few days ago, I told you that fiction writers don't just choose a story idea and go straight to writing a draft. Instead, fiction writers use strategies for bringing characters to life, strategies like imagining their characters in everyday scenes, considering the internal and the external characteristics of the main character, the protagonist. Writers go through their lives, thinking, 'What would my character do in this situation?' They give special attention to what motivates a character and the obstacles that get in the character's way.

"Writers postpone thinking about the details of what happens in a story, about the plot of a story, until they've done this other work. They postpone thinking about the sequence of events because eventually they take all they know about their characters—especially their understanding of their characters' motivations and obstacles—and they use this information to create a plan for their stories."

Before this point, perhaps students have drafted scenes that placed their characters in motion and revealed them as living, breathing people, but those scenes will probably not comprise the start of their story. Before a fiction writer can write her lead, the writer needs to know the character, to imagine him in action, and to have drafted, chosen between, and revised multiple plotlines for the story. Today then, after all their preliminary thinking and drafting, students will consider a variety of ways their stories could unroll.

❖ **Name the teaching point.**

"Today I want to teach you that after writers develop their characters, they draft possible plots for their stories. Fiction writers plan by plotting the arc of the story—and *specifically*, by aiming to intensify the problem. They do this by using what they know about plotting and then choosing from a variety of tools to help them plan."

TEACHING

Share an anecdote of a famous writer—Kurt Vonnegut—who plotted and explained two predictable story arcs.

"Many famous writers rely on story arcs to think through the plots of their stories. And, of course, there isn't just one way a story can go. Kurt Vonnegut once laid out five common story arcs that stories follow. One, for example, he calls 'man in hole,' and I revealed this arc (http://www.laphamsquarterly.org/voices-in-time/kurt-vonnegut-at-the-blackboard.php?page=all, Google search term 'Kurt Vonnegut at the Blackboard'). He described it this way: 'You will

Teachers, you can see how I teach story arcs within the context of a bigger focus—thinking about how the story will flow in general, across the pages. Only after stressing that the character will get herself into a growing tangle of trouble do I mention that this can be signified by the rising slope of the story arc. I'm trying to ensure that students understand how this graphic organizer functions as a symbolic representation for the story itself.

see this story over and over again. People love it and it is not copyrighted. The story is "Man in Hole," but the story needn't be about a man or a hole. It's this: somebody gets into trouble, gets out of it again. It is not accidental that the line ends up higher than where it began. This is encouraging to readers.'

"Here's another one," I said, as I revealed a second arc (http://www.laphamsquarterly.org/voices-in-time/kurt-vonnegut-at-the-blackboard.php?page=all). "See if you can guess what story this describes. It's a famous one. The arc begins way down here, with a truly despondent girl whose mother died and whose dad remarried a horrible woman with two horrible daughters who treat this girl like a servant. Things are about as bad as they can get for this girl." Some students registered looks of recognition on their faces.

"And then there's an invitation to a party, and everyone gets to go except the narrator! But then, a fairy godmother appears, and she sends the narrator off to the party, dressed to the hilt!" By now, most kids were nodding or whispering "Cinderella!" to each other.

"Things shoot way up from there, because Cinderella (yes, you guessed it!) attracts the prince's attention. And, of course, as you all know, when she leaves the party and drops her shoe, things go back to being rotten for her, except . . . they aren't as bad as they used to be because Cinderella now has memories of a perfect evening. And when the prince locates the girl who fits the shoe, things spiral to infinite amounts of 'happily ever after' for Cinderella." And I traced the line of the story arc pointing to infinity.

"Notice that these two arcs look very different from each other, but what overlaps is that things go up and down. Both arcs rise and fall as the plot rises and falls."

Explain why a writer would use a story arc to plan a plot.

"Story arcs can help you figure out the rises and falls of your own plot because they remind you that it's not just one event after another, with no real change or climb. It's like each scene in the arc is a whole new movement for your character. That's what makes readers want to keep reading, to find out how the character will get to the other side of this arc."

"The story arc also shows you that something is going to happen, and things are getting tough. Then something happens as the story curves, or arcs, that changes things or that solves your character's problem. After that, things change, your character is different, and there isn't a feeling of anticipation anymore."

Remind students of what they learned about how stories tend to go, and share your arc of the mentor class story.

"Writers, earlier this year, in reading workshop, we discussed how stories usually go—that usually the main character has wants, and something gets in the way of him or her getting these. So the character encounters trouble, or a problem. And today, we learned that usually after encountering the problem, the character has to deal with that problem somehow, which gives movement to the story. Often, the problem intensifies before getting resolved, with the character experiencing several challenges along the way. Or it gets resolved in a different way than the character

You may be wondering how this emphasis on story arcs will help those students who write stories with just two or three scenes. In fact, even the shortest of stories follows a rising/falling action. It is the arc that grips the reader and keeps him wanting to read on. The arc is what invests the reader in a character, and in a story, and what gives the reader that big "Aha!" or "Phew!" moment at the end. It is by creating this rising/falling action that your students will begin to understand the rhythm of story.

Here, my goal is not only to describe the predictable way that stories tend to go—their arc—but to also tuck in the fact that even though the story arc follows a clear shape, a character's journey through the arc may not. Things are often messy in stories; characters don't always get the things they want or solve problems as they set out to do. This messiness sounds a lot like real life—which adds richness, depth, dimension, and believability to characters.

imagined or hoped for. In this way, the story doesn't just go from one event to another in a flat way, but rather, each scene builds on the one before it.

"Students, you may recall that when we read 'Thirteen and a Half' together recently, we talked about how the story went, how the events fit together, what its shape was. If it were to be written up as an arc, it might look something like this," I said, turning to a chart where I had recorded the main events of the story on an arc.

You may want to use "Thirteen and a Half" as your class mentor text for this unit, or you may wish to choose another text. In either case, it's important to choose a story that your students have read several times, analyzed, and know very well.

The narrator goes to Ashley's big, fancy house.

Ashley gives the narrator a tour and makes up a lot of rules.

The narrator feels uncomfortable.

Ashley talks a lot about her getting older and also her exotic bird.

Ashley and the narrator find the bird dead.

The mother explains that the bird is not what Ashley thought it was.

The narrator wants to leave, but stays.

Ashley and the narrator hold a funeral.

Narrator is kinder to Ashley and more appreciative of her life.

Point out that when the author began writing this story, she probably didn't know *exactly* which choices the character would make—only that there would be some trouble—so she tried out different scenarios. Liken this process to the plotting of the shared class story.

"When Rachel Vail wrote this story, she probably knew that it would be about two kids having a bad play date. But she probably didn't know, when she started to write the story, exactly what would happen on every page. I bet she imagined one way the story might go, and another, and another.

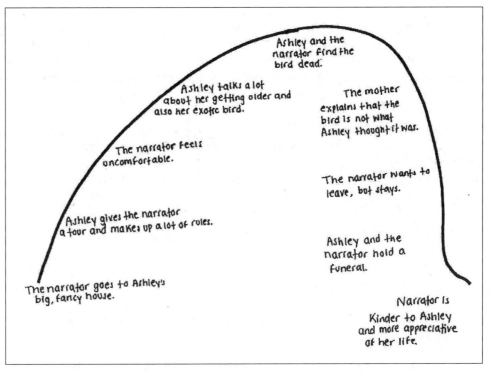

FIG 5–1   Story Arc of "Thirteen and a Half"

"Authors always know that the trouble will grow and that characters will make choices—some of which probably won't work out. And authors also know that *somehow*, in the midst of all the trouble, *somehow* there will be *something* that makes a difference. I bet Rachel Vail didn't start her book realizing all the little details—she probably didn't know before she started writing that Ashley would be someone the narrator feels just a little bit sorry for, or that the narrator would turn out to be the stronger, more put together one.

"When we plot our Esmerelda story, I know that our character will struggle to achieve what she yearns for, that our character will make choices. Some of these choices may not work out. Right now, we don't know which ones, exactly. But we *do* know that something will happen that makes a difference. Our character will find a way to resolve the struggle or she will change her sense of what she wants.

"And we know that just as a story arc climbs and then changes, Esmerelda will take actions, and things will happen that will result in a change."

ACTIVE ENGAGEMENT

Challenge students to work in partnerships to create a possible plotline for the first scene of the shared class story.

"Writers, let's plan the Esmerelda story together, keeping the story arc in mind. In the draft we've already begun, we have Esmerelda sitting on the steps of the school waiting for her bus to come and hearing everyone talk about this big party. She's wishing she could get invited, because everyone is going, but she also doesn't know what to do about it. Do we still want to start the story that way? Make it all about her wanting to go to the party and trying to figure out a way to go without being someone she's not?"

"Talk with your partner and think what the first scene in our arc should be. The starting scene must bring Esmerelda to life, show what she yearns for, and show the trouble (which we already know will be her conflicting feelings of wanting to be popular but not wanting to change who she is to become more well liked). And remember, things need to escalate and become more difficult before they change, so think about how we'll make Esmerelda's problem get worse. Turn and plan the start of our story arc."

Everyone started to talk. I moved among the partners.

"I think we should start with Esmerelda getting dressed in the morning, having a tough time deciding what she could wear to look cool," Jada said.

"Or," Annabelle added, "we could have her in the lunchroom, waiting for her friends and listening to the popular kids talk about the party that was coming up."

E. L. Doctorow once said, "Writing a novel is like driving a car at night. You can see only as far as your headlights, but you can make the whole trip that way. You don't have to see where you're going, you don't have to see your destination or everything you will pass along the way. You just have to see two or three feet ahead of you." Likewise, you'll convey to students that they don't need to have figured out the exact details of their characters' pathways. Rather, knowing that a little bit of trouble or yearning is coming, and then writing that, and then perhaps imagining it another way, and then writing that, is part of the process of crafting a story. The arc is a tool that can help guide students through this exploratory stage of writing.

This, perhaps more than anything else you teach during this unit, will make the difference between flat stories and robust ones. By asking students, "What's at stake for your character?" you remind them that in fiction, characters must struggle with something big, something deep, to change, to grow, to give the reader payoff. For Esmerelda, the protagonist of the shared class story, what's at stake is her image, her closest friendship, perhaps her own sense of identity—all very important things.

Convene the class. Report on overheard ideas for how the story could begin.

"Writers, I heard some great ideas. Some of you suggested we alter the start so that Esmerelda's already been invited to the party, and instead of her pining to go, she knows she's going so maybe we show her having a hard time deciding what to wear as a way to show how torn she is between wanting to be well liked and wanting to be true to herself."

Set students up to imagine what might come next. Then have them convene and add their ideas to the story arc.

"What do you think could come next? Keep in mind—you need to *show* (not summarize) her struggle, and the problems need to get worse. Turn to your partner and plan."

Again I listened in, and after a bit I again paraphrased what I'd heard a student suggest. Soon the story arc contained these scenes:

- Esmerelda receives an invitation to a party.
- She struggles to choose what to wear–something she likes, or something that she thinks will make people like her.
- Esmerelda's mom buys her a new outfit for the party–one that is decidedly not cool.
- Esmerelda hears that there may be a fashion "show" at the party where everyone walks down the catwalk.

Model for students that the story might also go another way.

"Great work! You now have one terrific story arc. But since you're familiar with the writing process, you know that, for sure, you'll need to give the story arc a few tries before deciding on the perfect arc. I heard a few other ways the story could go, too. I heard Miriam and her partner saying that the story could start right at the party," I drew a line under our first story arc and created a new arc with these points:

- Esmerelda sees some kids doing some dangerous stunts.
- She goes into another room only to hear a few people gossiping about one of her friends, Tilly.
- One of the kids tries to bring her into the gossipy conversation.
- She has to decide whether to join in or stand up for Tilly and not be popular.

"The first job of a story's beginning is to start at the right time. It should not start when things are quiet, when nothing's happening, when things are much the same as they always have been. After all, the whole reason we tell the story is because something about life is new and different, something's happening that stands out—and your responsibility, as the writer, is to begin the work at that point of change" (The Artist's Torah, Ebenbach, 60).

Philip Gerard, in his chapter "An Architecture of Light: Structuring the Novel and Story Collection," suggests that stories have a "signature that can be stated in a single sentence. The signature for Moby Dick is "Madman goes hunting for a white whale." This line defines what Gerard refers to as the "structural arc" of the story. He writes, "Think of the signature as the cable that hauls the rollercoaster cars up the long hill of suspense, round the hairpin turn of reversal, down the stomach-clenching fall" (Julie Checkoway, Creating Fiction, 152).

Most importantly, Gerard says that although writers begin with their structural arc and their characters clearly in mind, "almost everything will change" (153).

LINK

Remind students that as fiction writers plot story arcs, they understand that problems need to get worse before they get better.

"So, writers, remember that fiction writers plot their stories. They may not be sure exactly what will happen next, but they plan the start of the story against the shape of an arc, remembering that they can't just write anything that pops into their minds next. So in our Esmerelda story, after she finds out she's going to the party, we can't have her decide she doesn't care about being popular anymore and then just go to the party and have a great time. Instead, we need to think, 'Once she gets to the party, what will happen next?' We already know that Esmerelda's struggle to be both popular and true to herself will have to grow in intensity. Her struggle will have to get worse before it gets better."

Encourage students to explore and build multiple story arcs, each one better than the one before.

"Writers, I know many of you are pretty sure that you know exactly how your story should go. Still, it's important that you try a few different story arcs, just to make sure you have the best one possible—the one that you believe will make the most compelling story. Push yourself to come up with two or three different ones, each one an improvement over the one before it."

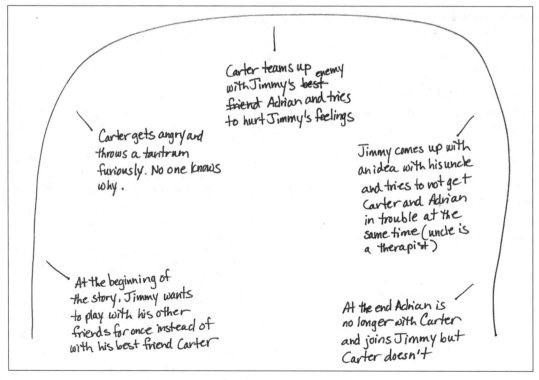

Carter teams up enemy
with Jimmy's best
friend Adrian and tries
to hurt Jimmy's feelings

Carter gets angry and
throws a tantrum
furiously. No one knows
why.

Jimmy comes up with
an idea with his uncle
and tries to not get
Carter and Adrian
in trouble at the
same time (uncle is
a therapist)

At the beginning of
the story, Jimmy wants
to play with his other
friends for once instead of
with his best friend Carter

At the end Adrian is
no longer with Carter
and joins Jimmy but
Carter doesn't

FIG. 5–2   Samee tries using a story arc to plan.

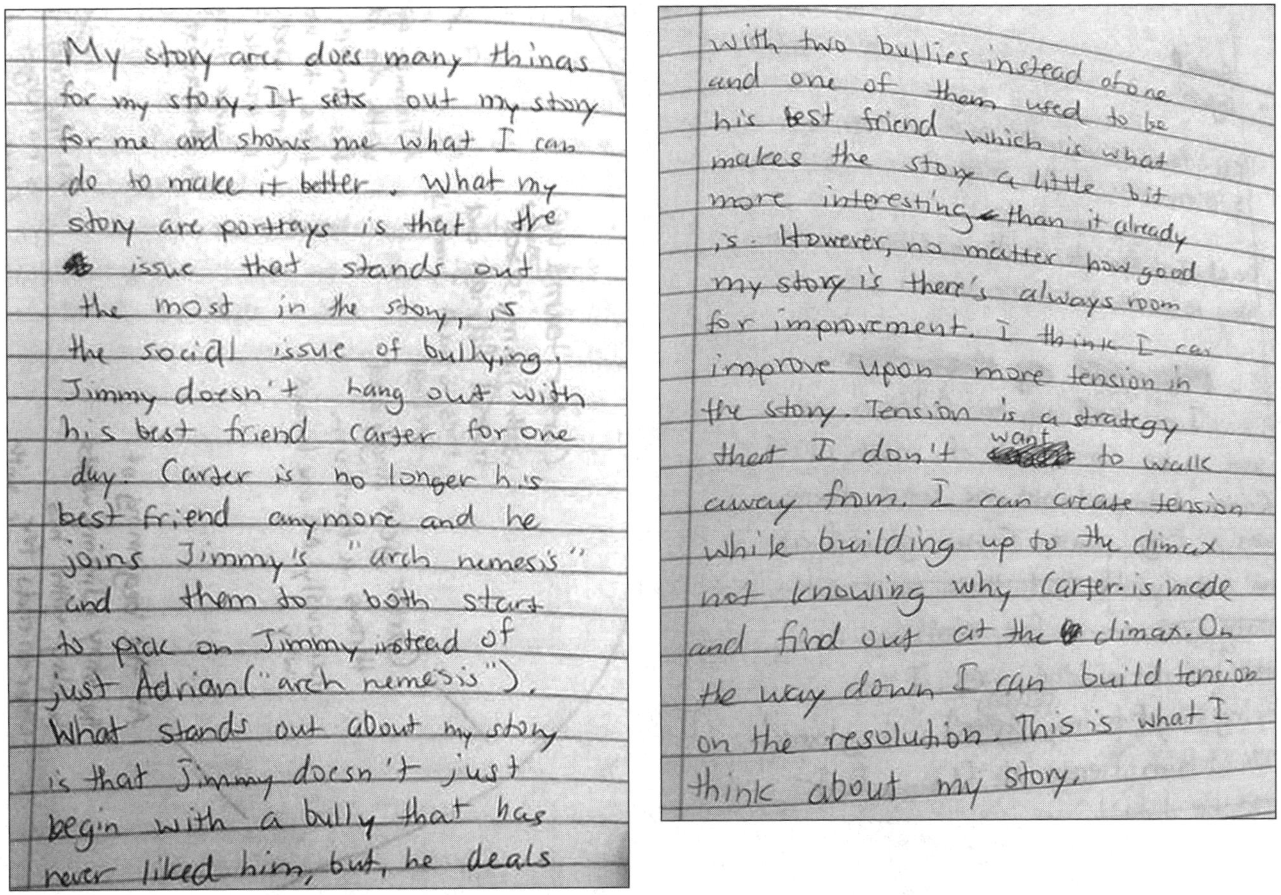

> My story arc does many things for my story. It sets out my story for me and shows me what I can do to make it better. What my story arc portrays is that the issue that stands out the most in the story, is the social issue of bullying. Jimmy doesn't hang out with his best friend Carter for one day. Carter is no longer his best friend anymore and he joins Jimmy's "arch nemesis" and them to both start to pick on Jimmy instead of just Adrian ("arch nemesis"). What stands out about my story is that Jimmy doesn't just begin with a bully that has never liked him, but, he deals with two bullies instead of one and one of them used to be his best friend which is what makes the story a little bit more interesting than it already is. However, no matter how good my story is there's always room for improvement. I think I can improve upon more tension in the story. Tension is a strategy that I don't want to walk away from. I can create tension while building up to the climax not knowing why Carter is mad and find out at the climax. On the way down I can build tension on the resolution. This is what I think about my story.

FIG. 5–3   As he reflects on his story arc, Samee decides to revise his original plan.

Invite students to try other story-planning tools, in addition to an arc, and to draw on other resources to plan, too.

"It's also important to point out that you don't have to draw an actual arc to plan if you don't want to. The arc helps us to remember that the story needs to change and develop, but it's not the only way to do this kind of planning. Some writers prefer to use timelines. Others like to make lists. Still others use different planning methods. What is important is that you choose a planning method that works for you.

"I've added today's teaching along with these planning options to our chart," I said, gesturing to our anchor chart. "You may notice a couple of points on the chart that look a bit shorter now, like 'Make your characters come alive.' I've summarized these points so our anchor chart won't grow too long to manage, but you still have 'clues' in the parentheses, and I think you'll remember what to do from earlier sessions."

How to Write Compelling Fiction

- Brainstorm a great story idea (think of small moments, places, events, issues, struggles, stories you wish existed in the world).
- Make your characters come alive (with traits, wants and challenges, self-attitude, relationships).
- Test-drive your character in scenes (envision and write actions, feelings, dialogue, setting, point of view).
- **Plot several versions of your story, aiming to intensify the problem (use arcs, timelines, storyboards).**

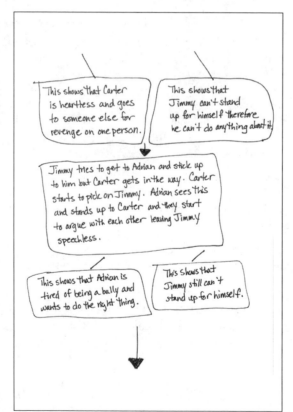

<u>Final Story Plan</u>

Jimmy plays with his other friends for one day instead of playing soduku with his best friend Carter. Carter gets angry at him and throws a tantrum. Jimmy still has no clue why Carter was mad but has yet to find out.

This shows that Carter is very sensitive and doesn't like being alone.

This shows that Jimmy doesn't know what happened to his friend but finds it best to leave it alone.

Jimmy's bully, Adrian starts picking on Jimmy and Carter starts to join in. Carter explains to Jimmy why they are no longer friends and how he is teaming up with Adrian to pick on Jimmy.

This shows that Carter is heartless and goes to someone else for revenge on one person.

This shows that Jimmy can't stand up for himself therefore he can't do anything about it.

Jimmy tries to get to Adrian and stick up to him but Carter gets in the way. Carter starts to pick on Jimmy. Adrian sees this and stands up to Carter and they start to argue with each other leaving Jimmy speechless.

This shows that Adrian is tired of being a bully and wants to do the right thing.

This shows that Jimmy still can't stand up for himself.

Carter approaches Jimmy and apologizes. He wants Jimmy to join him and team up against Adrian. Jimmy accepts the apology but refuses the offer. Carter gets mad and goes away. Adrian comes up to Jimmy and apologizes as well and becomes friends with Jimmy even though Carter doesn't want to.

This shows that Carter doesn't change and can't be friends with Jimmy because of how he acts.

This shows that Jimmy does change and stands up to Carter. He learns that he can't be liked by every one that makes friends with Adrian.

FIG. 5-4 After reflecting and a few more tries, Samee decides on a final story plan, this time using a flowchart style graphic organizer.

"I also want to remind you that you have other tools at your disposal for planning your plot. You can refer to our class mentor text, 'Thirteen and a Half,' for ideas. You can also think, as I asked you to do last night for homework, about the plots in your independent reading books or perhaps some short stories you've read in the past. And of course, touching base with your partner is always a good strategy to ensure that you're on the right track and that you are writing at your highest levels.

"You have lots of choices, strategies, and tools to help you create the best possible plot for your stories. Off you go!"

I cannot stress enough just how important it is to remind your students of the various tools and resources they have at their disposal— not only the ones in your classroom, but also ones they've used in past years. By now, seventh-graders should understand that learning is cumulative, and they should be able to draw on all the skills and tools they have acquired across their lives. Remind them of this again and again. And try checking in with students occasionally, to ask them which tools they are using specifically and how they are using these tools to develop and refine their writing.

Predictable Problems with Story Arcs

WHEN STUDENTS ARE WORKING ON THEIR STORY ARCS, I have discovered over the years that there are some very predictable problems that come up each and every time students reach this part of the process. I find that in my teaching I have a much lighter touch and am much less likely to get frustrated when I am expecting and prepared for those predictable problems. Depending on your students, you might find today's work session made up of mostly small-group work as you move about groups of students with similar issues. It is also possible that you will find yourself spending the first half of workshop time conferring almost exclusively with the squeaky wheels, while the rest of the students are working and giving you a sense of what they are doing. If your time with your students each day for writing is particularly short, you might find it better still to collect their work, make groups based on patterns you are seeing, and then teach into those groups the next day.

No matter which way you go, one predictable thing you will likely see is that many students will create story arcs that could very well be the plotting of a novel. Whether the length of time is a week or a year, there are so many characters and major events that it would not be possible for the students to complete these stories with anything less than hundreds of pages—or all summary! Depending on your students, you might approach this problem as one of time. Let them know they have ambitious plans, and perhaps these would work out into a novel. But for right now, perhaps they can choose one event on their arc that they can build into its own stand-alone story—perhaps one that could morph into a chapter in their novel, if that should come to pass.

Another predictable problem is common not just for seventh-graders, but for many amateur adult fiction writers as well: the plot hangs on a character who is passive; everything just happens to the character. The character plays no role in motoring his story along. These story arcs are rife with accidents and events befalling the characters. For this group, you might want to show them how a tweak here and there, making the character somewhat responsible for his fate, makes the story more interesting. For example, perhaps the marathon runner does hurt his ankle. But instead of it just happening, it happens because in his excitement to get started on the race, he went against his coach's advice and began running without a warm-up.

MID-WORKSHOP TEACHING   The Shape of the Story Can Be Part of Its Truth

I drew an arc on the board. As I did so, many students looked up to watch me. When I had most of their eyes, I started speaking. "While I know many of you have already moved past planning your stories and onto drafting, I know some of you are still working on your plans. No matter where you are, I think it's worth me sharing this one little tip I got from a writing teacher many years ago.

"That is, the shape of a story, where it starts and where it ends, says a lot about what matters to the author. If the story is about the importance of fitting in—or how much it really doesn't matter as long as you're true to yourself—then it makes sense to have the beginning of the story with the character grappling with fitting in, and the last scene showing some sort of nod, maybe even a scene that explicitly shows how the character feels *now* about fitting in. If the story is in part about growing up, learning to fly, it might begin and end with scenes that include that.

"While you're plotting your stories or revising your plots, you might want to stop and ask yourself, what is my story *really* about? What is the truth in what I am trying to say in this fictional story? How can the shape of my story—where it stops, where it ends, maybe even the peak of the arc—showcase the truth of what I am saying?"

Another common, predictable problem is when the story arc itself doesn't seem to hold up. The events don't seem to build, or the main conflict or crisis is just not in the right place in the story. In these instances, it is tempting to want to give students a formula. "A setup, a mix-up, and then a fix-up," I've heard well-meaning teachers instruct. However, while this might be helpful for some students if their story idea fits into the formula, it won't fit all story ideas. Moreover, it will also only fix today's problem and won't teach a student how to plot narratives for the rest of his life. So instead, I might opt for returning to a mentor text or two to study options for plotting. Have students plot alongside a published story, see how that author organized her story, then try similar plotting moves on their own.

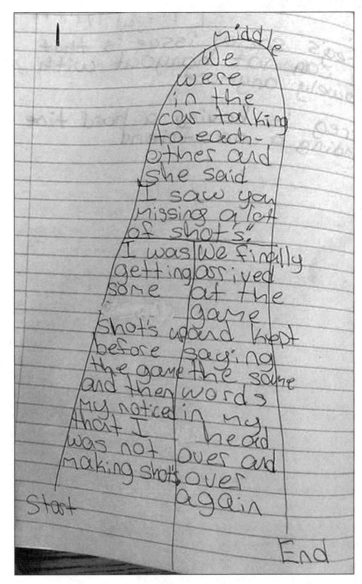

FIG. 5–5   A student tries a simplified story arc.

Taking Stock of What Students Are Doing Well—and Can Do Better

Celebrate the work students have been doing and tell them they are ready for the Grade 7 Narrative Writing Checklist.

"Writers, it's only been a handful of days since we started on this journey together of writing fiction, and already, you have grown leaps and bounds as writers! On the first day of this unit, I gave each of you a copy of the Grade 6 Narrative Writing Checklist, to remind you of all you learned in sixth grade and also to remind you to use that knowledge. Since then, you have churned out pages and pages of fictional scenes, and I know from reading many of those pages that you are ready to use the Grade 7 Narrative Writing Checklist."

I projected a copy of the grade 7 checklist alongside the grade 6 checklist and continued, "You will see right away that these checklists look very similar, in that they have the same categories. Of course what the grade 7 checklist asks you to do within each of those categories will be a little different—a little more sophisticated."

Narrative Writing Checklist

	Grade 6	NOT YET	STARTING TO	YES!	Grade 7	NOT YET	STARTING TO	YES!
	Structure				**Structure**			
Overall	I wrote a story that has tension, resolution, realistic characters, and also conveys an idea, lesson, or theme.	☐	☐	☐	I created a narrative that has realistic characters, tension, and change; and that not only conveys, but also develops an idea, lesson, or theme.	☐	☐	☐
Lead	I wrote a beginning that not only set the plot/story in motion, but also hinted at the larger meaning the story would convey. It introduced the problem, set the stage for the lesson that would be learned, or showed how the character relates to the setting in a way that matters in the story.	☐	☐	☐	I wrote a beginning that not only sets the story in motion, it also grounds it in a place or situation. It included details that will later be important to the story. These details might point to the central issue or conflict, show how story elements connect, or hint at key character traits.	☐	☐	☐
Transitions	I not only used transitional phrases and clauses to signal complicated changes in time, I also used them to alert my reader to changes in the setting, tone, mood, point of view, or the time in the story (such as *suddenly, unlike before, if only she had known*).	☐	☐	☐	I used transitional phrases and clauses to connect what happened to why it happened (*If he hadn't … he might not have, because of, although, little did she know that*).	☐	☐	☐
Ending	I wrote an ending that connected to what the story is really about. I gave the reader a sense of closure by showing a new realization or insight, or a change in the character/narrator. I might have shown this through dialogue, action, inner thinking, or small actions the character takes.	☐	☐	☐	I gave the reader a sense of closure by showing clearly how the character or place has changed or the problem has been resolved. If there wasn't resolution, I gave details to leave the reader thinking about a central idea or theme.	☐	☐	☐
Organization	I used paragraphs purposefully, perhaps to show time and setting changes, new parts of the story, or to create suspense for readers. I created a logical, clear sequence of events.	☐	☐	☐	I used a traditional—or slightly modified—story structure (rising action, conflict, falling action) to best bring out the meaning of my story and reach my audience.	☐	☐	☐

As students assess their writing, scaffold their work with the checklist and encourage them to set goals for themselves.

"As I pass out copies of these side-by-side checklists, look through your notebooks and find a couple of scenes you want to assess. Since you already know how to use these checklists from the work we did several days ago, you can get started right away. Remember to look back and forth between your writing and the items on the checklist, being honest with yourself about what you already do well, what you could better, and what you don't yet do at all." I circulated while students worked, prompting them.

"Move back and forth between your writing and the checklist."

"If you do something only once, consider whether you might work on it more."

"Remember to look for patterns. Think about what you do and don't know how to do as a writer, not what you do or don't do in just one place."

After a few minutes, I reconvened the class and said, "Tomorrow, most of you will start drafting your stories, and you'll want to be sure to use some techniques that you are not yet using or are just starting to use. Take a moment to star two or three goals for yourself."

Explain to students how to describe a story in one sentence.

"My writing teacher once said that one of the ways a writer know he's on the right track is if he can say what his story is in one sentence. Sort of like a one-sentence summary. It sounds easy at first, until you try it. If I were to try it with the Esmerelda story, I might say something like, 'Esmerelda is a girl who likes being different, but part of her wants to be popular, so one day she goes to a party and finds herself having to decide whether it is more important to be popular or to be true to herself.'"

WRITING A ONE-SENTENCE SUMMARY

"Tonight for homework, I want you to finish up your story arcs. When you've landed on the one you think describes how your story goes, I want you to try your hand at writing a one-sentence summary of your story. It will likely be a bit challenging, and you might have to have a few tries. But in the end, I think you'll find that it will help you hone in on what your story is *really* about. When you think you've got it, write it on an index card and then bring that index card with you tomorrow. With your story arc, your single sentence, and your goals in hand, you'll be all set to draft away tomorrow!"

Drafting and Revising with an Eye toward Meaning

From 2-D to 3-D

Planning and Writing Scenes by Including Evidence

IN THIS SESSION, you'll teach students that crafting scenes is, in a sense, about making the two-dimensional plans of the writer into a three-dimensional experience for the reader.

GETTING READY

✔ A bulletin board or chart titled "Coming Soon," with a space for students to post their one-sentence summaries (see Connection)

✔ A few examples of your students' story summaries that you will share (see Connection)

✔ Your writer's notebook (see Teaching)

✔ Two versions of the start of one scene of the shared class story—one told in summary and one as a detailed scene (see Teaching)

✔ One student's story summary that the class will help turn into a scene (see Active Engagement)

✔ Copy of "Thirteen and a Half" to display to class (see Mid-Workshop Teaching)

✔ "How to Write Compelling Fiction" anchor chart (see Link, Mid-Workshop Teaching, and Share)

✔ "Some Ways Writers Can Build Tension in Their Stories" chart (see Conferring and Small-Group Work)

✔ "List of Transitional Phrases" chart, leaving room to add more entries (see Share)

COMMON CORE STATE STANDARDS: W.7.3.b,c,d; W.7.5, RL.7.1, RL.7.2, RL7.3, SL.7.1, SL.7.2, SL.7.3, L.7.1, L.7.2, L.7.3

ODAY YOU TURN A CORNER. Your students will have done the rehearsal work leading up to this day; they will have generated and settled on a story idea that has meaning for them; created characters with distinct traits, motivations, and problems; mapped out a plan for how their story will unfold; and written a one-sentence story summary that captures the essence of the story. Now it's time to draft! Expect the excitement in your room to be sky-high today. You have likely been holding your seventh-graders back for days now, and they will be ready to dive in.

You will want to build off of students' enthusiasm and bring some fanfare to your teaching. This is, after all, a big moment. Meanwhile, know that the actual teaching you do today will have a direct result on the degree to which students draft with success or with difficulty. This means it is crucial that you deliver crystal clear instruction in what it means to story-tell versus summarize—as many kids will be apt to do the latter. You'll want to impress upon students the necessity of bringing their stories to life by showing and not telling. According to novelist James Thayer, telling explains, but showing *reveals*. To explain this concept to students, so that they are able to accomplish this task to good effect, we teach them to look at each bit of storytelling as an opportunity to leave evidence, like a criminal does. This is an image that might be a hit with seventh-graders, and it will stay with them as they sit down to do just that. Of course, if your reading and writing connections have been tight all along, you might instead connect today's work with your reading work, where you undoubtedly have been teaching your students to support all their ideas about their reading with evidence. Tell them that today they will be sitting on the other side of the desk, this time creating the evidence for their readers to find. No matter how you posit it, today is all about writing bit by bit, with details or evidence. This is how your students will create stories that sound like stories, ones that engage their peers, their readers. This is how they will get a feel for how this genre of writing goes. This will determine how they will ultimately share the message behind their stories.

By now, your students should have a clear plan for their stories—a story arc, timeline, or other plan. If some of your students do not yet have this, you may need to work one-on-one or in small groups with them. Fiction writing is challenging enough for young writers. To attempt this without a sense of how the story will rise and fall—how it will unfold on the page—will likely just bring frustration or a story that meanders with no clear direction.

"It is crucial that you deliver crystal clear instruction in what it means to story-tell versus summarize."

From 2-D to 3-D

Planning and Writing Scenes by Including Evidence

CONNECTION

Instruct students to post their one-sentence summaries in the space reserved for these.

"On your way to the meeting area today, can you hang your index card on our new bulletin board reserved for class 702? I want to be sure you all get a chance to read one another's ideas." Students stopped by the "Coming Soon" bulletin board, quickly tacking up their one-sentence story summaries before sitting down.

Congratulate students on their hard work and share a few kids' story summaries.

"First off, I want to congratulate you for landing on the story that you want to create—for doing the hard work of crafting a strong story arc and boiling your story down to its essence. That's not an easy task. I know you're dying to know what your classmates are writing about. And, of course, as part of a writing community, it's important that you become familiar with one another's work. Let me share just a few of your story summaries to give you a sense of the ideas percolating in this room.

"Annabelle's summary reads 'Lily wants to run for school elections but she realizes that in order to be a leader, she first must learn to stand up to the biggest bully in the school.'

"Yasmin's summary is: 'Cassie, an angry girl who lost her father, and takes it out on everyone around her, decides to be kinder to a new girl at school.'"

Samee read his, "My character wants to be friends with everyone. He comes across a personal fight and wants to fix it." Samee smiled, catching a mistake—"Well, actually that's two sentences, but I can fix it to be one." (See Figure 6–1 on page 57.)

"Now we get to the best part of this unit so far. Today we are going to put the meat on the bones of our stories. Today we are going to bring them to life. That's right! Today you get to draft."

Here, you not only celebrate the work students have done up until now; you also impress on your young writers the importance of having an open, supportive writing community, one in which sharing works in progress plays an active role. An added bonus: a bulletin board with student work in progress to show off!

❖ **Name the teaching point.**

"Today I want to teach you something fiction writers know: it's not enough to have good ideas for stories. To make the 2-D ideas feel 3-D, those stories need to come to life. Fiction writers can make this happen by asking, 'Is there evidence in my story's events? Does my writing show, not tell?' and then making sure that they story-tell, bit by bit."

TEACHING

Remind students of the difference between summary and scene by telling a familiar story in two contrasting ways.

"It's helpful to remember some of the things you learned in sixth grade, and even before that, about drafting stories, and to keep those things in mind as you move forward in your current stories. One of the most important reminders, of course, is that stories are a balance of summary and scene. For example, I could write this." I picked up a pen and jotted in my writer's notebook:

> On Friday afternoon, Mr. Covarubias's snake escaped from the tank in the science lab.

"Or, I could write":

> The breeze rattled the shades as it blew into our classroom windows. There was soft music playing in the background. The classroom was still except for the occasional turning of a page. Everyone was engrossed in reading. Suddenly, the door to the classroom swung open with a slam. Mr. Covarubias stood in the doorway, his glasses slightly crooked, his forehead beaded with sweat, "The snake escaped!"

"The first version is summary. It *tells* a lot of information really quickly, in not that many words. It sums up the action. The second version is storytelling; it's written in scene. It *shows* what's happening, bit by bit. Storytelling is what you will want to do when you draft."

Demonstrate how writers make sure they are creating 3-D writing by asking themselves, "Is there evidence?" and then adding that evidence if necessary.

"Another tip for helping you draft in a way that makes your stories come to life—makes them 3-D—is to not just *tell* the readers something and expect them to believe it, but rather, to be almost like a criminal who wants to be caught, by leaving evidence *everywhere* of the story you are writing."

"Let's think back to our Esmerelda story again." I turned to the section of my writer's notebook where I had begun working on Esmerelda's story. "In the scene where Esmerelda is listening to Liz and Maeve say mean things about Tilly, we *could* start like this":

> As the two girls talked, I felt uncomfortable. I didn't know what to do.

Again and again, you'll want to remind students of the strategies they learned in prior writing units that they can draw on now. This way, you convey that writing work is cumulative.

Here I am jotting quickly in my writer's notebook and reading aloud as I write. I use my voice purposefully so that students hear the difference between a summary and storytelling in a scene.

Likening storytelling bit by bit to a criminal leaving evidence everywhere is sure to be a big hit with seventh-graders. It is also memorable. Later, when kids repeat this process and recall tips for writing fiction, the evidence-leaving criminal is likely to jump quickly to mind.

"That's a fine first sentence. We're allowing the reader to see into Esmerelda's thoughts. But to make Esmerelda's state of mind bounce off the page—to make it 3-D—I can ask myself, 'Where's the evidence?' And then I can write in such a way that I'm leaving clues, leaving evidence that what I am telling the reader is true. So, here I want to think about how to show Esmerelda is uncomfortable and that she's unsure what to do. I can think a bit about what I do, or I know other people do, when they're uncomfortable. I know I fidget. My clothes feel weird, like they're too hot or something."

I picked up the pen and added to the story in my writer's notebook:

> The room felt really hot all of the sudden. I was beginning to wish I had worn a lighter shirt. This one was making me sweat.

"I think that works for the uncomfortable part. I think that's some solid evidence. Now, let's see . . . for the not knowing what to do, I could maybe make her fiddle with something, or start to do something just to look busy."

> As the two girls talked, I felt uncomfortable. I didn't know what to do. The room felt really hot all of the sudden. I was beginning to wish I had worn a lighter shirt. This one was making me sweat. I looked down at my phone, checking for text messages that weren't there. Then I noticed how dirty it was and made myself concentrate on slowly cleaning the screen with the bottom of my shirt.

"Writers, did you see how I made the opening of this scene pop? I didn't just summarize. Instead, I pushed my writing a bit more, asking myself, 'Where's the evidence?' and then adding that evidence in, story-telling it. You can do this with your scenes, too, to make them come alive!"

ACTIVE ENGAGEMENT

Set students up to summarize a moment from their stories to each other. Then share one student's summary, inviting the class to reimagine it as a story.

"Are you ready to try this out yourselves? With your partner, you're going to give just a summary of one moment from your story. This means you'll tell what happens in that part in just one or two sentences that sum up the action. Leave out the details. Okay, begin!"

As students talked, I circled the room, listening for a strong example I could share later—one that was clearly a summary but that I knew kids would have an easy time imagining as a story. After a minute, I called out, "If you haven't already had a turn, switch roles now."

Then I said, "Taylor, would you please share your summary with the class?"

Often, I begin with an example that falls short—and that mirrors the kind of work many students are currently doing. By showing students an "I could do it like this" example alongside a "but instead I want to aim for this" example, I hope to give them a clearer image of how their own work holds up and of what, exactly, they might do to lift the level of that work.

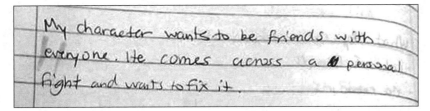

FIG. 6–1 Samee's original attempt at a short summary

"The bully, Billy, threw a pen at my main character's head after Zack told on Billy," Taylor said.

"Writers, do you see how that one sentence sums up the action of this moment in Taylor's story but gives us no details or sense of a story unfolding? That's a summary."

Remind students that when you turned your summarized tale into a 3-D story, you asked yourself, "Where is the evidence?" In this way, help your writers have success story-telling their classmate's summary.

"Now, I have a challenge for you. Can you help Taylor turn his summary into a story? Can you help him add evidence—details and actions and dialogue—so that this reads like a story?"

"Taylor could say, 'The pen almost hit him,'" Miriam offered.

"Tell it like a story," I prompted. "How might you begin? With a bit of dialogue? With an action? Story-tell that part."

"Zack ducked as a pen whizzed through the air, right past his ear." Miriam said. "He knew it was Billy, but he was afraid to look back to face him because he didn't want to see the other kids' faces."

"'Stop it!' he said, trying to duck, keeping his eyes focused on his desk." Jorge added.

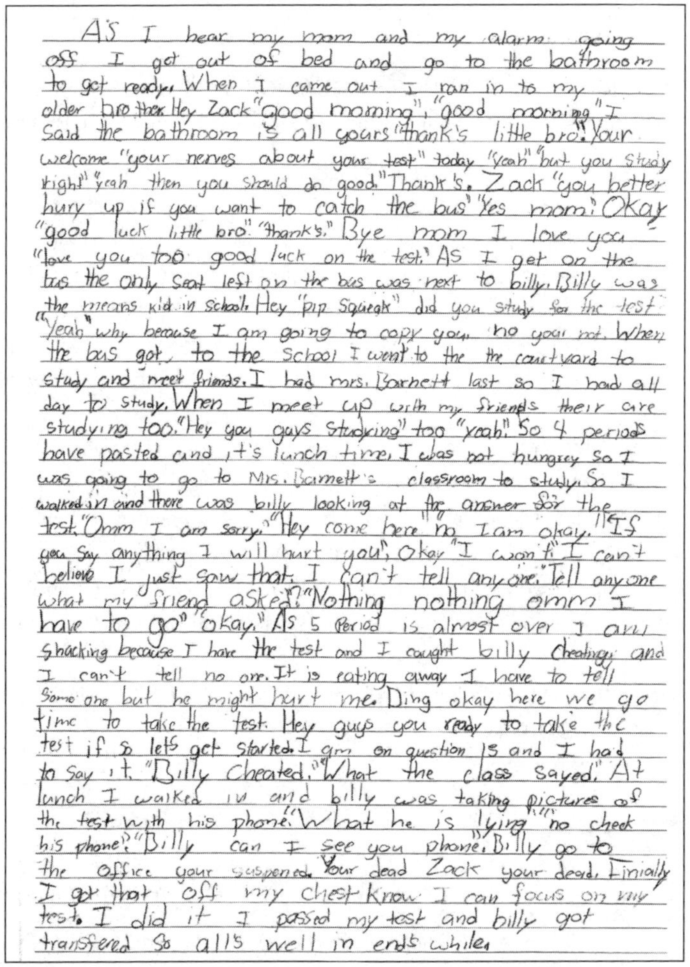

Debrief by reminding writers to show their characters by putting them into action.

"Nice work. I can tell you're getting the picture of this scene. You brought the story from 2-D to 3-D with detailed evidence—with movement, thinking, feelings, and dialogue. I want you to notice that in both my example and Taylor's, actions big and small were great ways to bring the stories to life."

FIG. 6–2 Taylor's first, fast draft approximates some of the ideas others gave him.

Again and again in this series, I take an active role whenever students are trying new work. Never do I say, "It's your turn to try," and then sit back and passively watch what students do. To the contrary, I am constantly assessing and coaching on the fly, helping students rise to the next level. Also critical is the fact that I coach with transferable prompts that students can carry as reminders to any story they might work on next.

LINK

Send students off to work, reminding them of the various components of today's teaching. Remind them that they can draft out of order, beginning with the scene they feel most inspired to write.

"I know that some of you will be meeting with me or with each other during writing time today to talk through your plans for your stories. Others of you will be putting the finishing touches on your plans. Most of you, however, will be moving into drafting. Whether you are drafting today or sometime in the future, I want to remind you that it's always a good idea to start drafting in 3-D," I said, pointing to the new additions on our anchor chart. "Just like the best 3-D films were *filmed* in 3-D (instead of having the 3-D effects added post-production), the strongest stories are *drafted* in 3-D. Writers don't wait until revision to add the evidence that makes the story pop. So get in your evidence now, as you draft. Story-tell, bit by bit, your characters' actions, feelings, descriptions, and thoughts.

"I also want to remind you of something that you may remember from years past. Once you've planned your story, you have the option to draft your story not chronologically, from beginning to end, but scene by scene, starting with the scene you feel especially motivated to write, the moment you think you have the most energy for and can write the best today. This allows you to see a lot of progress quickly, of course, and also keeps you from running out of steam for writing scenes you're not as sure of at this stage. But most importantly, by writing what you know best first, you will have a solid scene that you can use to mentor yourself to your own best work.

"One more thing. Remember to work toward the personal goals you set for yourself yesterday when you used the narrative writing checklists to assess your writing!"

Follow-up is critical. Whenever I ask students to set goals for themselves, I make a note to myself not to let the work drop into oblivion. Similarly, when I hang a chart in the room, I refer to it often. When I ask students to practice something I taught in a conference or small group, I record my teaching, so the next time I work with students I can say, "Show me how you've been practicing X." If I want students to take seriously what I ask them to do, I need to follow up, even if it is with a quick reminder like the one I give here, to work toward their personal goals.

How to Write Compelling Fiction

- Brainstorm a great story idea (think of small moments, places, events, issues, struggles, stories you wish existed in the world).
- Make your *characters* come alive (with traits, wants and challenges, self-attitude, relationships).
- Test-drive your *character* in scenes (envision and write actions, feelings, dialogue, setting, point of view).
- Plot several versions of your story, aiming to intensify the problem (use arcs, timelines, storyboards).
- **Draft a 3-D story (story-tell bit by bit, include evidence of your characters' actions, thoughts, feelings).**

Increasing Tension by Developing Action

A VERY COMMON TENDENCY with student writers is *not* to propel characters into action, whether physical or otherwise. Instead, in many young writers' stories, the characters are observers of the world around them. Stuff happens *to* them, not the other way around. This may be, in part, because so often young writers don't actually feel in control of their *own* worlds. How, then, could they possibly try to exert control over a fictional world? This results in stories that lack not only action, but also tension or drama.

Perhaps one of the best ways to address this issue is explicitly. I have often found with topics such as these that the typical seventh-grade response is denial. "No, there's action," they'll say. "See, here she's picking up a pencil?" To preempt that response, I like to teach the concept of developing tension through action in a small group (as I do below), showing the kids a few explicit ways to increase action, and then having them experiment with how these choices might affect the action in the story. This way, all of the students are in the same boat, and they often help to keep each other honest.

I gathered four students together at an empty table and said, "You all have some very deep and clearly well-cared-for characters. I can feel the importance of these characters in the way you have included the tiniest of details about them in your stories." I paused to let them half-smile. "However, I feel like the one thing we haven't really seen from them is much action. And when there isn't much action, there's not much tension. And as you all know, the best stories have action and conflict. What I'd like to show you are just a few ways to add tension to your stories. By doing this, you should have an easier path toward getting in more action. I got these ideas from a writer who writes for professional writers, Noah Lukeman." I gave each student a half-sheet handout of a quick chart I had created and talked off of it.

Some Ways Writers Can Build Tension in Their Stories

- Increase the obstacles (or the difficulty of the obstacles).
- Make it challenging for the character to act.
- Create a time crunch.
- Raise the character's motivation.
- Add danger.

"There are others, of course. And I can tell from talking to you now that you have more ideas. But I'm sure you can imagine how any one of these could be built up a bit in a story in a way that would then create not only more tension, but also more action."

Gobin jumped in, "Yeah, like how in my story, Philip is playing an online video game tournament. And there's a lot of action on the screen. But not a lot in real life."

"Are you imagining a way to increase tension, and maybe add some action to boot?" I asked.

"Yeah. I was thinking I could do two things. I could make it that there's a little sister or somebody who interrupts his playing all the time. Maybe she's threatening to turn the console off. So she would be running around and he would have to stop playing to chase her." The other kids in the group nodded. "And maybe the mom could be yelling that he only has fifteen more minutes or something," added Ali. "That would create a time crunch."

"Excellent ideas," I chimed in. "Do you think you are all ready to give this a shot with your own writing?" The group nodded. "Okay, why don't you all stay here and get started on this work. Feel free to use these strategies, and each other, as resources."

"Can I get everyone's eyes up here?" Once everyone was looking, I said, "I noticed that almost all of you are doing a fantastic job making sure that you are writing in scenes that bring the drama to life, being sure to story-tell, bit by bit—to include action and dialogue, and thinking, too.

"But it's also true that sometimes fiction writers need to write summaries, as well as drawn-out scenes. Sometimes writers can move a character across space or time with just a sentence or two. They can cover a bunch of events that happened in just a short paragraph. Can everyone direct your eyes to the board?"

I projected a piece of the mentor text, "Thirteen and a Half." "Look with me at this excerpt from 'Thirteen and a Half.' Notice the places where Rachel Vail decides to write in scene, story-telling the action, bit by bit, and when she writes in summary, taking the characters across space or time with just a sentence or two. Tell your partner where you see scenes and where you see summary, and why you think Rachel Vail made those decisions."

"What do you want for a snack?" asked Ashley.

I didn't know.

Ashley climbed up onto one of the counters and opened a cabinet. "Let's have Mallomars," she said. "I think you can tell a lot about a person by the way she eats Mallomars, don't you?"

She brought down the box, and held it open for me to choose one. I picked one in the center of the back row, wondering what that revealed about me. She took one from the far right front and said, "Come on and meet my bird, Sweet Pea. Did I tell you I've had him since I turned three?"

My Mallomar was melting a little on my fingers as I hurried to keep up with Ashley, around corners and then up, up, up a steep flight of stairs with dark red carpeting worn out in the center of each step. My house is just regular.

"Sweet Pea is a budgie," Ashley was explaining. "People think that's the same as a parakeet, but it's not. Budgies are slightly larger and much more exotic. Do you like exotic animals?"

"Um," I said.

"I got Sweet Pea when I was three years old and though tragically he never learned to talk people-language, he is still able to communicate, at least to me. I can tell his chirps apart. You'll see. This is my brother's room—don't go there," she warned, indicating a closed door. "This is the bathroom—do you have to go?"

"No."

"OK. Tell me when you do."

I took a bite of my Mallomar, maybe revealing that I was a hungry type of person.

(continues)

Ashley gripped a doorknob on a tall white door. "And this—this is my room."

The students turned and talked. I listened in and then gathered them back, inviting students to share what they discovered about summaries and storytelling.

"The part where Ashley's on the counter, getting the Mallomars and talking about them is all in scene," Miriam said. "There's a lot of information we learn about Ashley and her bird, and it's definitely better to get it with dialogue and action."

"And, I was saying to my partner," Ali jumped in, "that one part that was summarizing was, 'My Mallomar was melting a little on my fingers as I hurried to keep up with Ashley, around corners and then up, up, up a steep flight of stairs with dark red carpeting worn out in the center of each step. My house is just regular.'" Ali read from the text. "We thought that was because we didn't need to see every little step, or hear the whole conversation. The author just wanted to get us to the room."

"I've added this tip about knowing when to use summaries to our anchor chart," I said, pointing to the new bullet. "A wise writing teacher named Barry Lane once said that fiction writers 'explode the moment and shrink a century.' Keep that in mind as you draft today."

How to Write Compelling Fiction

- Brainstorm a great story idea (think of small moments, places, events, issues, struggles, stories you wish existed in the world).
- Make your characters come alive (with traits, wants and challenges, self-attitude, relationships).
- Test-drive your character in scenes (envision and write actions, feelings, dialogue, setting, point of view).
- Plot several versions of your story, aiming to intensify the problem (use arcs, timelines, storyboards).
- Draft a 3-D story (story-tell bit by bit, include evidence of your characters' actions, thoughts, feelings).
- **Manage space and time**
  - **Use summary to quickly move a character across space and time.**

Using Transitional Phrases to Signify Passage of Time or Change in Place, or to Summarize Parts of the Story

"WRITERS, some of you are starting to get the hang of how to move seamlessly from scene to summary to scene again. You know when to slow down, story-telling in 3-D, and when to get the character—and reader—to move quickly from one moment in time or place to another. If you're still not sure how to do this—or even if you are—I want to remind you that transitional phrases are a helpful tool to make these *transitions*. Take a look at some of these you've learned in past years." I projected a short list.

Transitional Phrases

All of a sudden

And suddenly

Afterward

Meanwhile

"Can you help me grow this list? Take a second to think what other phrases would help you to move your characters and story, quickly through time or to a new place—or to summarize a part of your story. Put your thumb up when you have a suggestion."

With the students' help, soon our list looked like this:

Transitional Phrases

All of a sudden

And suddenly

Afterward

Meanwhile

The next day

That night

Last year

Earlier that day

After what seemed like forever

In the distance

To the left/right

On the other side

If only

"Nice job, writers. I will add this bit about transitional words to our anchor chart. I want to point out something here, and that's that not only did you include transitional phrases or words that take the action *forward* in time, but you also included some that take you *backward*, like *earlier that day*, and *last year*. Time doesn't always move linearly in stories. Sometimes action is recalled, or characters have memories that provide important information for the reader."

How to Write Compelling Fiction

- Brainstorm a great story idea (think of small moments, places, events, issues, struggles, stories you wish existed in the world).
- Make your characters come alive (with traits, wants and challenges, self-attitude, relationships).
- Test-drive your character in scenes (envision and write actions, feelings, dialogue, setting, point of view).
- Plot several versions of your story, aiming to intensify the problem (use arcs, timelines, storyboards).
- Draft a 3-D story (story-tell bit by bit, include evidence of your characters' actions, thoughts, feelings).
- Manage space and time
  - Use summary to quickly move a character across space and time.
  - **Use transitional words and phrases to show changes in time or place.**

SESSION 6 HOMEWORK

USING TRANSITIONAL WORDS AND PHRASES

"Tonight, as you work on your drafts, see if you can play around with transitional words and phrases. Try these on for size. Experiment with when and how in your stories you move from summary to scene and from one place or time to another—either in the action itself or in your characters' heads. And as you do this, pay attention to which parts of your story feel important to stretch out—which parts make you want to slow down and story-tell, bit by bit—and which you think are better told as summary. Tomorrow we'll be focusing on when it's especially key to slow a story down."

Stepping into the Drama of the Story to Draft

IN THIS SESSION, you'll teach students that fiction writers create their best drafts when they experience the world through their characters' skin, letting the story unfold as it happens to them, and highlighting the most meaningful parts of the story.

GETTING READY

✔ Example of a familiar text, such as "Thirteen and a Half," in which students have probably experienced "becoming" the character (see Teaching)

✔ Current lead for the class story, written on chart paper or projected for the class (see Teaching)

✔ Current story arc chart for the class story (see Teaching)

✔ Idea for a scene for the class story that you can use to demonstrate writing by pretending to be the character (see Active Engagement)

✔ "How to Craft Compelling Fiction" anchor chart (see Link and Homework) ✎

✔ "Writing Critique Group Protocol" chart (see Conferring and Small-Group Work)

✔ A passage from "Thirteen and a Half" or whatever published story you are using to demonstrate using paragraphing for dramatic effect (see Share) ✎

COMMON CORE STATE STANDARDS: W.7.3a, W.7.5, W.7.10, RL.7.2, RL.7.3, RL.7.10, SL.7.1, SL.7.2, L.7.1, L.7.2, L.7.3

E ARLIER IN THE UNIT, we emphasized the fact that writers rarely sit down before the blank page, think up an idea, and then magically produce a story. To the contrary, we emphasized the need to *plan*. To pause and plod and reflect and revise before diving into a draft. Today, then, may come as a surprise, because today, we say, "Actually, magic *does* happen."

In this session, you will try to convey to students the experience of losing oneself in a draft. You will teach them that there comes a time when, rather than pausing to study classroom charts or continuums, rather than pausing to re-envision a particular scene or sequence of events, rather than pausing to check in with a writing partner or a mentor text, writers just write—long and fast.

"Walking in the character's shoes allows writers to record the story as it happens."

One way we lose ourselves in a story—whether it is one we are reading or one we are writing—is by empathizing with the characters, so much so that we walk in their shoes, feel their feelings, think their thoughts. As readers, this keeps us turning the page. As writers, this keeps our pens moving. Walking in a character's shoes allows writers to record the story *as it happens*, to let the story flow from the pen almost without thinking. Teach students to write with their plans in mind, to write with the intention of facing increasingly challenging obstacles and overcoming some of those challenges to experience relief of some kind. But essentially, to let their stories write themselves.

Stepping into the Drama of the Story to Draft

CONNECTION

Celebrate that your students have begun bringing their stories and characters to life.

"Writing fiction it's a rather amazing process, isn't it? You plan, list, choose, sketch—then suddenly it's as if everything has just taken on a life of its own. I don't know if any of you have had that strange feeling of characters speaking and acting in ways that surprise you, even as you are writing them with your very own hand. Yes, you have your plans, but they seem to have gone further than you could ever imagine. This is the magical power of writing fiction. At some point, your stories take you by the hand and drag you along for the ride."

Name the teaching point.

"Today what I want to teach you is this: before writers get going on a draft, they think a lot about ways to make a draft into a really good story. But once they're in the midst of the story, they try to lose themselves in it. They *become* the characters, and writing is a bit like a drama, happening to them."

TEACHING

Remind students of the experience they have as readers, of losing themselves in a story, becoming the character.

"You all know how, when you read, you feel almost like you *become* Katniss or Ponyboy or Melanin Sun or the narrator in 'Thirteen and a Half?' You read the words and suddenly you are that girl kneeling in the dirt next to her classmate at a bird funeral. You know what she's thinking as she awkwardly waits, her legs going numb. You hardly need the words of the story to tell you that the girl is going to step up and say just the right words to help Ashley feel better."

Tell students that readers can more easily walk in the shoes of a character if the writer has done this first.

"Readers can do that. They can read words on the page and suddenly be in the shoes of the character because *writers* first do the same. In a book called *The Stuff of Fiction*, Gerald Brace (1972) says it this way":

 COACHING

Ray Bradbury once said, "First, find out what your hero wants, then just follow him!" Obviously, this is easier said than done. The message, though, is at the heart of this session. Today the goal is that students will go for it—that they will follow their main character, letting the story they've spent days planning flow from their imaginations and onto the page. Later, they'll have time to revise. Today, though, is about fast-drafting. It's about letting themselves go, letting their pens fly, letting their imaginations soar.

Whenever possible, I suggest you make the connection between reading and writing explicit for your students. For one thing, making connections helps with transference by sending the message that what we learn and do in one context has relevance in others. For another, making connections allows for deeper understanding as students experience the same concept from multiple angles and perspectives.

It is not enough for a writer to tell us about a person or a place; he must give us the illusion of being the person ourselves . . . the basic failure in much writing is the failure of the writer's imagination: he is not with it . . . not trying hard enough to live from moment to moment in the very skin of his characters.

"As writers, you need to try to do this work—to live in your characters' skins as you draft their stories!"

Demonstrate how you go from envisioning to enacting to drafting, using the shared class story.

"And so today I'm going to reread the latest lead to our Esmerelda story, and as I do so, I'll try to put myself into her skin. In the lead we've settled on, Esmerelda is already at the party. I revised it a bit since you last saw it. Today I'm not going to be rethinking the lead so much as writing more. To do that, I'm going to pretend to *be* Esmerelda." I reread the latest draft, written on chart paper:

> I was finally at the party I wanted so badly to be at. Yet, there I was, sitting on the floor next to the television that was blaring some reality show. I couldn't make out anything that was being said on the show because the stereo was also blasting. All of the sudden I heard a crash. I looked away from the tv just in time to see a kid, I think from my science class, pick himself off the floor.
>
> "Who's next?" he asked. He gestured to the couch. "I am," another guy said and hopped up to stand on the back of the couch, balancing on his toes. "1-2-3" the crowd called. All at once the new kid, who I didn't recognize, jumped off the couch and landed with a thud on the coffee table.

"I'm going to keep in mind that the next dot on the story arc says, 'She goes into another room only to hear a few people gossiping about one of her friends,'" I said, referring to the chart showing the story arc.

"But mostly I'm just going to try to be Esmerelda." I picked up my pen and began scrawling on the paper, saying aloud the words as I wrote. Then I stopped and said, "I just now made up the idea that Esmerelda was sitting there trying to fit into the conversation when the other kids started talking about her friend. I have no idea what, exactly, will happen next, so I'll reread what I just wrote and just let something come to me."

Soon I added (and voiced) this scene:

> "I mean, did you see what Tilly wore tonight?" Liz snorted. "No one wears that color anymore."
>
> I just sat quietly on the edge of the chair. I didn't think I even knew what Tilly was wearing. I never paid attention to those sorts of things.
>
> Another girl, I didn't know her name, rolled her eyes, "She's always wearing and saying and doing the wrong things. It's like she doesn't care what people think."

"Let your story move as naturally and as easily as possible," Shirley Jackson urges young writers in *"Notes from a Young Writer"* (Come Along with Me, 1995). *"Suppose you are writing a story about a boy and a girl meeting on a corner; your reader wants to go to that very corner and listen in; if, instead you start your boy and girl toward the corner and then go off into a long description of the streetcar tracks and a little discussion of the background of those two characters—you will lose your reader and your story will fall apart."*

I was shocked. They had to know I was friends with Tilly. We ate lunch together everyday and, if she hadn't been late to the party, we would have been sitting together. Why would they talk about my friend in front of me?

Recap specific tips you hope students gleaned from the demonstration.

"Writers, do you see that when you write—when any fiction writer writes—you keep in mind the big plan for how a story will probably go, but you let the details emerge from the specific, exact actions the characters take? Usually, our scenes involve two or three characters, and one does or says something and then the next one reacts."

ACTIVE ENGAGEMENT

Set students up to extend the class story by putting themselves into the unfolding scene. Then call on one set of partners and add their work to the class story.

"To continue writing our Esmerelda story, you need to *be* Esmerelda, sitting uncomfortably in a room with people you thought you wanted to be friends with, but now you're not so sure. You need to keep in mind that Esmerelda really wants the people at the party to like her. But, on the other hand, she is also very loyal to her friend who has stuck with her.

"Right now, pretend *you are* Esmerelda. Picture her. She's sitting all awkwardly in that chair while these people she wanted so desperately to be a part of are acting like jerks. What does Esmerelda do? (Remember—actions matter, not just talk.) Turn and tell your partner the next bit of the story." To get them started, I reiterated the last scene:

> I was shocked. They had to know I was friends with Tilly. We ate lunch together everyday and, if she wasn't late to the party, we would have been sitting together. Why would they talk about my friend in front of me?

As students talked with their partners, I scaffolded their work with transferable prompts. "*Be* the character. Actually, put yourself in this scene, act it out. Then describe the character's tiny actions in writing." And, "Don't summarize. Slow down the scene so we can see exactly what the character is doing, feeling, thinking." Soon I called on one partnership and added this to the story:

> Suddenly, I wished that I wasn't in the room anymore. I decided, as impossible as it might sound, to try to sneak out of the room without anyone noticing. I stood up, and as I did, somehow knocked my chair over. Now they were staring at me.

"I bet you didn't plan for Esmerelda to knock over that chair. I bet it just happened as you put yourself in her shoes and reacted to what was happening around her. That is the beauty of 'being your character.' The story will often just pour out of you in ways that bring your character and the scene perfectly to life."

Because this is Day Two of drafting, whatever you teach should arise from your informal assessments of their drafts in progress. Very likely, you will find that many students are largely summarizing rather than writing in scenes, in which case you'll probably want to teach a minilesson like this one that focuses on "showing, not telling." You'll notice as I model and then coach students that "being the character" is really another way to slow a story down and write it bit by bit. So if another more pressing issue than "show, not tell" rises to the surface as your students begin to draft, you may choose another focus for your teaching today.

LINK

Remind students that drafting is a form of acting on the page, and send them off.

"Writers, I want to remind you that writing is a lot like drama. Once you've written your lead, you need to reread it and become the main character. You need to stand in the character's shoes, to see through her eyes, to blush with her, and to hope with her. This way your readers will also be able to experience the story you put onto the page."

How to Write Compelling Fiction

- Brainstorm a great story idea (think of small moments, places, events, issues, struggles, stories you wish existed in the world).
- Make your characters come alive (with traits, wants and challenges, self-attitude, relationships).
- Test-drive your character in scenes (envision and write actions, feelings, dialogue, setting, point of view).
- Plot several versions of your story, aiming to intensify the problem (use arcs, timelines, storyboards).
- Draft a 3-D story (story-tell bit by bit, include evidence of your characters' actions, thoughts, feelings).
- Manage space and time.
  - Use summary to quickly move a character across space and time.
  - Use transitional words and phrases to show changes in time or place.
- **Become the main character, living through the drama of the story—and then allow your writing to unfold.**

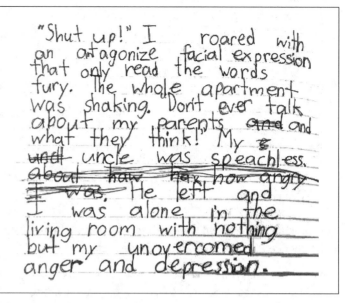

FIG. 7–1 Gabriel uses evidence, a strategy from the previous lesson, to bring drama to his story.

Teaching Students How to Work within Critique Groups

ONE OF THE STRUCTURES that has been instrumental in my development as a writer is belonging to writing critique groups, changing groups only a few times, for over two decades. We meet on a regular basis, usually weekly, and share our writing with each other. Each member gives and receives feedback and support. There is something different in a small group doing this work because it's not just a discussion between one writer and one reader, but rather a group of readers who can give feedback, providing a great opportunity for richer conversations. Of course, being a participating member of a writing group wasn't something I naturally knew how to do when I started. It was something I learned how to do by observing, receiving, and giving responses in a group over time. It is also something you can teach to your students.

You might, of course, opt to teach your entire class how to give and receive feedback in small groups. But, this early in the year, it might be wise to just choose a couple of groups of students who could be your proverbial test balloons. You might choose two partnerships that seem to be already working very well and put them together in a group of four, or else pay close attention to interactions during minilessons and other talk opportunities to see who has complementary skill sets and personalities.

Once I pulled my group, Miriam, Taylor, Jada, and Javi, together I said, "A lot of famous writers say they are better writers because they belong to a writing critique group: John Green, Laurie Halse Anderson, Jacqueline Woodson, and Linda Sue Park, to name a few. Writing groups offer their members critique, as well as support. They give the writer a fresh set of eyes on their work, so the writer can get a better sense of what's working and what's not. They also can help the writer problem solve if there are tricky parts in their stories." I could tell Taylor was interested, mainly because he likes anything that smacks of possible fame.

The rest of the students looked interested but not overjoyed. I continued on. "Most writing groups follow a ritual of sorts. I thought I would take the liberty to write down the one I use with my adult writing group." I held up a small chart.

Writing Critique Group Protocol

1. Each member has a turn sharing his or her work.
2. The person sharing reads his or her piece, or an excerpt of the piece, out loud.
3. Members of the group take turns giving feedback.
   a. They start with specific compliments.
   b. They offer tips or suggestions to improve the writing.
4. The writer jots down notes and asks questions in response to the member's feedback.
5. The writer thanks the group.
6. The next writer takes a turn.

"There are a couple of areas that might be tricky. It can be nerve-wracking to share your writing, and some people are very sensitive to other people's comments. So, for the writer it's good to take notes on what people say so you won't forget what was said, but also to know that you don't have to take *everybody's* advice. When you are the one giving feedback, it's important to remember that the best compliments are the most specific ones. Instead of saying, 'It was funny,' I would try to say something more specific, such as, 'The situations you put your characters in are so absurd that they are funny. I can completely picture them, and they are so odd they make me laugh!' Also, while suggestions are important, and you can certainly use the tools in this room (charts, checklists, mentor texts) to come up with tips, a gentle hand goes a long way.

"Does this sound like something you might want to try?" Miriam smiled. The rest nodded. "Before you begin, it might also help for you to think if there's anything in particular you'd like the group to listen for that you'd like feedback on. If not, that's fine, but it can help the members of your group to give more useful feedback if they have a lens to look through."

I stepped away from the group and watched them arrange themselves. Then I planted myself nearby to listen in and swoop in to give quick tips if needed. I knew that if this group was successful, a buzz might form, and before too long, I would have many critique groups helping each other to develop and improve their writing exponentially.

MID-WORKSHOP TEACHING

Creating Patterns as a Means of Cohesion

"Seventh-graders, I need to stop you for just a quick minute," I said, disrupting the almost-silence, save for the soft music playing in the background. "I know so many of you are just filling up page after page of writing as you draft your scenes. I am so excited about that. One thing, though, that might be easier to start considering now, rather than later, is the idea of how to create cohesion in your pieces. That is, how do writers make sure the various pieces of their stories feel connected and integrated—cohesive? I know you all know about transition words. But another way you might consider doing this work of cohesion is through creating interconnected patterns throughout your stories. For example, let's look again at Samee's story. I want you to notice as we look at it how he mentions certain names and details often so that the pieces of the scene all fit together."

"Hey Jimmy, want to play tag?" "Sure, why not?" I replied. We joined a group of other kids getting ready. It was a beautiful day outside and I felt more excited than any other old recess period. Today was unusual though. I wasn't bored today. Today was a day that I didn't play with my best friend, Carter. I'm sure he wouldn't mind me just hanging out with a couple of friends just this once. "Tag, you're it!" some kid exclaimed to me. I ran and chased people as fast as I could. I saw Carter walk outside. He looked at me in a strange manner as I ran and jumped past people who were it. He stomped infuriatingly to a moldy corner and started to do his math homework. A fairly shorter kid walked up to him.

"Want to jump some rope? I'm sure it'll be fun." "Leave me alone!" Carter shouted back. Many kids stared at him. I'd never seen him act like this before. Slowly, everyone went back to what they were doing. I was worried about Carter but I left him alone, worried he would throw a tantrum.

FIG. 7–2 In this scene, Samee works to show cohesion by repeating certain words, actions, and ideas.

Paragraphing to Structure Fiction

"I WAS TALKING TO YASMIN TODAY about her draft, and one thing she noticed was that the way she organized her paragraphs, how she broke them up, helped focus attention on different parts of her work. She noticed that placing information about one part of a setting in one paragraph—like her description of her room—then breaking off into another paragraph to describe a new part of that setting—like the snowglobe—helped to highlight different aspects of this setting and this scene. It also helped to move the story along. Yasmin also noticed that if she really wanted certain ideas or moments to go together for the reader, it helped to keep them all in one paragraph."

"After talking to Yasmin, I started peering over your shoulders, noticing specifically how each of you was paragraphing—and what techniques you were trying that others could try too—and I noticed that Yasmin was not only using transitional phrases to move her story from one place or time to another, but she was also using paragraphs to do that. (See Figure 7–3.)

"For example, here, she wrote:"

Forcing myself to get up and do something productive. Sighing, I slowly lifted up my duvet savoring the warmth beneath my sheets. I stood up slowly heading to my dresser.

I took the snow globe that sat on the corner of my dresser immediately turning the round object upside down. I reached into the broken rubber base pulling out my silver key. I took my time getting to my closet. Inserting the key into the keyhole and then twisting the knob. I sighed relief washing through me as hi scent filled my nose.

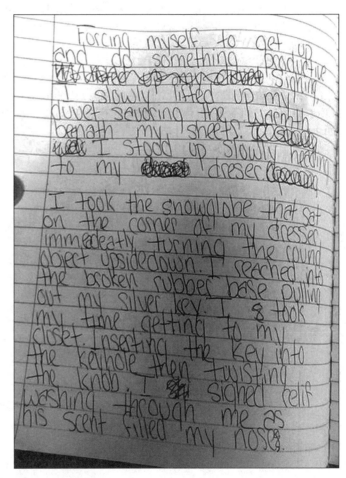

FIG. 7–3 Yasmin works at using paragraphs to help structure her draft.

"There's another way that fiction writers use paragraphs to great effect, and that's for dramatic impact. Take a look at this passage from 'Thirteen and a Half,' and you'll see what I mean."

> *Ashley started sobbing again.*
>
> *"Maybe I should call my mom," I whispered.*
>
> *"Don't leave!" screamed Ashley.*
>
> *So I didn't.*

"The lines of dialogue are indented to indicate a new person is speaking, but do you see how the last line, 'So I didn't,' is set off, with no real reason for it to be? That is Rachel Vail's way of creating a dramatic impact. Here, she is showing that the narrator is really there for this kid Ashley—someone she doesn't know well, whose own mother has, in a way, not been there for her. This is a big moment in the story, so Rachel Vail shows this by setting it off as its own paragraph. You can try this too, in your stories. It's another way to structure key parts."

How to Write Compelling Fiction

- Brainstorm a great story idea (think of small moments, places, events, issues, struggles, stories you wish existed in the world).
- Make your characters come alive (with traits, wants and challenges, self-attitude, relationships).
- Test-drive your character in scenes (envision and write actions, feelings, dialogue, setting, point of view).
- Plot several versions of your story, aiming to intensify the problem (use arcs, timelines, storyboards).
- Draft a 3-D story (story-tell bit by bit, include evidence of your characters' actions, thoughts, feelings).
- Manage space and time.
  - Use summary to quickly move a character across space and time.
  - Use transitional words and phrases to show changes in time or place.
- Become the main character, living through the drama of the story—and then allow your writing to unfold.
- **Use paragraphs wisely (to move in place and time, to highlight something, for dramatic impact).**

SESSION 7 HOMEWORK

APPLYING PARAGRAPHING MOVES TO HELP ORGANIZE YOUR STORY

"Writers, for homework tonight, could you make a point of looking at your draft through the lens of paragraphs? See if you're using your paragraphs as a tool for organization, letting them help you separate some things and connect others. If you find yourself having a hard time imagining how that would go, look at a mentor text and study its paragraphing moves."

Studying Published Texts to Write Leads

STARTING IN THE EARLIER GRADES, we teach students a repertoire of strategies for crafting leads. But we also teach them to craft *many* leads for a single piece. We show students the importance of trying on this lead, then that lead, much like someone might try on various pairs of shoes or ties when searching for the perfect way to present an outfit. Even when a lead seems "just fine," we push students to write anew, until they create the lead that shines. The Common Core State Standards assert that seventh-graders should "engage and orient the reader by establishing a context and point of view and introducing a narrator and/or characters" (CCSS W.7.3.a). In line with this standard, we teach students to draw from their repertoire of strategies as they draft many leads, until they unearth the one that beckons to readers and sets them on the proper course.

Students need to consider two things when writing leads. On the one hand, they must bear in mind the larger context. Students must ask themselves, "What do my readers need to know early on? How might I orient them in my first few sentences?" At the same time, they must attend to craft. Students must ask themselves, "How might I write these opening sentences in a way that grabs my readers' attention? What strategies do I have at my disposal for writing with beauty and power?"

We ask students to revise their leads before forging ahead with the rest of the draft for two reasons. First, re-envisioning an opening paragraph allows students to re-envision the larger context—to imagine various courses their stories might take before settling on one. And second, it is much easier to revise the course of a piece from the beginning than it is to revise after churning out pages of writing.

In this session, you will turn to published authors to teach and inspire. For a writer, beginning strong does more than just lure in readers. Beginning strong buoys writers to keep writing well. And so you turn students' attention to favorite leads with the intention of stirring their hearts and setting them off with a soaring start.

IN THIS SESSION, you'll teach students that writers draw from their repertoire of strategies for writing effective leads, especially ones that allude to important events and lessons that will unfold. You will also remind students that writers reread literature to learn techniques for writing.

GETTING READY

✔ The lead of a story other than "Thirteen and a Half." Here we use the lead to "Ribbons" by Lawrence Yep. (see Teaching)

✔ The lead of "Thirteen and a Half" or of whatever story you and your class are using as your mentor text (see Active Engagement)

✔ Chart paper and markers (see Active Engagement)

✔ A student's writing to analyze the lead (see Active Engagement)

✔ "How to Write Compelling Fiction" anchor chart (see Link and Mid-Workshop Teaching) 🌀

COMMON CORE STATE STANDARDS: W.7.3.a,d; W.7.4, W.7.7, RL.7.3, RL.7.4, RL.7.10, SL.7.1, L.7.1, L.7.2, L.7.3, L.7.6

Studying Published Texts to Write Leads

CONNECTION

Celebrate that students have begun their stories, and do so by conveying the essence of a couple of stories to the class.

"Writers, something extraordinary is happening in this classroom. Stories are coming to life in your drafts. You need to know each other's stories!

"You need to know that in Annabelle's story, the main character, Lily, is developing the strength to become the kind of leader she believes would be worthy of student council. Then there is Samee's bullying story with a twist—his main character's bully used to be his best friend! I could go on and on—each of you are writing such individualized stories in such incredible ways. If you get some free time, you should ask to read each other's drafts. And not just in this class! All the seventh-grade classes are doing fantastic work on fiction."

Here, you highlight the learning that can happen within a writing community. Your message in this connection is that your seventh-graders can learn as much from their peers' work as they can learn from your work, or from a published demonstration text. This is an important reminder that you'll want to make again and again.

❖ **Name the teaching point.**

"Today I want to teach you that just when writers are most fired up to write—when they have just written their lead—they force themselves to pause. They review what they've written, and they revise it. They revise the lead because by doing so, they revise their entire story. Sometimes they do this with help from a pro."

TEACHING

Tell students that to write leads that draw readers into a story, it helps to study the leads published authors have written.

"You already know that the beginning of a piece of writing, any piece of writing, is called a *lead* because this opening is the way an author *leads* readers into the text. The lead entices people to walk through the doorway and into the story.

"I often think that leads are one of the most important things for writers to work on when they revise, because a lead is what ushers readers through the door and gets them to read the rest of the story. That said, you might be saying to yourself, 'Well, that's all well and good, but how do I create a great lead?'

Notice the concrete image this description conveys. My hope is that down the line, whenever students are writing fiction and they recollect what they know about leads, they'll recall a bit of text leading the way through a door and will understand the importance of those opening lines to a story. Notice, too, that here I try to capture a term and a bit of teaching students have likely learned in prior years in a novel way. This keeps the instruction fresh while reinforcing the skill.

"Of course, you know how to answer that! When you want to learn how to do something, you can study texts written by authors you admire. After you look really closely at exactly how other authors pull something off, you can try the same techniques in your own writing."

Tell the class about the experience one student had studying the leads of familiar stories. Read one aloud, listing what the student noticed about it and then showing the resulting revisions in her own lead.

"Miriam was trying to figure this out the other day, so she decided to study the leads of some stories she knows well. First, she reread the lead to Lawrence Yep's short story, 'Ribbons.' It starts like this:

> The sunlight swept over the broad grassy square, across the street, and onto our living-room rug. In that bright, warm rectangle of light, I practiced my ballet. Ian, my little brother, giggled and dodged around me while I did exercises.
>
> A car stopped outside, and Ian rushed to the window. "She's here! She's here!" he shouted excitedly. "Paw-paw's here!" Paw-paw is Chinese for grandmother—for "mother's mother."

"Looking at this story reminded Miriam of things she'd learned earlier: it often helps to start with the exact words one character is saying (or with a small action); and, in a short story, it's important to start close to the main event. If there's a waterfall in the story, start when you can hear the falls. The main tension in this story revolves around Grandmother and Stacy. Notice that the lead of the story hints at what will come later."

Set the class up to listen to and then talk with a partner about what one student did as she wrote her lead.

"Here's Miriam's first lead—the one she was inspired to write after reading 'Ribbons' and thinking about what she already knows about leads (see Figure 8–1)."

> It was a normal day in the life of Maya Young Winters (me). I had had a loud noisy breakfast which included two twin sisters screaming as my mother brushed their hair, a dog howling for a piece of bacon and my father, putting ketchup on toast like it was a normal thing to do. Then I'd left at promptly 7:27 to catch my bus. I'd laughed at Anna Lou's bad jokes, gotten through homeroom, first and second period and lunch with my posse of friends: May, Luna, and Ruby. Then around came sixth period.
>
> Ms. Gulch was my science teacher and even her name was terrible.

Science fiction and horror writer F. Paul Wilson has said, "I don't know how it is with other writers, but most of the time when I finish [reading] a story or novel, I may be pleased, I may even be impressed, but somewhere in the back of my mind I'm thinking, 'I can do that.'" The act of apprenticing oneself to a respected and more experienced practitioner is an age-old tradition.

FIG. 8–1 Miriam's first attempt at a lead for her story

ACTIVE ENGAGEMENT

Share a second lead, this time asking the class to work with a partner to list what they notice about the lead that all of them could try.

"Then Miriam looked at a second lead, this time from Rachel Vail's 'Thirteen and a Half.' She was pretty sure this story would teach more techniques, so she read it really closely. Reread it with me now, and think, 'What has Vail done that we can learn from?'"

> *All I knew about Ashley before I went over there yesterday was that until this year she went to private school and now she sits next to me in math. But she asked me over and since I couldn't think of a good no, I said OK.*
>
> *Ashley lives near school, so we walked. We didn't have a lot to talk about on the way, but she didn't seem to mind. She was telling me that when she grows up she wants to be a veterinarian and a movie star, and travel all over the world very glamorously and live life to the hilt. She asked if I like to live life to the hilt.*
>
> *"I mostly just hang around," I admitted.*
>
> *"But when you get older, and you can do anything," she whispered, as we began climbing the steep steps up to her huge stone house. "What do you like to imagine?"*
>
> *I was a little winded from the steps, so I just shrugged.*
>
> *"Like, I am constantly imagining I can fly," said Ashley, spreading her arms wide. "Do you ever imagine you're flying?"*
>
> *I stopped for breath. "I sometimes imagine I'm in a bakery."*

"Vail's used lots of techniques here; the way in which she's crafted the lead is one we could examine and talk about for hours. So let's reread it again. As you listen this time, pay attention to what part of the lead stands out for you, and then when I finish reading it, turn and point out that part to your partner. Name what Vail has done that you could emulate."

I reread the lead and reminded the students of what they each needed to do in their own minds. After giving them a moment or two of silence, I asked, "Ready?" and when they nodded yes, I directed them to share with a partner, and listened in as they talked.

Notice that when teaching strategies, I am careful to describe each step in a sequence. I don't simply suggest that students "talk about what they can learn from this author." Instead, to set them up to make a reading-writing connection, I list the steps they will follow, so that the process is clear and replicable.

Convene students to talk as a group about what they noticed in the lead, and insert your own questions and observations to lift the level of talk.

After a moment, I said, "Who can get us started on a conversation about the techniques Rachel Vail has used in her lead?"

"It has less dialogue. The dialogue starts later down the lead," Yasmin offered.

"Hmm, . . . that's interesting," I said, looking at the text. "That's a sharp thing to notice. Do you also see that if there's *less* talk, there is *more* of something else?" I asked. Then I named the larger principle.

"Writers, when I try to learn from other authors, I push myself to name what a writer *has* done, not just what he or she *hasn't* done, because it's easier to emulate something positive. What *did* Vail do instead of writing lots of dialogue?"

"She introduces the characters?" Gabriel asked.

"She shows the narrator's thoughts and a bit of her personality," Annabelle added. "Well, actually, we learn more about Ashley, but it's mostly through the narrator's thoughts as she walks with Ashley up her steps."

"And Vail also gives us information about Ashley's house. It's a huge stone house, and since the narrator is a little winded from the steps, we know the steps are either really big or else there are a lot of them, which is something that's not spelled out," Samee said.

"This author does some subtle work with the setting right away, so that the reader needs to infer here," I confirmed, providing Samee with the words he seemed to be reaching for. "But also, even before we see the house, as Annabelle mentioned, we see the narrator, walking alongside Ashley, a person the narrator doesn't know very well. It's not the author who describes the setting, is it? It's the narrator who notices it. And what do you make of the huge house with the big (or endless) steps? Why did the author write the setting in such a way that there is a mention of how big and fancy Ashley's house is right from the start?"

Set students up to repeat this work, this time as partnerships, and then share some of their observations.

"Try this again, but this time, instead of a class conversation, talk with your partner. Try to push yourselves to name what Rachel Vail has done in this lead."

After a couple minutes, I convened the class, and a few kids shared.

José said, "I think there is action, but it is really only them walking and the narrator heading up the steps. It's not like big exciting action."

Inviting a student to launch a whole-class conversation during the active engagement, rather than simply retelling what I hear students discuss, is unusual. Because the teaching component of this minilesson was brief, I saved enough time for this, knowing that my goal was not only to share students' thinking, but to challenge them to reach for more precise, sophisticated ways of talking about the process of writing.

Jada jumped in, "Yeah, I agree with José, but I think some stories start by showing or creating a mood. That's what this lead does because we get that it's meant to be funny."

"And flying is mentioned," Samee added. "Which, when we first read it, I didn't pay much attention to, but now I know it connects to a major theme in the story. So I guess you could say that the author also hints at something about theme in her lead."

"You've noticed a lot of techniques!" I said, as I jotted a list on a sheet of chart paper:

Techniques for Crafting Leads

- Sometimes stories begin not with a big action but with a small action, which can be against the backdrop of a setting, like when the narrator climbs up the tall steps to Ashley's house.
- Some stories begin by conveying a mood, and only afterward does the sequence of actions begin.
- Sometimes the time and the place are revealed slowly, bit by bit, as the character sees or moves into the setting.
- Some stories foreshadow a central theme or idea by including a telling image, piece of dialogue, or action.

Channel students to use what they notice an author has done in order to help one student revise her lead again.

"Let's all listen again to Miriam's first lead and think whether the techniques we've learned from Vail could help her as she gets ready to revise this lead. Listen again, then tell your partner if you have suggestions for Miriam."

It was a normal day in the life of Maya Young Winters (me). I had had a loud noisy breakfast which included two twin sisters screaming as my mother brushed their hair, a dog howling for a piece of bacon and my father, putting ketchup on toast like it was a normal thing to do. Then I'd left at promptly 7:27 to catch my bus. I'd laughed at Anna Lou's bad jokes, gotten through home-room, first and second period and lunch with my posse of friends: May, Luna, and Ruby. Then around came sixth period.

Ms. Gulch was my science teacher and even her name was terrible.

After the students talked with their partners, I looked at Miriam. "So what did you decide to do?" I asked. Miriam shared her piece and walked us through the revisions she had made.

"I decided to start even more in the action, the way Rachel Vail gets them right at Ashley's house. Even though I liked all the stuff about Maya's family, especially her Dad using ketchup on his toast, I decided it was more important to set

You might have noticed that a few items on the chart were not ones mentioned by the students. I find that I can tuck in a few extra tips when doing this sort of brainstorming lesson, either claiming them as my own or as other "over-heard" comments that weren't shared with the whole class. That way I can ensure that the content I think is most important is included in the class chart, even if students don't supply it.

I deliberately selected a student whose lead invited further revision. I wanted to make it easy for students to imagine ways they could incorporate more setting. I also carefully chose a student who enjoyed collaboration, was viewed as a strong writer by classmates, and would find this whole experience a positive one.

up Ruby and Maya's relationship right away and get them to science class as fast as possible." Miriam put the new lead up on the document camera (see Figure 8–2).

> *Ruby has been my best friend since we were in diapers, as my mom would say. She is the most tender hearted person you could ever know, and is scared of many things: spiders, disappointing anyone in any way shape or form, and Ms. Gulch.*

Miriam stopped and said, "Then I would go back to the rest of my first lead and the next sentence would be,"

> *Ms. Gulch was our science teacher. Even her name was terrible.*

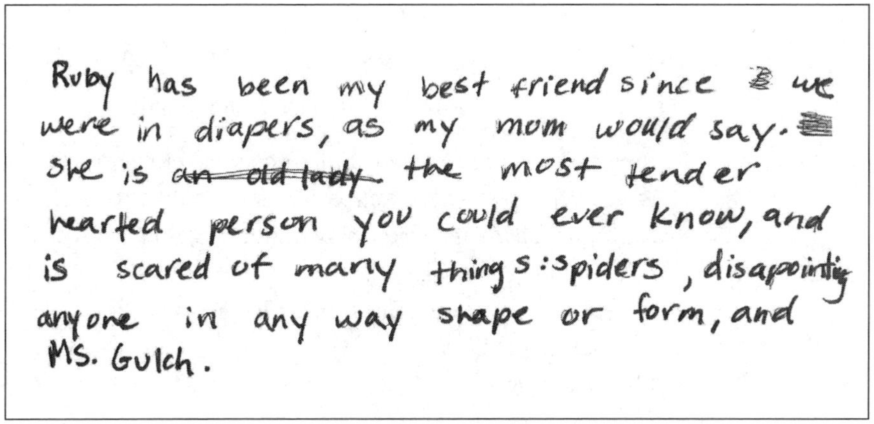
Ruby has been my best friend since we were in diapers, as my mom would say. She is ~~an old lady~~ the most tender hearted person you could ever know, and is scared of many things: spiders, disapointing anyone in any way shape or form, and Ms. Gulch.

FIG. 8–2 After getting help from a mentor text, Miriam tries her lead again.

LINK

Restate the options your kids have for today, reminding them of one step-by-step process they might take to revise their leads.

"Do you see what Miriam learned from other authors to try in her own lead? Today, each one of you needs to decide what you will do. Some of you are probably realizing that to write with this sort of detail, you need to rethink your story plan, figuring out how you can zoom in more on your scenes. Some of you may decide that you need to do some revisions that are similar to those Miriam has done. Some of you will want to study published leads for yourself, learning more techniques. All of you will be drafting and revising in some way, but you'll need to decide how to go about doing that. Remember, you can always use the resources at your disposal—the anchor chart, narrative checklist, mentor texts—to help."

How to Write Compelling Fiction

- Brainstorm a great story idea (think of small moments, places, events, issues, struggles, stories you wish existed in the world).
- Make your characters come alive (with traits, wants and challenges, self-attitude, relationships).
- Test-drive your character in scenes (envision and write actions, feelings, dialogue, setting, point of view).
- Plot several versions of your story, aiming to intensify the problem (use arcs, timelines, storyboards).
- Draft a 3-D story (story-tell bit by bit, include evidence of your characters' actions, thoughts, feelings).
- Manage space and time.
  - Use summary to quickly move a character across space and time.
  - Use transitional words and phrases to show changes in time or place.
- Become the main character, living through the drama of the story—and then allow your writing to unfold.
- Use paragraphs wisely (to move in place and time, to highlight something, for dramatic impact).
- **Revise the lead—and hence the entire story (small action, mood, time and place, foreshadow).**

Throughout these books, you will notice how I repeatedly turn students' attention to the resources in the room, regardless of the focus of the minilesson. If you want them to use the anchor charts and mentor texts and writing checklists, you also need to use them, incorporating them into your teaching and referring to them often.

Crafting Leads that Foreshadow and Connect

YOU HAVE NO DOUBT DISCUSSED FORESHADOWING in your reading workshop by this point in the year—if not with the whole class, then with some of your students. It is one of those literary devices that kids relish knowing as readers and enjoy pointing out at every opportunity. You might decide that one great way to complement the work you are doing in today's minilesson and the work you are doing with reading is to look at foreshadowing from the other side of the desk—the writer's side.

You can guide your students who already have strong leads to make their leads better still. Teach them how to make their leads subtly gesture toward something that is still to come in their stories. You, of course, can point them to the class mentor texts, or even their independent reading books (hint: almost all well-written texts have foreshadowing somewhere in their first chapter). You might also have them read past students' writing and practice adding strings of foreshadowing on someone else's work. But probably the strongest way to teach this would be to model the decisions to be made with your own piece or the class's piece.

You might talk through how an author often adds foreshadowing as a revision move, once he knows how his story is likely to go. He can think of this foreshadowing as little clues he is sprinkling throughout his piece, leading to the most important event. You might model how to choose which parts of the story to foreshadow (the big fight) and which not to (what the character will eat for lunch). You might also think aloud about the kinds of things that make good fodder for foreshadowing: character actions, quirks, habits, and idiosyncrasies, or objects that will become instrumental in the plot.

Teaching the techniques of foreshadowing to struggling writers can also be enormously helpful. Foreshadowing at the beginning of the book can offer the writer an anchor to help connect the rest of the disparate events in the story. If, for example, a student is very attached to a particular scene or image in a story, one way to help that student integrate it into the story is through the use of foreshadowing. Insert that special sweatshirt or a glimpse of a key character into the beginning of the story, and voila!

MID-WORKSHOP TEACHING   Researching in Fiction

"I'd like to stop you for just a minute," I interjected into the quiet classroom. "You might have sneaked a glance over at Taylor, who is sitting at a laptop right now. You might even have noticed that he's not using a word processing program to work on his draft, but he's on a website." A few students smirked, certain I was going to call Taylor out on this. "I think the work he's doing right now is so inspiring."

A few quizzical looks surfaced. I continued, "Taylor was working away on his story and realized that there were a few details for his story that he didn't know—things like the types of technology the kid who is cheating in his story might use and the specific questions about math that he might need to include in the test. What Taylor did that was so brilliant was that he realized that even though he was writing fiction, which is made up, he was trying to make it accurate and believable. That means he will want to use facts whenever he can, so the details about settings, objects, the world his characters live in, can be real, even though the characters and the plot in the story are entirely from Taylor's imagination.

(continues)

"And writers don't just jump online to get these little facts to up the reality quotient. They also look in books, ask friends, or even do some observational research. Like for our Esmerelda story, I might decide to go to the mall and see what the fancier stores are selling to wealthy teenagers these days so I can see what Liz and Maeve might wear—or might want to wear. Or if you're writing about a scene in a soccer field, you might want to go visit one to take in the sights, sounds, even smells. These little realistic, true details can help make your fiction stories feel more believable to your readers." I added another bullet to our anchor chart.

How to Write Compelling Fiction

- Brainstorm a great story idea (think of small moments, places, events, issues, struggles, stories you wish existed in the world).
- Make your characters come alive (with traits, wants and challenges, self-attitude, relationships).
- Test-drive your character in scenes (envision and write actions, feelings, dialogue, setting, point of view).
- Plot several versions of your story, aiming to intensify the problem (use arcs, timelines, storyboards).
- Draft a 3-D story (story-tell bit by bit, include evidence of your characters' actions, thoughts, feelings).
- Manage space and time.
  - Use summary to quickly move a character across space and time.
  - Use transitional words and phrases to show changes in time or place.
- Become the main character, living through the drama of the story–and then allow your writing to unfold.
- Use paragraphs wisely (to move in place and time, to highlight something, for dramatic impact).
- Revise the lead–and hence the entire story (small action, mood, time and place, foreshadow).
- **Research key facts to make the story more believable.**

Taking Charge of Writing Decisions to Realize Your Vision

"THERE WAS SOME INCREDIBLE WORK HAPPENING TODAY. I'm not speaking specifically about the writing so much as the way in which you were making your own decisions today. You decided what you would work on, you set an agenda for your work, and then you went about ticking off the items on your agenda. It was inspiring to see you all working toward making your writing match your vision for it.

"In a few minutes, you'll have a chance to finalize your plans for work tonight. Right now, brainstorm with your partner some of the resources you might use to realize your plans—or just to get stronger as a fiction writer. What can you do to take charge of this growth? Glance around the classroom, think about tools you've used in the past. Are there things you have at home—or that you have access to in or outside of school—that you might reference or study to help you do what you hope to do to develop your fiction writing skills—and your current story?

DIRECTING YOUR OWN LEARNING

"Writers, I'd like you to continue your self-propelled work tonight for homework. Take a few minutes to write down your own homework assignment. What are you going to do to make your piece better, stronger, to become what you envision it to be? Will you study a mentor text closely and try a few techniques? Will you return to the checklist and remind yourself of some of your goals and then work toward them? Will you try some research online or observationally, or finish up some work you started today? Set your agenda for your own work for tonight—and keep in mind that you are the expert on what will best ensure that your vision for your piece is realized."

Grounding Dialogue in Scenes

IN THIS SESSION, you'll remind students that writers "stay in scene," by making sure scenes are grounded in dialogue, action, and setting.

GETTING READY

✔ "Scenes" chart from Session 3 (see Teaching)

✔ Two versions of an excerpt from a previous student's work, copied onto chart paper or projected for the class. The unedited excerpt should be dialogue-heavy and should fail to be grounded in scene; the edited version should include action, thoughts, feelings, and setting to create a fully formed scene (see Teaching).

✔ Class shared story on chart paper or projected for the class (see Active Engagement)

✔ "The House on Fire Test: Keep What's Important, Get Rid of What's Unnecessary" chart (see Mid-Workshop Teaching and Share)

✔ "How to Write Compelling Fiction" anchor chart (see Mid-Workshop Teaching)

COMMON CORE STATE STANDARDS: W.7.3.b,d; W.7.4, W.7.5, RL.7.2, RL.7.3, SL.7.1, L.7.1, L.7.2, L.7.3, L.7.6

AFTER BEING A MEMBER of a writing group for adults for almost two decades, and teaching for nearly as long, it never ceases to amaze me that professional adult writers regularly struggle with the very same issues, on a different scale, that adolescent writers contend with. Case in point: staying grounded in scene. For some adult writers, the tendency is either to oversummarize or overinternalize. They might write pages and pages of the character's deep inner thoughts or pages and pages that are *telling* about something, rather than showing it. Both of those things are often in evidence in the short realistic fiction stories written by seventh-graders. But young writers, in their urgency to get their story from point A to point B, are much more likely to overuse dialogue and underuse other aspects of scene writing.

Throughout the whole of this unit, you have no doubt noticed, again and again, the emphasis placed on scene writing. It is so crucial to fiction that students were practicing the craft of scene writing even before they had settled on a story idea. As one of my writing teachers, the best-selling author Jennifer Belle, often says, scenes are the bricks that make up the story. They are the raw material writers use, stacking one upon the other, to create an arc. When a scene is not fully realized—when the characters are not grounded in scenes—the bricks can crumble.

In this session, we will face head on the predictable and very common issue of dialogue-laden scenes. Even if your students are not writing dialogue-heavy scenes today, know that they will very likely go down that path someday, and your teaching will be there to guide them, even far off in the future. In fact, much of what the Common Core Standards ask for in terms of narrative writing can be witnessed in one well-crafted scene.

If you feel, based on your knowledge of your students, that some or all of your students don't need to work on the fine art of scene refinement, you might want to move on to the work described in the mid-workshop teaching point regarding honing in on what matters most in the story. Quite frankly, both the main teaching point and the mid-workshop one are focused on the same central concern: knowing the truth of what you are trying to say and aiming to show it as well as possible.

Grounding Dialogue in Scenes

CONNECTION

Tell about a time you were awakened in the dark and felt disoriented. Compare this to the disorientation some readers feel when drafts are made up almost entirely of dialogue.

"A few nights ago I was visiting a friend who lives far away, so I slept over at her house. I was asleep in her guest room, and my cell phone rang. I woke up completely discombobulated. When I reached for my phone where it usually is, by the bed, it wasn't there. I opened my eyes and it was pitch dark. For a minute or two, I didn't know where I was. The phone was still ringing. So that was familiar. But the rest was in darkness, so I had no idea where I was. Has that happened to you before? You wake up in the middle of the night and because you can't see anything, you don't know where you are? I was completely disoriented. I found a light switch and flicked it on. Once the light was on, I remembered I was at my friend's house.

"The whole thing made me think about how often that can happen in writing, too. Sometimes when I'm reading your writing, or you are reading each other's writing, I'm asking, and your other readers are asking, 'Where am I? What's going on here?'"

Your teaching takes on special immediacy and intimacy when you highlight the events of your life. Teachers sometimes say to me, "But I'm not a writer. My life doesn't contain writing lessons!" So I try to show them that even waking up in the middle of the night can bring new life to a minilesson.

❖ **Name the teaching point.**

"Today I want to teach you that you need to be sure that you 'turn on the lights' in your stories by grounding your characters in scenes. That is, writers make sure to show characters' actions as well as the place and time, so that their readers don't have that disoriented feeling, asking, 'Wait, where is this? What's going on?'"

TEACHING

Give students an example of a former student's dialogue-heavy scene, in which the characters are not grounded in a scene, leaving readers feeling disoriented.

"We all know what makes up a scene." I flipped to our "Scenes" chart from the boot camp in Session 3.

Scenes

- Are small moments, or mini-stories
- Include a clear setting that is woven throughout the moment
- Have characters who are thinking, talking, acting, or perhaps doing all of those things
- Contain a character motivation and obstacle of some sort

"When you're writing a scene, it's easy to get so caught up in the dialogue that you forget everything else that makes up a scene—the things that keep the reader grounded and knowing what's happening. Let me give you an example. One of the kids in one of my classes a couple of years ago, Nick, wrote this." I showed a short, almost generic excerpt that I'd copied onto chart paper.

> I was so embarrassed. I didn't know what to say. "Um . . ."
>
> "Just apologize," she said.
>
> "I'm sorry," I said.
>
> "You're forgiven. Let's go get a slice," she said.

"Some things work in this section. Characters are talking. We can tell how they're feeling. But the characters are floating. The story produces the same feeling I had when I woke up in the middle of the night and I didn't know where I was. We can't tell where the characters are, and we're not sure what they are doing. We're disoriented."

Tell the class that the writer revised this scene by adding action, thoughts, feelings, and setting, and show the resulting next draft.

"To make sure the lights are on for readers, it's essential to ensure the character is actually in a fully formed scene. In other words, the character will not only be talking; he'll also be thinking, feeling, and moving within a setting. In fact, those other things are so important that a scene can have all of those things and *not* have dialogue and still be a scene. Watch how Nick's draft became much clearer—and emotionally richer—when he added action and setting.

"Nick didn't actually know what his characters were doing. When he wrote the draft, his characters were just talking. He hadn't envisioned the action, thoughts, feelings, or setting yet. So he decided to revise his draft to add these elements. He decided to make his characters walk home from school. It would be a crisp, fall day. That way, one of the characters could do stuff with falling leaves and acorns, and the other character could be fiddling with his jacket. Nick expected these things to be fillers, really, to hold up the talk, but the actions ended up revealing the real story in a very important way. Listen to Nick's next draft, the one he wrote after thinking about where the characters were and what they were doing." I read an excerpt from Nick's revised draft aloud.

Here, I deliberately choose a very brief excerpt, knowing its revised version is more than double in size and that my teaching point will therefore be all the more dramatic—and effective—when students see the enormous impact that adding action and setting has on the story.

Notice the return to earlier teaching about letting characters lead (from Session 7) and about not knowing the exact choices characters will make—or the trouble that may ensue from these (from Session 5). Again and again, I weave in earlier instruction with new teaching, to offer additional context for these steps.

I was so embarrassed. I didn't know what to say. "Um . . ." I kicked a pile of leaves that had gathered at the base of one of the trees on Bergen Street. My face felt like it was so hot it would melt.

A breeze wooshed and leaves danced on the sidewalk. "Just apologize," she said. She pulled her collar tighter and buttoned the top button. I snuck a glance at her face. She was biting her bottom lip. I knew it was hard for her to ask for an apology.

An acorn fell off a tree and ricocheted off a car parked on the corner. The smell of tomato sauce and garlic wafted in the cool late October air. My stomach growled. I snuck another peek at her and now she was stomping every leaf on the sidewalk. Moving intentionally to them and then crushing them under her boots as she walked. My heart pounded. What if I apologized and she didn't forgive? What if I didn't and she never spoke to me again. "I'm sorry," I said.

She turned her head and smiled. "You're forgiven. Let's go get a slice," she said. She pointed to the pizza shop, two doors down. I raced ahead, stomach still growling, so I could hold the door.

Debrief, tucking some extra tips into your description of what the student did to revise. Point out that when he added setting and actions, the writer discovered important new interactions and meanings in his story.

"Writers, do you see how the characters are not in the dark anymore? We can really picture them. We can see what they're doing and where they are. And you know what? When Nick wrote this, his only plan was to have the two of them walking home together. He chose to make it a fall day only because it was fall when he was writing this story, and he thought he could describe it well. Then, as he wrote the scene, adding in the actions and other things, stuff started happening between the characters that Nick never planned for at all. It just happened on the page! It surprised Nick that his main character was taking so long to apologize when his friend was clearly upset, and Nick was totally surprised when she started crushing leaves, violently. There was a lot more feeling between them than Nick had realized. All this drama came out in the story, simply because Nick decided that he needed to get his characters out of the dark and to rewrite the story, showing the characters as they moved and interacted in the setting."

FIG. 9–1   Brian works at grounding his characters dialogue in action, setting, and thought.

In this minilesson, I tucked in an extra teaching tip that is clearly more challenging than the main teaching point itself. In this example, Nick has done writing-to-discover work that is beyond what most writers in this class can do. He is actually a high school student, and this is skilled work. But I do still want to expose all writers to the richest and deepest ideas, because who knows what will "click" for a kid! When I do this, however, I am confident that my main teaching points are within reach and pertinent for everyone. The little subordinate tips one weaves into a minilesson are one of the ways our minilessons become multilevel, providing various pathways for students.

ACTIVE ENGAGEMENT

Ask students to reread the class story from the chart paper while asking, "Will this make sense to readers?" When they encounter a passage that might be disorienting, ask them to revise it with their partner, adding setting.

"So let's try it. Let's read this section of our Esmerelda story (I've been writing some more of it), and as we read, let's ask ourselves, 'Will this make sense to my readers? Is this clear?' If you come to a place in the story where the words seem to come out of the dark, a place where you suspect that readers might feel disoriented, you and your partner will have a chance to write-in-the-air, adding references to the setting, characters thoughts and feelings, as well as any small actions that characters do, into our next version."

I retrieved the draft and read a section of it aloud—a section that I knew was well lodged into the setting, plenty of character thoughts, and amplified with actions. I read:

> "So, Esmé," Maeve interrupted. She was looking at me, calling me a much cooler version of my name than I was used to.
>
> I couldn't help myself, I smiled. She had given me a cool nickname. It was almost like we were friends. My eyes left the spot on the carpet I had been staring at and looked at Maeve. "Yeah?" I said, in what I hoped was my coolest voice.
>
> Maeve leaned forward on the beanbag chair, her perfectly painted fingernails planted on her knees. "You know Tilly better than anyone in this room, why does she dress like that?"

"Could you picture what was going on?" I asked. "Did you see the place?" Students nodded. "So let's read on," I said, and this time read the upcoming section (a part I knew was underdeveloped).

> "I mean, she never looks good," Maeve said.
>
> "Worse than that," Liz jumped in. "She looks like she doesn't even care."
>
> I wasn't sure what to say. "Uh—well."
>
> "I mean, look at you—look at us. We clearly care. We look good," Liz said.
>
> "I know. You completely look like you should be hanging out with us. Not with Tilly."

The students talked to their partners, and after a moment I intervened. "Writers, please don't simply *comment* on how you'd go about rewriting this to add setting and actions. Actually talk as if you're writing, or as some people say, write the new text 'in the air.'"

Notice that instead of beginning the active engagement by saying, "Could you rewrite this scene so that . . . ," I instead ask readers to begin by rereading a fairly large passage of the Esmerelda story by using the lens of "Is this clear?" By backing up and starting with this, I not only get the chance to synthesize all the points I have made in this minilesson, but I also demonstrate to writers how they might position themselves to do this work in the first place.

Because I initially asked students to "write-in-the-air," I am careful to hold them accountable to my instructions. Otherwise, I inadvertently send the message that they do not need to listen closely when I speak or follow my directions.

Ask one partnership to share their new version.

"Let's listen to Brendon and Annabelle. While they write-in-the-air, I'll record it."

> "I mean, she never looks good," Maeve said. She tucked her hair behind her ear, a diamond earring peeking out. It was the largest diamond earring I had seen on a kid. And I could tell from the sparkle it was real.
>
> "Worse than that," Liz jumped in. "She looks like she doesn't even care." Liz sat up straight on the bed, her own painted finger nails flashing.
>
> I wasn't sure what to say. "Uh-well," I stammered. I felt like anything I said would be the wrong thing. I suddenly felt as if someone had turned the heat up. I was sweating.
>
> "I mean, look at you—look at us. We clearly care. We look good," Liz said. She hopped off the bed and signaled to Maeve to stand next to her. They posed back to back, showing off their perfect looks. I don't think I ever realized just how obsessed they were with looks—their own and other people's.

Debrief, highlighting the sequential steps you hope writers use with their own texts. Emphasize that revisions that begin as corrections can become entirely new creations.

"Writers," I said, "you've done some amazing revision. You reread this part of our draft and realized that readers might feel disoriented, as if the scene were taking place in the dark. So you included a little information about the characters' exact actions in the setting, and as you did this, you—like Nick—ended up surprising yourselves and finding that things are happening between the characters that we didn't even realize when we planned the story!

"This is what writers do. Their revisions start out as corrections and end up as creations!"

LINK

Remind writers that today they'll shift between drafting and revising, and that to revise, they'll want to reread their drafts with specific lenses—perhaps including what they just learned.

"Writers, today you'll continue to draft and revise your stories, shifting between the two processes. And when you revise, you'll reread for all the goals that have become important to you. You'll make sure your characters feel real. You'll keep an eye on the deeper meaning of your story. You'll make sure you don't leave your readers in the dark. If there is a section of your story that seems disorienting, you can revise it like you've done today, grounding it in scene by including actions, setting, thoughts, and feelings. Please be sure that if you expect to *correct* your draft, you do so, knowing that revisions that begin as corrections often take on a life of their own and become creations. Let your characters do things that you'd never expected they'd do. Be prepared to be surprised and to capture all that new stuff!"

I make today's teaching even more significant by highlighting for students how addressing one issue in a piece often yields additional accomplishments.

Especially (but not only) toward the end of the unit when students are moving between drafting and revising, it is critical that we remind them to use everything they have learned to guide their work. In other words, the message is "Do what makes the most sense for you and your piece at this time," not "Do what I just did."

Using the Narrative Checklist to Set and Support Personal Goals

I FEEL LIKE THERE'S A FINE BALANCE when using the checklists with students. On the one hand, they can be incredibly powerful tools for self-assessment, as well as transparent for my expectations and the expectations of their grade level. On the other hand, there is the danger of students feeling as if they are just another hoop to jump through—another way they are writing for someone else. One of the ways I try to combat that is by bringing the checklists periodically into my conferences and small-group work.

MID-WORKSHOP TEACHING   Including What's Important

"A few years ago I got a chance to study with James Howe, the author of *The Misfits*, and he had us do this really interesting exercise, in which we had to make a list of things we'd have to take if our homes were on fire. When we looked over the lists, he noted that we only took what was necessary—whether practically necessary, like shoes or important papers, or emotionally necessary, like photos and sentimental objects. He said that as writers, when we draft and revise, we need to do the same sort of work. We need to read our work, making sure we've included what's important but gotten rid of any of the extra stuff, the stuff we don't need. By doing that work, we create stories that are not filled with fluff and distracting stuff, but only the most crucial things.

"Can you do that right now? Can you just take a sweep through your pieces and see if you've included what's most important, but also gotten rid of stuff that's just weighing the story down? This is something you want to check on all the time as a writer, not just today, and not just this piece. This chart can help you think about some lenses that might help you decipher what to keep and what to get rid of. I also added a new point to the anchor chart, a point that summarizes 'the house on fire test.'"

The House on Fire Test: Keep What's Important, Get Rid of What's Unnecessary

What's Important to Keep (or Include)

- Actions, thoughts, and dialogue that move the story
- Actions, thoughts, and dialogue that develop character
- Descriptions and moments that highlight theme
- Images and metaphors that pop out meaning
- Scenes that are significant
- Summaries that explain important information

What Can Probably Be Cut

- Actions, thoughts, and dialogue that don't do any work
- Adjectives and frilly language that could be replaced with strong nouns and verbs
- Descriptions that don't give important information
- Distracting details (no matter how fun they are!)
- Scenes that don't give important information, or could be easily summarized
- Summaries that give background information that the reader doesn't need

How to Write Compelling Fiction

- Brainstorm a great story idea (think of small moments, places, events, issues, struggles, stories you wish existed in the world).
- Make your characters come alive (with traits, wants and challenges, self-attitude, relationships).
- Test-drive your character in scenes (envision and write actions, feelings, dialogue, setting, point of view).
- Plot several versions of your story, aiming to intensify the problem (use arcs, timelines, storyboards).
- Draft a 3-D story (story-tell bit by bit, include evidence of your characters' actions, thoughts, feelings).
- Manage space and time.
  - Use summary to quickly move a character across space and time.
  - Use transitional words and phrases to show changes in time or place.
- Become the main character, living through the drama of the story—and then allow your writing to unfold.
- Use paragraphs wisely (to move in place or time, to highlight something, for dramatic impact).
- Revise the lead—and hence the entire story (small action, mood, time and place, foreshadow).
- Research key facts to make the story more believable.
- **Get rid of extra stuff that weighs the story down!**

When I met with Gobin, his desk was covered with written-upon sheets of paper, all clearly organized in some fashion. I could just make out the pages of his writer's notebook open to his story arc underneath the piles. And underneath it all, his writing folder. "I see you're up to your eyeballs in writing!" I said as I pulled up a chair.

Gobin smiled, clearly quietly proud of his industriousness. "I've already drafted one scene today and have started working on my next." He pointed to his story arc, which, now that I was looking at it, I could see he was also using as a checklist of sorts, checking off each scene as he drafted it.

I let him know I was impressed by his diligence and his thoughtful planning. He wasn't letting a moment go to waste. "So, what exactly are you working on in your drafting?" I asked. When he looked at me blankly, I soldiered on, "You know, what work are you doing as a writer? Are you crafting something? Doing something with dialogue? Something with structure? That sort of thing."

"I'm just working on drafting. I'm writing my story."

I smiled to let him know I was still impressed, but also pressed forward, "I think that's great. I also think that while you're working, you're not just going forward, one step at a time. You are following goals you set for yourself as a writer within that drafting. Much like, on that television show, 'Dancing with the Stars,' people don't just 'do the foxtrot.' They work on certain moves, tricks, ways to make it their own. That show has judges and coaches to help them decide what to work on. You have other tools you can use to help you pick something to work on, like charts, the lessons I teach, mentor texts."

Gobin interrupted me, "And the checklist," he shuffled through his papers to his folder to pull it out.

"Say more," I said.

"I can go back and look at my checklist to see what things I knew I needed to work on, and keep them in mind now as I draft."

"Oh, I like that idea," I said, giving no indication that this was the fulfillment of exactly what I hoped to teach him. "Tell me more about that."

"Well, I know I have most of the things under structure." I watched Gobin's finger run down the category, eyes skimming as he went. His finger paused, "Except in my ending, I'm really not showing much change. I mean big change. I'm telling about it. But I could do more to *show* it."

"You certainly don't need me to sit here anymore, do you? You are completely in control of how your piece goes, and are even using tools in ways that will make your work stronger and more sophisticated. Good for you!" And with that I disappeared, wanting to show him that I trusted his judgment and the choices he was making for his piece.

Celebrate that Students Are Using What They've Learned to Move Ahead with Revisions and Drafts

"THERE WAS A LOT OF WORK HAPPENING TODAY. Lots of lights going on for a lot of writers today. I know many of you are done with your drafts and have already started revising. Others of you are drafting and revising at the same time. You are becoming skillful, self-sufficient writers of fiction. I see a lot of you are checking on points on the 'House on Fire Test' to get rid of stuff your stories don't need, to lighten them, streamline them, to get to the points you want to make faster. And some of you are choosing a bullet or two on the anchor chart, and then you're assessing your leads or checking how your stories are moving along in time and space. Referring to these tools gives you a focused, logical way to plan how you're going to revise."

Explain that fiction writers draft quickly.

"I want you to know that the fact that so many of you are drafting so quickly is a really good thing. It means you are getting lost in your stories. It means you're letting your characters take you for a ride, which means, you in turn, will be taking your readers on a ride. As the famous mystery writer Raymond Chandler once said, 'The faster I write, the better my output. If I'm going slow, I'm in trouble. It means I'm pushing the words instead of being pulled by them.'"

PUSHING AHEAD TO COMPLETE YOUR DRAFTS

"No matter where you are in the process, try to get yourself to the end of your draft by tomorrow. Even if there are tons and tons of other revisions you know you want to do, and plan to do. In fact, if as you're writing you know what revisions you will do, and don't have the time to include them as you draft, just start a To-Do list for yourself right now, so that you can get to the end of your story for tomorrow. As you might have guessed, you'll be focusing on endings tomorrow, and I'd like everyone to have something to work with.

"Also, if finishing up your story does go quickly, and you have time, go back and revisit some short fiction texts, or even television shows, movies, or music videos. Look especially at the endings. This is only worth doing if you know the piece really well. We want to get a sense of how endings can fit into the whole of a piece."

Session 10

Writing Endings that Make Readers Swoon

A FEW SUMMERS AGO, I became mesmerized by the women's gymnastics competition at the Olympics. I was glued to the screen, watching gymnast after gymnast throw her body across the mats or pommel horse or balance beam—leaping, twirling, diving. No matter how complicated and flawless their routines were, if they did not "stick" their landings, their performances felt ruined.

It is the same way with stories. We've all had the experience of reading and getting lost in a story. We fall in love with the characters, get swept up in the plot, then we reach the end, and—bam!—it's as if a door is slammed in our face. The ending is too sudden, or unbelievable, or just plain unsatisfying. We all know, too, that our students often fall into these same traps when they are writing their own endings. We've all read students' stories about a kid who toils away at a job to earn enough money to buy her mother something—a valentine, a charm bracelet—and then suddenly she learns she's won the lottery. We've read about the unpopular girl who is ridiculed at the start of the story and elected class president at the end of the story. Those kind of endings simply disappoint the reader.

Today, the goal is to teach students that in real life, solutions don't usually fly in from outer space (or from left field). No one arrives on the scene at the final moment, solving everything in an instant. Each of us, as a person and as an author, can find small solutions in the everyday truth of our all-too-human existence. No, we do not usually win the lottery. The girl who is ostracized one day doesn't usually become class president the next day. But in real life, that girl can find a place for herself and come to realize that there's more than one way to realize her dreams.

The Common Core Standards expect students to "provide a conclusion that follows from the narrated experiences or events." This is a simple thing to do if students truly understand the concept of the story arc—that the ending is where the story has been heading all along. For this to be the case, students must internalize cause and effect, not just in their science, math, and reading life, but also as writers. When they are in charge of the cause, students need to make sure the effect (in this case, the ending of a fictional story), follows a logical and satisfying path.

IN THIS SESSION, you'll teach students that writers of fiction craft the endings that their stories and their readers deserve. In particular, they make sure their endings connect with the hearts of their stories and help to create a satisfying feeling for the reader.

GETTING READY

- ✔ "Some Principles of Crafting Quality Endings for Fictional Narratives" chart, which you will create prior to the minilesson (see Teaching)

- ✔ A video clip from the ending of a movie students will be familiar with, such as *Harry Potter and the Sorcerer's Stone* (see Teaching)

- ✔ Drafts of class shared story (see Active Engagement)

- ✔ "How to Write Compelling Fiction" anchor chart (see Link)

- ✔ Mentor text, "Thirteen and a Half" (see Share)

- ✔ Students' writers notebooks (see Share)

COMMON CORE STATE STANDARDS: W.7.3.d,e; W.7.5, RL.7.2, SL.7.1, L.7.1, L.7.2, L.7.3

There is no one way to write a wonderful ending. An ending may be happy, sad, funny, or thoughtful. It may contain dialogue and action, or it may be a bit of setting. What all good endings have in common is that they address something essential in the story. Today's session aims to show children that writers and characters alike can find turning points in the details of their lives. Today's session also marks the end of this bend, a bend that focused primarily on the blurry lines between drafting and revision, and this session positions students to prepare for publication with an eye toward audience.

"Teach students that in real life, solutions don't usually fly in from outer space. No one arrives on the scene at the final moment, solving everything in an instant."

94

Writing Endings that Make Readers Swoon

CONNECTION

Get students to recall how they felt when a story, a movie, or a game ended in disappointing fashion—and prepare them to write satisfying endings to their own stories.

"Have you ever had the experience of reading a book, watching a movie, or even playing a video game, and you're completely loving it. You're so into it that even if your stomach growls, you don't get up to grab food. Then you get to the end and you're so excited to find out how it all wraps up, and then . . ." I mimed complete disappointment, verging on anger and disbelief. "You think, 'What just happened? That was a *horrible* way to end!'" Students nodded their heads emphatically. "I can tell as I look at your faces that this has happened to you, too.

"So obviously, the last thing you want to do is make your readers angry when they get to the ending of your story. You want to make them feel satisfied when they get to the end. Even better, you want to get them to swoon—make them count the days until they can read something else you wrote."

❧ Name the teaching point.

"Today I want to teach you that writers take their time with endings, weighing and considering and revising until they find one that fits. They know a satisfying ending will tie up loose ends, resolve the unresolved difficulties, and bring home the story's meaning."

TEACHING

Remind students that they're ready to move way beyond a simple "The End" ending to the stories they're writing.

"When you were little—around five or six—if you were anything like the little kids I know, you probably ended your stories like this." I projected a page of kid writing with big bubble letters and curlicues that read "THE END!"

"As you got older, maybe third or fourth grade, you knew that wasn't the way to end—that usually there would be some final action that brought your stories to a close. But sometimes you would create a big mess in your stories that

Often I begin my lessons with something that is not directly about writing but that nonetheless reflects a principle of writing. Doing so allows me to engage students before leading their attention to the day's teaching.

you weren't sure how to clean up, so you just plopped in something magical or unbelievable to end your stories, like Superman flying in and saving the day. If I were a fourth-grader writing our story, I might have a parent enter the scene and interrupt Esmerelda's uncomfortable conversation at the party with a line like this: 'Stop saying mean things about people!' That way, the discomfort would end, and Esmerelda wouldn't have to do any of the hard work that comes from getting into that kind of a jam.

"But you're older now. You're adolescents—almost adults. And you've lived more, read more. And you know life doesn't work like that. Sometimes stories end happily. Sometimes they end sadly. But no one swoops in at the last minute to save the day. The main character, whether it's you in your life or a fictional character in a book or a movie, must *do* something at the end of the story to make it end in a way that feels satisfying. These moments can be big or small."

Provide some principles to guide the writing of good endings.

"Of course, there are other things writers do as well to craft strong endings, ones that make readers swoon and call for more. To write those sorts of endings, it helps to know a few principles of good endings. To write an ending worthy of all the work you've put into your writing, you can do a few things." I pointed to a chart I'd created in advance.

Some Principles of Crafting Quality Endings for Fictional Narratives

1. Keep in mind what your story is <u>really</u> about and make sure the ending helps to show that.
2. Pay attention to the structure of the story and make sure the ending fits the arc:
    a. Has the character evolved?
    b. How has the plot developed?
3. Ensure that all loose ends are tied up.

Offer an example of a video that illustrates a satisfying, quality ending.

"Let's take a look at a clip of a famous ending from a film that you probably know from a few years ago: *Harry Potter and the Sorcerer's Stone*." I turned to my laptop and cued up the clip. "As you watch, I want you to think with me about the ending. If you recognize the use of some of the strategies from this chart, notice which specific ones were used.

"Just a quick reminder: *Harry Potter and the Sorcerer's Stone* is the first book and movie in the series. At the start of it, Harry lives with his aunt and uncle and cousin Dudley, relatives who treat him unkindly. Under Professor Dumbledore's orders, Hagrid takes Harry to Hogwarts School of Witchcraft and Wizardry, where Harry befriends Hermione and Ron. Together, the friends get involved in a mysterious battle with Voldemort, who is acting through a Hogwarts teacher to get at the Sorcerer's Stone. Okay, take a look at the ending, and keep the items on this chart in mind as you watch."

I showed the final clip of *Harry Potter and the Sorcerer's Stone*, in which Harry, Hermione, and Ron say good-bye to Hagrid for the summer, and Hagrid gives Harry a photo album with a picture of Harry, as a baby, with his parents.

We are suggesting that you use a clip from the film Harry Potter and the Sorcerer's Stone *here, but if you don't have easy access to this video, feel free to use any movie ending that your students are familiar with. You just want to select a movie with a conclusion that embodies the principles of a strong, well-crafted, fully satisfying ending—something that will get your kids to "feel" a great ending and then write one.*

Notice how quickly I summarize the story I use to exemplify powerful endings—just enough so that students have a context for what they are about to watch.

"Writers, what did you notice? Quickly, turn and talk to your partner."

I gave students just a minute to do this, then said, "Did you notice how this ending scene, which captures the connection between Harry and his family and between Harry and his friends, highlights one big thing that this movie is about—the power of love? That goes to the first point on this chart. And did you notice, too, that by presenting a confident, happy Harry in this final scene, the film shows him evolved from the miserable kid he was at the start? This gets at the third point. The film's ending also addresses point three by giving Harry something he didn't have at the start of the story, and desperately wanted—knowledge of his parents, which the photo from Hagrid represents. This, then, develops that big part of the plot. The choice to end with the image of Harry and his friends at the train station, leaving Hogwarts, ties back to the beginning of the story. Harry didn't get on the train in the very first scene of the movie, but it was in the first third of the movie—toward the start, which reminds us that endings can connect back to the beginning, without being exactly the first paragraph. The scene also provides resolution because we get to see Harry surrounded by love and friends, which he wasn't when he was living under the stairs at the Dursleys. We know also, through the waving photo album, that his parents' love is always with him, even if they can't be physically with him. Harry's problems aren't all solved, but there is a satisfying feeling of a closure of sorts."

Debrief, summing up the elements of a quality ending to a story.

"See how finely crafted stories have finely crafted endings? Every single decision surrounding this final scene was carefully made with consideration for wrapping things up—for bringing the character and plot to the end of their arc, for bringing out the story's message, and for giving the viewer a satisfying conclusion. This goes right alongside what you now know makes a good ending!"

ACTIVE ENGAGEMENT

Ask students to generate possible endings for the class story, bearing in mind the "Principles of Crafting Quality Endings for Fictional Narratives" chart.

"So let's imagine some possible endings to our Esmerelda story, putting what we just learned to practice. Recall that the ending should relate to the story's real message, or theme. So we need to remember what the story, at its heart, is about." I flipped through drafts we'd written on chart paper.

"Would you agree that our ending needs to somehow address Esmerelda's need to do the right thing but also her desire to be more popular?" Students nodded, so I said, "Keeping this in mind, work with your partner to come up with two possible endings."

Recruit students' thinking and coach in, as needed.

After a bit, I asked Kerri to begin the conversation by sharing her idea. She said, "I think Esmerelda can be torn about what to say—whether to defend Tilly or not. But then, just as she's about to stand up to say something, Liz has second thoughts. Maybe she changes her mind. Maybe she remembers Esmerelda is friends with Tilly."

I create ways for students to be active participants in their own learning, even during the teaching portion of a minilesson, which is why I give them a lens for viewing and some time to brainstorm ideas with a partner. However, I also use the teaching to relay the information I think is critical for students to have, which is why I quickly shift from students sharing their observations to me highlighting key information for them.

Don't worry if your students don't grasp the full complexity of today's teaching. Endings are something professional writers struggle with every day, and one minilesson will not be sufficient to teach kids all they need to know about the art of ending a story. Do expect, however, that this lesson leaves them thinking about their endings, rather than letting a series of actions dictate some finite place where their story must end.

Turning to the whole class, I said, "What do you think of Kerri's suggested ending? Does it address—even resolve—Esmerelda's need to do the right thing? Does it link to her desire to be popular? Does it show that she's changed internally?"

José chimed in, "I'm not sure if it does the last thing, but yeah, it links to her desire to do the right thing. I mean, at least it shows her wanting to stand up."

Keisha added, "But Esmerelda kind of gets saved if we end the story this way. I mean, she isn't forced to do anything, one way or the other." Others in the class agreed.

Then Javi said, "I want Esmerelda to get over wanting to be popular. I want her to realize that she has good friends and that's all she needs. Maybe we can have Tilly walk in at just that moment, and Tilly's just found out she's on the cheerleading squad. The other girls try to kiss up to her, but Tilly knows Esmerelda is her only true friend. Esmerelda realizes she did the right thing not saying horrible things about her friend *and* she gets to be popular."

I said, "I know Javi's not alone in thinking that in a story, a character should change—so it makes sense that Esmerelda should stick to her conviction, become strong, and get rewarded for that. But I want to remind you that people—both in real life and in fiction—tend to change and grow in small ways. Realistically, Esmerelda is not going to get over her desire to be popular in the blink of an eye, nor will she become popular that fast, even if she were able to get what she wanted. So, Javi, can I steer you toward considering the much, much smaller changes that human beings actually make?"

"Okay," Javi said, "well maybe she *does* stand up for Tilly, then, and the girls are kind of impressed, so they give her attention, but not the kind she expected."

"Yeah, so she's still craving more from them, but she's also glad she stood up for her friend," Samee added.

"What do all think?" I asked. "Does this ending feel realistic? Does it show character and plot development? Does it tie up loose ends and satisfy you?" The class indicated that the ending did all these things.

"Nice job, writers. I agree."

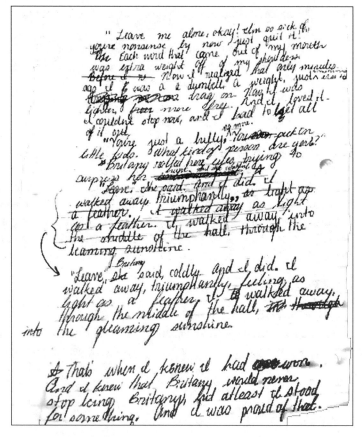

FIG. 10–1   Annabelle revises her ending to ensure that it carries the meaning she wants for her story.

When I guide students to try to practice the work of a writer, I am careful to walk the fine line between letting them do the work themselves and offering scaffolds to lift the level of that work. Making sure that my scaffolds are transferable to other pieces and giving students the final decision-making power are two ways that I ensure that I don't simply take over a piece from students.

LINK

Acknowledge that students are at various stages of the writing process, and suggest that when they are ready, they have ways to craft the very important story ending.

"Writers, you are at different stages of this process, which is fine. Some of you may begin to write the first draft of your ending today, and others of you will do this tomorrow. No matter where you are in your work, when you get to your story's ending, remember that writers always consider whether an ending matches the story. And they look for solutions and resolutions that come from the grit, the specificity, the truth of the story. Remember that endings *matter*. As you work on your own—whether you do so right now or later tonight or tomorrow, think about the endings you considered and analyzed last night for homework, to see if you can cull any inspiration from there. Write a few different endings. Weigh which one you like best. Experiment a little. Getting an ending right takes some thought."

Update the anchor chart with the bullet on crafting an ending.

"I'm going to add this new thinking about endings to our chart."

Notice that I did not explicitly teach the students how to write and experiment with different endings. I assumed that the students would hold on to that strategy from our earlier work on leads and revision. If you feel that your students need that work explicitly taught, by all means do so.

How to Write Compelling Fiction

- Brainstorm a great story idea (think of small moments, places, events, issues, struggles, stories you wish existed in the world).
- Make your characters come alive (with traits, wants and challenges, self-attitude, relationships).
- Test-drive your character in scenes (envision and write actions, feelings, dialogue, setting, point of view).
- Plot several versions of your story, aiming to intensify the problem (use arcs, timelines, storyboards).
- Draft a 3-D story (story-tell bit by bit, include evidence of your characters' actions, thoughts, feelings).
- Manage space and time.
  - Use summary to quickly move a character across space and time.
  - Use transitional words and phrases to show changes in time or place.
- Become the main character, living through the drama of the story—and then allow your writing to unfold.
- Use paragraphs wisely (to move in place or time, to highlight something, for dramatic impact).
- Revise the lead—and hence the entire story (small action, mood, time and place, foreshadow).
- Research key facts to make the story more believable.
- Get rid of extra stuff that weighs the story down!
- **Finish strong—make sure the ending shows what the story is really about, fits the story arc, ties up loose ends.**

Helping Students to Write Well about What Matters to Them (Even When they Might Not Know What That Is, at First)

WHEN I WAS A YOUNG TEACHER, during one of the first keynotes I ever saw Lucy Calkins give, she spoke about the importance of treating students' writing as we would if they gave us a crumpled Valentine. We would look past those wrinkles and the sweat and see the intent, the heart, behind the gesture. She taught me that children, whether in first grade or seventh, have a hard time saying exactly what is in their hearts. Sometimes they don't even exactly know that it's there, just that they feel compelled to write about certain topics, certain moments. They are gesturing toward the meaning but can't quite wrap their fingers around it. Our job, arguably our most important job as teachers of writing, is to help them uncover that treasure and then bring it to light in the best possible way.

The first secret to doing that work, according to Lucy, is that we have to believe, despite the scowl, the rolled eyes, the badly punctuated sentences, that every young writer has something important to say. And that important something is in this piece—it is in every piece—just as there is a pulse in every part of our bodies, even though it is stronger in some places than others. The second secret is to make sure the student feels as if she made that discovery, so that it is very clear that her story really is her own.

Over the years I have had to remind myself over and over again that every student has that truth to share. When I spotted Rahm, legs spread out, head hanging backward off the back of his chair, I found myself repeating that mantra in my head—but aloud, I asked, "What's going on?"

"I'm done," he said.

I let a smile light up my whole face, "Wow—so exciting to be done with your draft. You must feel great to get that story out on paper!"

"Uh, I guess so, yeah." He sat up a bit.

MID-WORKSHOP TEACHING
Crafting Surprising but Inevitable Endings

"Writers, eyes up here for a second. As I was walking around speaking to those of you who are working on your endings, I was reminded of something one of my writing teachers once said to me, that the defining characteristic of a short story—that's what you're writing in this unit—is that it has a surprising, yet inevitable, ending. That is, when we read a short fictional story and get to the end, we experience an element of surprise, but when we think about it, we can't imagine the story ending any other way. For example, in 'Thirteen and a Half,' we are surprised that the narrator says kind things at Sweetpea's funeral and is also nice to Ashley even though she's eager to go home—that she almost feels sorry for her. But when we really think about it, we can't imagine the story going any other way. The narrator is an intuitive, sensitive person, so it's fitting that she would start to feel sorry for Ashley, especially as she comes to understand Ashley's circumstances. In fact, as the reader, we start to feel sorry for Ashley, too.

"So when I say *surprising*, I mean that there's a twist—something new is presented—not like a Superman comes out of nowhere twist, but a 'Let me give me reader something to think about' twist. And meanwhile, this twist should feel like one toward which the story was heading all along. Think about the ending of *Harry Potter and the Sorcerer's Stone* again. That picture from Hagrid, of Harry's parents holding him—it's not what Harry wanted. What he wanted was to have his parents back. But that's not realistic, is it? Instead, the end gives him a connection to his parents. It gives him relationships with people who knew and loved them, and a concrete memento of his time with them. This is a twist in Harry's journey in that first book, but it also feels inevitable that he should have this, right?"

I scanned the story, called "Christmas." It was about a family, told almost entirely in summary. It started with the opening of presents, moved into Christmas dinner, and ended with the whole family on the couch watching videos. Quite frankly, it was very weak and seemed not to be about much of anything at all. No wonder he felt done. But I repeated Lucy's mantra and leaned in close, "This seems so big, Rahm. This seems like a very important story. I'm really, really—wow. There's a lot here." Rahm was sitting up a little, looking vaguely interested. "It is important, isn't it?"

"Yeah," Rahm said.

"Now, I see there are a lot of scenes here, each one sort of a story unto itself. If you were to point out which one you think really captures what you're trying to say here, the meaning behind your story, which scene would it be?" I was guessing he was going to pick the presents. But I was sort of pulling for the meal. I thought there were a lot of family-delving possibilities there.

"The videos. Definitely the videos," Rahm said, picking up his pen. I was, quite frankly, a little disappointed. In my mind, I was letting go of all the teaching points I had set up for if he had picked the other two. So instead, I reminded myself of the mantra, "Yes, of course. They are so important aren't they? So important. I can see that now. How you were gesturing toward that. That's the longest section of your story. Tell me about it."

Rahm looked me right in the eyes, "This isn't just fiction. It's based on my life. You know how you said we could do that?" I nodded. "Well, this is how my family spends Christmas every year. We open presents and eat a big meal, then go and sit and watch videos on the couch the rest of the night."

"That seems so important. That's the heart, isn't it?"

"Yes. You see, my family always takes videos of our Christmases so we can watch them. But we only watch those videos on Christmas day. And since my dad died, it's the only time that I get to see him." Rahm looked at me, dry-eyed, sort of smiling. I, meanwhile, was fighting back tears.

"I see. So it's not really about the videos. It's really about this kid who lost someone close to him. I'm not sure about who it is in your story, but this scene—it's about missing someone, loving someone even after they're gone, isn't it?"

"Yeah," Rahm was really smiling now.

"So, I'm imagining, you probably already had this planned, that in the revision process it's going to be all about cutting away the things that get in the way of telling the story of the kid reliving his memories of that lost loved one on Christmas."

"Exactly," Rahm said, his head already bent to the paper.

Conducting a Close Reading of Endings

Name the work students have accomplished today, and liken the close reading work they do in reading workshop with the work you hope they will try now in their mentor texts.

"Writers, you've accomplished quite a lot today—from tiny detailed revisions to big swaths of revision! A lot of you have spent a good portion of time also leaning on others to help make your writing better, which is really wise. Whether you work with a partner or a small group of writers, or turn to a mentor author, it helps to look at your writing in the company of other writers.

"It's worth noting that some of the close reading work you've been doing in reading workshop is work you can also do with your mentor texts. You can reread and study, bit by bit, whole pieces, or else focus on specific sections, investigating these closely."

Invite students to try this out by selecting and jotting a line from the ending of the class mentor text that stands out to them—one they hope to study closely.

"Let's try this with the ending of 'Thirteen and a Half.'" I projected the ending of the story. "This is the very last scene, right after the funeral, during which the narrator says a few really poignant things about Ashley.

> *"Thanks," she said, as we headed back toward her house. "That was really beautiful, what you said."*
>
> *I shrugged.*
>
> *She held the back door open for me. "Is this the worst playdate of your life?"*
>
> *"It's up there," I admitted.*
>
> *We waited out front for my mom to pick me up. I sat between my stuff and Ashley. We both tilted our faces up toward the sun. When my mother's car pulled up and she beeped, I turned to Ashley. "Happy half-birthday," I said.*
>
> *"Thanks," she answered. "Thanks for, you know, being here today."*
>
> *I grabbed my stuff and ran down the steps to my mom. I slipped into the car, buckled my seat belt, and leaned over to get my kiss.*
>
> *"Did you have a good time?" Mom asked.*

FIG. 10–2 This student tries out a classic romantic ending.

I shrugged. I looked out the window. Up the hill, on the front lawn, Ashley was running around in big, loose circles, her arms spread straight out.

"Now, hone in on a line that you want to study really closely. Then copy just that line into your notebook."

Share the line you selected and your thinking about its significance.

I gave students a minute to do this, then said, "The line I copied was 'I sat between my stuff and Ashley.' In that line, the narrator does something so small that if we weren't studying it, we probably wouldn't notice it. She sits *next* to Ashley while she waits for her mom. This proximity shows the reader that she feels closer to Ashley than she did at the start of the story—something has shifted for her. Maybe she'll even continue showing Ashley the kindness that she extended to her with the funeral speech. Maybe these two will be friends."

Suggest that partners work together to study the line they selected and to name what it does for the story. Listen in as they talk.

"Right now, go ahead and share your line with your partner, and then read it together really closely, to name the work that line does and what it means for the story." As students turned and talked, I circulated, listening in. A lot of them had pinpointed the line in which Ashley pretends to fly, including Jada and Samee. After nudging this duo to cite the text specifically, I guided them to talk long about the line.

"This line shows that Ashley is still young, even though she feels so grown up," Jada said.

"But more than that," Samee interrupted. "The narrator watches Ashley pretend to fly, which circles back to the beginning of the story. It makes me think more about all the imagery of birds and flying. And how Ashley's budgies never flew because they were trapped in a cage."

"Oh yeah! I see that too," Jada said. "Maybe Vail wants to show us that Ashley feels free here. Or maybe she's sad and that's her way of making herself feel better."

Notice that the line I pick conveys an important, but subtle message. When I model a skill for students, I usually try to pick a harder, more sophisticated example to showcase, leaving slightly easier ones for them to then discover and try out during the active engagement. Here, my goal is also to convey one of the story's bigger messages, knowing that students will likely pick up on this and extend it when they give this task a go themselves.

SESSION 10 HOMEWORK

CLOSE READING

"Writers, today when you go home and think about the work you are doing here at school, I want you to bring your reading skills to the forefront. Try some close reading of a short story. It can be the one we're studying together, or it could be another one you like. Pick a section to read closely, then mark it up with your thoughts and ideas, either in the margins or on Post-it® notes. Bring it in with you tomorrow. The work you do as a close reader will help you become a more aware and skillful writer."

Reading Drafts like Editors

IN THIS SESSION, you'll teach students that writers become their own editors using a variety of tools to raise the level and quality of their writing.

GETTING READY

✔ Grade 7 and 8 Narrative Writing Checklists (see Teaching and Active Engagement) 💿

✔ An excerpt from the shared class story (see Active Engagement)

✔ "Four Major Types of Sentences" chart (see Mid-Workshop Teaching)

✔ "Ways to Create Conflict" chart (see Share)

✔ "How to Write Compelling Fiction" anchor chart (see Share) 💿

A NYONE WHO TEACHES WRITING (or writes themselves) knows well the challenges of revision. Once students have done the hard work of collecting and developing ideas and turning them into a working draft, it is hard to muster the energy—or the vision—to rework that draft. All too often, students change a few words here, a couple lines there, then sit back in their seats and claim, "I'm done!" Today, more than ever, then, your young writers will need you to rally their engagement. To do that, you will not only provide them with a tangible tool for success. You will package your teaching in shiny paper that begs to be unwrapped.

Though by now your students are well versed at using the Narrative Writing Checklist, you'll likely find that, as with many things you teach, they need reminders to transfer their learning—in this case, reminders to use this invaluable tool to guide their work. The beauty of using the Narrative Writing Checklist during revision is that the guidance it offers is concrete and doable. And "concrete and doable" are exactly what students long for during revision, when their eyes struggle to see an alternative way to structure or craft what is already on the page.

However, it is not simply the tool that rallies students' commitment to revision in today's lesson. It is also how you market that tool. For one, you will acknowledge the tough spot students are in today. For another, you will connect the work they do with the work of real-life writers—ones who turn to editors at this critical juncture in the writing process. And then, once students feel your understanding and know they are not alone, you will hold out the silver tray and say, "I have just the thing to get you over the hurdle."

The best part is that what you have to offer really works. So even if students initially look at you with skepticism in their eyes, they will soon have in hand a list of specific ways to improve and strengthen their drafts, which will in turn give them the direction and the energy to hunker down for the final stretch of the unit.

COMMON CORE STATE STANDARDS: W.7.3, W.7.5, RL.7.10, SL.7.1, SL.7.2, L.7.1.b, L.7.2, L.7.3

Reading Drafts like Editors

CONNECTION

Acknowledge the challenging work that students face and connect it with the work that real-life writers do.

"Most of you are in that really tough place in the writing process—the most dangerous spot, if you ask me. You're done with your drafts. You've done a little revision. It's tempting to say, 'Good enough.' But, you have come too far and worked too hard to stop at 'good enough.' In the professional publishing world, the stage you're in is often when a good editor steps in. Good editors help a writer locate the places where she can elevate her writing from okay to fantastic.

"If you've ever looked at the acknowledgments in a book, the place at the front or back of a book where an author thanks the people who helped her write the book, you'll see she always thanks her editor. That's how important a role editing is!"

"I thought editors only checked small stuff, like punctuation and grammar—that sort of thing," Yasmin barged in.

"Those are done more typically by copy editors or proofreaders. They play a key role, too, but much later in the process, right before the piece is published. The editor I'm talking about is the type that helps you make decisions about craft, structure, meaning, and word choice, and a lot of that work begins fairly early in the writing process. Sometimes I play the role of editor for you. Sometimes your classmates do. Sometimes you will want to be that person for yourself."

I take any opportunity to connect the work that students are doing with the work that writers in the real world do. Doing so gives purpose to what students learn and do in the classroom and feeds the bigger goal of nurturing lifelong writers versus students who write because a teacher gave them an assignment.

❖ Name the teaching point.

"Today I'm going to teach you that the best writers are their own best editors. Writers can support their drafting and revision work by using tools, such as checklists, resource books, and support from peers to ensure that they are working at the highest level."

TEACHING

Use a quote or example from a famous editor, then connect it to the checklist—to show how the checklist can help writers until they develop the innate sense that editors have.

"Some of you might have heard of Ernest Hemingway or F. Scott Fitzgerald. They were very famous writers who worked with an incredible editor named Maxwell Perkins. He was fantastic about not only discovering great writing talents, but also giving incredible feedback to help a writer make his piece the best it could be. Max knew how to read closely and intelligently and had a deep understanding of what made writing great. That sort of understanding doesn't happen overnight. It takes time and practice. And, of course, we also don't all have Max Perkins living in our desks, so we need to figure out ways we can be our own best editors. Tools, like checklists, can help you to lean on that knowledge until it becomes your own."

Explain that the checklist can be used throughout the writing process.

"I know some of you looked at the checklist while you were in your notebook phase. Others of you used the checklist after you finished your first draft and were getting ready to revise. Some of you had it alongside during the entire process. You are sort of using it like a shadow writing teacher, nudging you and reminding you of what you already know how to do and the goals you have planned for yourself. Those of you who have been doing that consistently will be the leaders in this work." A few students shrugged or nodded to show they were game to share.

Discuss the ways students could use the checklist to be their own editors and to elevate the level of their writing, and how using this tool can set them up for work today and into the future.

"If you decide to try to use the checklist in this way, you can place it next to you as you draft, highlighting the places where you want to be especially aware. You could look for the places where you checked 'yes' where you accomplished certain things or made certain moves and see if you really did those things consistently—if you're being hard enough on yourself. And if you are, can you look at the next grade level up? Are there things you can do that would raise the quality of your writing to an even higher level—à la Max Perkins? Can you push yourself to the edges of your very best work and be your own editor?"

ACTIVE ENGAGEMENT

Have students use the checklist on the class story, with your coaching. Choose an excerpt of the story and an excerpt of the checklist for this work.

"Why don't we see if we can do this work with the class story? Let's take a look at another piece of the draft. A section near the end of the story when Esmerelda finally says something. As we read it, let's just look at the string from the seventh- and eighth-grade checklist about description and craft." I hung an enlarged section of the checklist next to where I was projecting the excerpt. "As I read this section out loud, try to go back and forth between the story excerpt and the checklist, thinking of what we could do to be our own best editors, our own Maxwell Perkins."

My teaching feels "light" in this minilesson, because by now, students are well versed at using the Narrative Writing Checklist. Today's minilesson acts more as a way to tell students that what they already know how to do in one context (i.e., use a checklist to set goals) can serve them in others, as well (namely, to guide their revision). Though I tuck in little tips about how to do that work well, I don't feel the need to demonstrate for students before guiding them to practice it on their own in the active engagement.

I couldn't take it anymore. As much as I wanted to be liked by them, I didn't want to be like them if they were going to be mean like this.

"Seriously, guys, you need to check yourselves first," I said.

"What?" Maeve said, a snarl showing up on her perfect nose.

"Tilly's my friend. I won't let you say stuff that's rude about her," I said. I wished my voice was louder and stronger, and my face wasn't burning. But I was glad I was speaking up. I forced my eyes up from the rug to look them in the eyes. They both looked shocked. Liz was leaning all the way forward on the bed now, mouth hanging open.

The students barely let me finish reading before they burst into a flurry of talk, pointing at the checklist.

Refocus students when they get concerned with simply checking things off, and not seeing patterns or the bigger picture (improving the work). Make big the next steps they can see.

Narrative Writing Checklist

	Grade 7	NOT YET	STARTING TO	YES!	Grade 8	NOT YET	STARTING TO	YES!
	Structure				**Structure**			
Overall	I created a narrative that has realistic characters, tension, and change; and that not only conveys, but also develops an idea, lesson, or theme.	☐	☐	☐	I not only created a narrative with well-developed characters who change, I used the story to comment on a social issue, teach a lesson, and/or develop a point of view.	☐	☐	☐
Lead	I wrote a beginning that not only sets the story in motion, it also grounds it in a place or situation. It included details that will later be important to the story. These details might point to the central issue or conflict, show how story elements connect, or hint at key character traits.	☐	☐	☐	In establishing the situation and place, I hinted at a bigger context for the story (revealing issues that have been brewing, showing how the setting affects the character, contextualizing a time in history, and/or developing one out of many points of view).	☐	☐	☐
Transitions	I used transitional phrases and clauses to connect what happened to why it happened (*If he hadn't … he might not have, because of, although, little did she know that*).	☐	☐	☐	I used transitional phrases and clauses, grammatical structures (for example, paragraphing, descriptive phrases, and clauses) and text structures (such as chapter divisions and extended italics) to alert my reader to changes in the setting, the mood, the point of view, or the time in the story.	☐	☐	☐
Ending	I gave the reader a sense of closure by showing clearly how the character or place has changed or the problem has been resolved. If there wasn't resolution, I gave details to leave the reader thinking about a central idea or theme.	☐	☐	☐	I gave the reader a sense of closure by revealing character change(s) that followed from events in the story, or perhaps a resolution. If there wasn't resolution, I wrote to convey how the events of the story affected the characters, and to circle back to a central idea, issue, or theme.	☐	☐	☐
Organization	I used a traditional—or slightly modified—story structure (rising action, conflict, falling action) to best bring out the meaning of my story and reach my audience.	☐	☐	☐	I modified a traditional story structure, dealing with time in purposeful ways, to best suit my genre, bring out the meaning of my story, and reach my audience.	☐	☐	☐

"We're doing everything and on an eighth-grade level!" said Taylor. "I see that we're totally showing character change and complications and hopes and dreams."

"Hold on. Don't just say when you see it. This isn't 'Where's Waldo!' Talk about what you see that we're doing and what might be next steps."

Miriam jumped in. "I think we show a lot of internal conflict in her thinking. And we confirm it with her words. So we're good with the character work. But the setting—our setting work doesn't really reflect the same kind of change. Maybe we can show how the fancy room that at first had so impressed Esmerelda looks either faded or tacky or overdone, now that she sees the kind of people they really are. You know, like that beanbag chair, maybe has some pellets coming out—like you can see the cheap insides. Or that huge, framed mirror has a couple of cracks along the edge. Sort of representing how Esmerelda is now seeing Liz and Maeve."

In some minilessons, especially when students are practicing a new strategy, I create a teaching text that contrasts starkly with where I want students to take it. In other words, I make it easy to see the holes in the before and the growth in the after. In this lesson, however, I use a teaching text that is fairly strong, because I want to emphasize for students that effective self-assessment takes work. I want to push them to look beneath the surface—to read their drafts expecting to find something they can make better, even when there is already a lot of good writing in place.

LINK

Remind students of other drafting and revision strategies they have learned, and suggest that the checklist is something they should consider as a valuable tool to add to that repertoire.

"I think you're getting a good handle on this, guys. I think you are going to be amazing editors for yourselves. You will not fall into the trap of thinking you're done when the work is really just getting started. Today when you go off to work, I think many of you will do some great stuff being your own editors. I want you to remember, you don't just have your checklists, either. You also have the charts in the room, your mentor texts. Even each other. Some of you have been checking in a lot with your partners, even forming writing critique groups. All these tools will go a long way toward making sure your writing will be at the level you most want it to be. After all, my favorite quote from Max Perkins is, 'I believe the author should always be the final judge.'"

Partnering Like an Editor

S O MUCH OF THE WORK your students have likely done so far with their partners has been using their partners more as a listener or sounding board than as a resource for editing. You might decide that today you could teach students who are ready for

more, but perhaps not quite ready for writing critique groups. You could pull those students together and show them that there are many ways to partner like an editor.

(continues)

MID-WORKSHOP TEACHING   **Choosing Sentence Types and Ways of Connecting Thoughts within Sentences**

"Writers, can I stop you for a minute?" I waited until all eyes were on me, then walked over to a chart I had created. "I was listening to a few of you in partnerships talking about your writing, and I overheard one of you say, 'I'm pretty sure that's not how that sentence is technically supposed to go. But I'll just fix it when we get to editing.'" I feigned horror, "How can that be? How can it be that seventh-graders are saying to each other that they know their sentences are probably not right—but 'whatever'?"

The students exchanged sheepish looks: one part guilt, one part accusation that someone got them all in trouble. "So, just to make sure you're not waiting until editing to fix your sentences, and just to make sure you don't waste a second looking for the text or person who might help you answer your questions about sentence construction, I thought I would share this chart with you about sentences. Can you follow along as I talk about each type?"

Four Major Types of Sentences

1. Simple sentences:
   - Contain a subject and predicate (also called an independent clause) and convey a complete idea
   Example: My teacher loves sentences.
2. Compound sentences:
   - Contain two or more subjects and predicates (or independent clauses) and convey more than one complete idea.

They are connected by punctuation, like a semicolon or a conjunction (and, but, so, yet, or, etc.).
Example: My teacher loves sentences and she loves to write them.

3. Complex sentences:
   - Contain one independent clause, with a subject and predicate, and one dependent clause (a group of words that couldn't stand by itself) with a subject and predicate
   Example: Because my teacher loves sentences, I want to write her a good one.
4. Compound-complex sentences:
   - Contain at least one dependent clause and two independent clauses
   Example: After we talk about sentences, we will write some and our teacher will be happy.

After going through the chart with the students, I asked them to try their hands at crafting their own sentences of all four types in their writer's notebooks. After a few minutes of writing, I asked them to share with a partner and added a few class favorites to the chart. I ended with, "So, writers, I hope this settled a few of you who were unsure about what makes up a sentence—or how to make sure your sentence follows accepted conventions. The next time you're in that quandary, feel free to refer back to this chart."

For example, you could teach partnerships how they can read each other's work with various lenses. They could read with the lens of clarity or word choice or tone. They could look to see if they could identify the themes the writer was working toward and spot the places those themes are suggested or inferred. They could also read with the lens of craft, looking for places that could be buoyed up and made stronger, richer, more engaging.

Another move you could teach partnerships is how to give positive, constructive feedback that fuels the writer. You could offer a few suggestions for this type of feedback, such as, "Compliment in such a way that the writer feels that you saw what they were working on—and how you were affected or moved as a reader." And, of course, teach them strategies for offering helpful advice, such as, "Be gentle. Make clear it is only your opinion. However, the more practical the advice, something concrete that the writer can work on right then and there, the more helpful it is. Look to see if you can offer resources or examples to help the writer follow through with the advice." After giving your tips, listen in on partners' conversations, feeling free to whisper in to coach as needed.

Some partnerships find it helpful to observe other partnerships to see how successful partner talk might go. This is especially helpful if you have students who are English language learners or simply struggle with expressing themselves verbally. If this is the case for any of your students, you might consider fishbowling a strong partnership, even from another class, so that students can observe what other kids do when being supportive partners. If that's not possible, you could show them a video clip of writing partners giving feedback. No matter if the observation is live or on video, give students time to name and record the partner moves they observe and then plan ways they could try those moves in their next writing conversation.

Developing Conflict

Congratulate students on the revision work they have done.

"There has been a tremendous amount of work going on in this classroom today. In fact, I would say, I've been impressed with all my seventh-grade classes lately, for the hard work and ways students are sticking to revision—even when the going gets tough. But this class has been especially impressive with its persistence, even when there's been some challenging work to do. Now you're working like real-life writers do. Congratulations on that!"

Share what a published writer suggests about the importance of conflict to fiction—as well as several ways to create conflict.

"I wanted to talk also about something I've seen in your work. This work you've been doing, the stories you've been writing, often involve a kind of conflict. And conflict is what makes things, well, particularly stories, more interesting. There are all sorts of conflicts that show up in fiction. These are things that make characters clash so that there's more tension, more obstacles, more trouble—and all this tension and trouble build and build like a pressure cooker, and just beg to be resolved, one way or another.

"Noah Lukeman, a writer that some of you have heard me talk about before, says there are a few common types of conflicts that writers can use to add some energy to their stories. Follow along on this chart as I discuss some ways to create or build conflict in your stories. One way you might do this is by creating characters who don't like each other. Another way is to force characters who don't like each other to be together—maybe stuck in an elevator or on a bus stuck in traffic. Another way to create conflict is to play with family relationships: parents, grandparents, siblings. They can all cause conflict. What about inner conflicts—wanting one thing, but then wanting something else, too? And of course romance or crushes can cause some interesting conflicts."

Ways to Create Conflict

- Create characters who don't like each other.
- Make characters who don't get along have to be together.
- Highlight family relationships and tensions (mother-daughter, brother-sister, cousins).

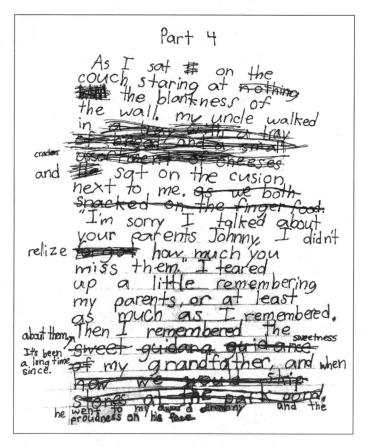

FIG. 11–1   Not a word or sentence is left unexamined in Gabriel's piece.

- Develop inner conflicts (wanting two different things, wanting one thing, but doing something else).
- Introduce a romance or a crush.

"I'm adding conflict to the anchor chart as a key ingredient of well-written stories. This is something you should consider whenever you write a story," I said, gesturing toward the chart.

How to Write Compelling Fiction

- Brainstorm a great story idea (think of small moments, places, events, issues, struggles, stories you wish existed in the world).
- Make your characters come alive (with traits, wants and challenges, self-attitude, relationships).
- Test-drive your character in scenes (envision and write actions, feelings, dialogue, setting, point of view).
- Plot several versions of your story, aiming to intensify the problem (use arcs, timelines, storyboards).
- Draft a 3-D story (story-tell bit by bit, include evidence of your characters' actions, thoughts, feelings).
- Manage space and time.
  - Use summary to quickly move a character across space and time.
  - Use transitional words and phrases to show changes in time or place.
- Become the main character, living through the drama of the story—and then allow your writing to unfold.
- Use paragraphs wisely (to move in place or time, to highlight something, for dramatic impact).
- Revise the lead—and hence the entire story (small action, mood, time and place, foreshadow).
- Research key facts to make the story more believable.
- Get rid of extra stuff that weighs the story down!
- Finish strong—make sure the ending shows what the story is <u>really</u> about, fits the story arc, ties up loose ends.
- **As you revise (or draft) your stories, keep in mind these points:**
  - **Develop or increase conflict (tension, obstacles, trouble—between, among, or within characters).**

LOOKING FOR WAYS TO ADD OR DEVELOP CONFLICT IN YOUR STORY

"Tonight for homework, I want you to consider your story with the lens of conflict. Read through your draft and see if there's any way you can add or heighten conflict to strengthen your story, make it more compelling. You might look especially for the places in your story that might feel like they're dragging. Try adding or developing conflict to see if that makes your writing stronger. I do caution you though—too much conflict can also weaken a story. So make sure not to overdo it!"

Revision

Weaving in Symbolism and Imagery to Bring out Meaning

IN THIS SESSION, you'll teach students that when revising, writers hold onto their intended meaning and use a variety of strategies to ensure that meaning is popped out for their audience.

GETTING READY

✔ "When Fiction Writers Revise to Include Symbolism or Imagery, They . . ." chart made prior to the minilesson (see Teaching)

✔ Draft of shared class story (see Teaching and Conferring and Small-Group Work)

✔ Draft paper (see Teaching)

✔ Excerpt from a student's draft (see Active Engagement)

✔ "How to Write Compelling Fiction" anchor chart (see Link)

✔ "Tips for Writing Realistic Dialogue" chart, one copy for each student (see Share)

COMMON CORE STATE STANDARDS: W.7.3, W.7.5, RL.7.4, RL.7.5, SL.7.1, L.7.1, L.7.2, L.7.3, L.7.5, L.7.6

116

TODAY YOU DRAW an important connection between the work students do as readers and the work they do as writers. You will, of course, have done this prior to now, perhaps without giving it much thought, but today you do it with a particular purpose. Today you spotlight the connection to give students a concrete vision of what is fairly sophisticated work—creating meaning-laden imagery and symbolism in their stories.

First, a suggestion: this session should be fun, not daunting! Don't expect your seventh-graders to do this work perfectly. They won't, and mastery isn't the goal. Rather, the point is to give students the time and space to play around with one craft technique authors use to convey meaning to their readers. Of course, to do this, students will need to first identify what that meaning is, which is why you begin the session by reminding them that they are already doing this work as readers.

Your teaching will be accompanied by a chart that lists a step-by-step way to find and then develop meaning through objects, settings, and actions, and you may find that some kids are pros at this—that they add just the right touches to their stories. Others will have less finesse; they may add an overabundance of clocks (to show time passing) or flying birds of many shapes and sizes (finding "inspiration" from Rachel Vail's "Thirteen and a Half," if you use this as your class mentor text). Expect this, and welcome their approximations.

Meanwhile, recall that adding symbolism to a narrative, while not a craft technique specified by the Common Core State Standards for writing, is one that students will have learned to do as sixth-graders—and to self-assess for if they have been in classrooms of teachers who used the Narrative Writing Checklist ("Craft: I wove together precise descriptions, figurative language, and symbolism to help readers picture the setting, actions, and events and to bring forth meaning"). If so, today's teaching will be a reminder of instruction your students have had in the recent past and will offer them yet another opportunity to practice this technique. And if it's their first time learning this in the context of a writing workshop, they can draw on all that they have learned about spotting symbolism and imagery in stories they have read to now convey meaning in their own. In this way, you can tap the high-level interpretive demands of the Common Core Standards through the side entrance of writing.

Revision

Weaving in Symbolism and Imagery to Bring out Meaning

CONNECTION

Point out the symbolism and imagery that authors have created in some familiar stories—and the meanings these highlight—and suggest that students can use this technique in their stories, too.

"A couple of days ago, during reading workshop, I overhead a few of you talking about our mentor text, 'Thirteen and a Half,' after doing some close reading of another text in your book club. This group had noticed some similarities between the class mentor story and the novel they were reading, *Wonder*, by R. J. Palacio. Both texts have compelling images, like Ashley pretending to fly (in 'Thirteen and a Half') and the boy's face in *Wonder*, as well as symbols—the bird and the jewelry box coffin (in 'Thirteen and a Half') and a mask the main character wears when he is small (in *Wonder*). The club was talking about how these images and symbols helped them understand some of the central ideas in these two stories—like being torn between wanting to be a kid and wanting to grow up.

"I immediately thought of the work we were doing in writing workshop. How you, too, are writing meaningful stories, like the ones Rachel Vail and R. J. Palacio wrote. And that you could do some of the work they and other authors like them do all the time by using imagery and symbolism to highlight your meaning."

❖ **Name the teaching point.**

"Today I want to teach you that fiction writers have tools to clarify the meanings in their stories for their reader. They can spotlight what's most important by including imagery and symbolism. They do this by focusing on key objects, settings, or actions."

Because the teaching of today's minilesson may be difficult to grasp, I begin by citing concrete examples of imagery and symbols in familiar stories that relay meanings I imagine students may want to convey in their own stories—like the desire to hold onto parts of childhood while also wanting to grow up. In this way, I scaffold the work they will try out today even before they begin.

TEACHING

Convey to students some ways they might revise their stories to include imagery and symbolism that spotlight meaning—and reveal a premade chart naming these.

"Some of you may be thinking that imagery and symbolism are too complicated for you to incorporate as writers. After all, you've just started to get good at spotting these as readers. But, the truth is, in some ways, creating imagery and symbolism that spotlight the meaning in your own stories is almost easier than finding and studying these as readers. It's the same thing as when you hide something from someone. It is so much easier to be the hider than the finder.

And, really, when you use imagery and symbolism to highlight meaning in your stories, you're doing a sort of literary hiding. Here are some ways you can use imagery and symbolism in your own stories," I said, pointing to a premade list on chart paper.

When Fiction Writers Revise to Include Symbolism or Imagery, They . . .

1. Reflect on what the story is really about—the deeper meanings/central ideas
2. Reread the story looking for objects, settings, actions that reflect this meaning to develop as symbols/images:
   - Describe these in detail
   - Increase the importance of these to characters
   - Repeat these in a few places throughout story to make them pop for the reader
3. Reread to make sure that those choices clarify, rather than distract from, the meaning

Demonstrate how you follow these steps to revise one of the scenes in the shared class story.

"Now, if we were to add symbolism to our Esmerelda story, we would start by thinking, 'What is this story really about?' That meaning has evolved a bit, hasn't it? If we'd answered this question when we began writing the story, I think we would have agreed it was about fitting in. But lately, the story has felt more and more about how the choices we make can affect us and the people in our lives. And also about the idea of knowing the kind of person you are and recognizing the importance of standing up for yourself and the people you care about, not just compromising who you are to fit in." I laughed. "That's a lot!"

"I'm going to reread our story, and as I do, help me look for objects, settings, or actions we could develop to reflect this meaning." I turned to a projected copy of part of our class draft.

> As I walked down the hallway, I listened for other kids' voices. I knew some of my friends must have been somewhere, but I also really want to find the popular kids, like Liz and Maeve.
>
> "I know! That is so funny!" I heard from a doorway on the left. I was pretty sure it was Maeve's voice.
>
> I walked a few more steps, not sure if I should go into the room or not.
>
> "I have never laughed so hard in my whole life," said Liz, her voice sounding so happy.
>
> I turned to the doorway and saw them in a room that must have been Liz's bedroom.

"So, based on what I know about the meaning of the story, a couple of objects, well, setting pieces really, jump out at me. The long hallway and the doorways. Are you guys seeing that too?" A few students nodded. "I think I could make the doorways themselves a bit more important because they could represent choices. Do I choose this door or this one? And I could also really do some work with the hallway, describe it more so that it is elevated from a set piece to

Here, I do two things: first, I convey the message that a story's meaning may shift. A writer might begin with one big idea in mind and later discover that, in fact, she is writing about something else—in this way underscoring the fact that authors revise not just their writing, but their ideas. Second, I demonstrate how to articulate some central meanings in the class story, so that students will have a model for how they might articulate the central meanings that are evolving in their own stories.

You'll notice throughout these units that even when the focus is on me teaching, I set students up to be active participants. Often it's simply by telling them how I want them to read or listen or watch and by asking questions that I expect them to ponder without answering aloud—questions that I will answer aloud as I exemplify my teaching point.

an image. The long hallway, especially if I show it as dark and a little confusing, can be a nice transition image for her choices." I picked up the pen and wrote.

> I headed into the hallway. It was much longer than my hallway at home, and sort of empty. My hallway at home was covered with family pictures and filled with light. This one was plain, nothing hanging on the walls. And, since someone had turned out the lights, it was a bit dark. As I walked down the hallway, I listened for other kids' voices. I knew some of my friends must have been somewhere, but I also really wanted to find the popular kids, like Liz and Maeve.
>
> "I know! That is so funny!" I heard from a white trimmed doorway on the left. I was pretty sure it was Maeve's voice.
>
> I walked a few more steps, not sure if I should go into the room or not. There was light pouring out of that doorway.
>
> "I have never laughed so hard in my whole life," said Liz, her voice sounding so happy.
>
> I turned to the glowing, beckoning doorway and saw them in a room that must have been Liz's bedroom.

ACTIVE ENGAGEMENT

Invite students to practice the revision work you just modeled, by imagining what imagery and symbolism might bring out the intended meaning of a former student's story.

"Writers, let's practice this. Max told me he was really trying to write a story about a kid with bad self esteem trying to get comfortable with himself, no matter what other people said. Here's a short piece of his story. Take a quick look at this and think a bit about ways we might use imagery and symbolism to elevate the meaning if we were Max." I projected the excerpt onto the board.

> I sat in the middle of the bus. The cool kids sat in the back. The nerdy kids sat in the front where the bus driver could keep an eye on them. I sat in the middle with all the sort of regular kids. The ones who just wanted to be left alone. I sat by myself, wishing, like I always did, that my mom would let me walk home like Rick. But she always said, "One more year. When you're in High School you can knock yourself out." Then she laughed like she had made the funniest joke in the world.
>
> Anyway, I was sitting on the bus, bored and trying not to be noticed when I took out my phone. I went to swipe to turn it on and it flashed red battery sign. It was dead!! Now what? I had a long bus ride home with nothing to do. I could do my homework, but why would I want to do that?

"He could add something about the phone. You know, like how you can use the phone as a mirror. That would be a way to show he's thinking about himself—that he's self-conscious," Shane said.

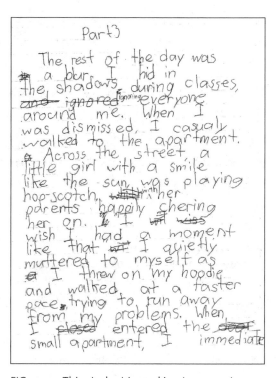

FIG. 12–1   This student is working to pop out contrasting images.

"Yeah," Ryan chimed in. "He can look in the phone like it's a mirror and not like what he sees. Then the phone could be a symbol for what he feels about himself and a symbol of how he doesn't feel connected to the world because, you know, it doesn't work." Ryan grinned.

"Or," Yasmin chimed in, "Max could work on the imagery a bit more. The imagery of Rick being gone. Maybe focus on the fact that the seat next to him is empty and almost every other seat on the vehicle has two people sitting together."

"All of these are great ideas," I said. "I can tell from all the hands that are still up that you have a lot more, but I think you're getting the hang of this. You don't actually have to add a lot to develop symbolism and imagery in your stories."

LINK

Challenge students to think through their next steps, making a plan of the work their stories would benefit from next.

"When you go off to write today, I know you might be tempted to do the most exciting thing you can think of to your piece—in this case, adding symbolism and imagery and metaphors. But I want you to restrain yourself a bit. You wouldn't jump to throwing sprinkles on a cupcake without first baking it and icing it. It's the same thing with writing fiction. You need to make sure you've done all the foundational work first, so that the sprinkles have some place to stick. So before you head to your seats, make a mental plan of what your draft needs you to do first." I paused to give them time to think.

"Now, think of what should come next, after that." I waited again.

"And of course, you can always refer to our handy anchor chart to help draft, plan, and revise your writing. In fact, while I'm thinking of it, let me add a point about symbolism, imagery, and metaphors."

The hall was dim, taking in the dark light from the overcast sky. I walked through it silently, my shoulder brushing against the wall. That's when my eyes caught at the bright neon yellow poster that said—

"Vote for Lily!" followed by
- I will encourage more afterschool activities
- I will encourage kids to show good character
- I will ~~stop the bullying~~ *stand up to bullying*

The last idea made me swallow. Was I really honest when I wrote that? I asked myself. Or was it just a cheat to get elected? Either way, as student council representative, I was responsible for keeping my promises, right? But how was I supposed to keep this one? My head was mixed up with all these questions, all these thoughts crying for a break. I looked around me to see if anyone was looking and <u>viciously</u> tore the poster off the wall, digging my fingernails into the top of the hard paper. *(adds tension)*

"It needed to come down anyway," I mumbled.

For the first time in a while, the hall filled with sunshine. The beams of bright light shooting through the windows. ~~The hall~~ was buzzing with kids talking about their weekend plans. But I talked to no one. I had too much on my mind. My heart pounded, and I was left wondering if I'd really do what I said I'd do…stand up to Britany. What was I thinking? I couldn't do it! But I promised, I sighed with regret.

Then a thought occurred to me ⟶

FIG 12–2 Annabelle uses setting to match her characters' feelings and the story's plot.

By now, you are accustomed to the fact that, at the end of a minilesson, I do not send students back to their seats with a directive to practice here and now what I just taught. Today's lesson goes a step further in that I almost discourage students from practicing the teaching point! My message to students is manifold and actually one of the most important ones I can send—that writers don't do things just to do them. They constantly broaden their repertoire of techniques but aim to use them purposefully. Which also means that writers constantly check in with their current writing and with themselves to make those thoughtful decisions.

How to Write Compelling Fiction

- Brainstorm a great story idea (think of small moments, places, events, issues, struggles, stories you wish existed in the world).
- Make your characters come alive (with traits, wants and challenges, self-attitude, relationships).
- Test-drive your character in scenes (envision and write actions, feelings, dialogue, setting, point of view).
- Plot several versions of your story, aiming to intensify the problem (use arcs, timelines, storyboards).
- Draft a 3-D story (story-tell bit by bit, include evidence of your characters' actions, thoughts, feelings).
- Manage space and time.
  - Use summary to quickly move a character across space and time.
  - Use transitional words and phrases to show changes in time or place.
- Become the main character, living through the drama of the story—and then allow your writing to unfold.
- Use paragraphs wisely (to move in place and time, to highlight something, for dramatic impact).
- Revise the lead—and hence the entire story (small action, mood, time and place, foreshadow).
- Research key facts to make the story more believable.
- Get rid of extra stuff that weighs the story down!
- Finish strong—make sure the ending shows what the story is <u>really</u> about, fits the story arc, ties up loose ends.
- As you revise (or draft) your stories, keep in mind these points:
  - Develop or increase conflict (tension, obstacles, trouble—between, among, or within characters).
  - **Reflect on deeper meanings/central ideas of your story and consider objects, settings, actions that you can develop as symbols, images, or metaphors.**

"Once you have that plan, go ahead and make it public by telling someone near you what you will do today. Then off you go!"

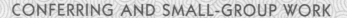

Tucking in Character History to Create Character Depth

AT THIS POINT IN THE UNIT, most students will have their drafts well on their way. There will certainly be a lot of troubleshooting in your conferences and small groups. However, it is also crucial that you remind yourself to teach to not only "fix," but also to elevate. Encourage students to carry through on their plans to add symbolism, imagery, and metaphors, to take risks and experiment with vivid images and language, but at the end, to always make sure their efforts have a purpose and deepen the meaning that is conveyed to readers.

You might decide to pull a group of students together who all have solid drafts but who could all benefit from another layer of depth in their pieces. These writers could range from your strongest to some of your more struggling writers. As long as their drafts have a clear trajectory and are hitting the key points needed in a fiction story, they would be candidates for today's small-group work. You could even decide to pull a mixed-ability table group, because the chances are pretty high that students have yet to experiment with your teaching point: fiction writers often add a bit of back story or personal history to create character depth and believability.

"Writers, when I teach, often I refer to my life. Particularly when I was your age, right?" They all nodded. "When I do that, what does that do for you as a listener and learner?"

Jada looked up, "It lets me that you were once our age. That you can relate to us." I nodded.

Brandon jumped in, "It also tells me that you're real. That you have a real life."

"What Jada and Brandon are saying about telling stories in teaching actually is the same reason many writers include a bit of history or back story about their characters. We all have histories. When our characters do too, it makes them more relatable. It is also true that having a past makes things feel more real. It helps our readers suspend disbelief.

MID-WORKSHOP TEACHING   Creating Metaphors

"Writers, I need to interrupt for just a few quick minutes," I said, moving toward Harriet. "I was just talking with Harriet. She is thick in the world of symbolism and imagery, like many of you are. But she also talked a bit about another thing writers might do to elevate their writing and give good work for their readers to do. That is, you can create metaphors for different ideas in your story.

"As many of you know, metaphors are a way of talking about or describing something by comparing it to something else. So, as many of you already know, Harriet's character is trying to make the track team. Harriet decided to try to describe her main character's hard work in getting ready for the tryouts with a metaphor. First, she thought of what she wanted to say, just in plain language. She was working as hard as she possibly could at what felt like an impossible task. She wasn't sure if she was strong enough or not, but she wasn't going to give up.

"Next, she thought of other things or people that are that way too. She started to think about things that are little that do big things and ended up deciding on a tugboat—those little ships that tug huge cruise ships and barges through the harbor. This is what she came up with."

April ran up the stadium steps, her breath ragged, her legs aching, her whole body telling her to quit. She didn't. She was a tugboat pulling the largest barge in New York Harbor, and she was going to use all her strength to pull that huge, heavy barge all the way to the dock.

"The great thing about trying this out in your stories is that it doesn't take a whole lot to have an effect. Just a line or two make a difference. Look at me try it with our class story."

> I couldn't take it anymore. As much as I wanted to be liked by them, I didn't want to be like them if they were going to be mean like this.
>
> "Seriously, guys, you need to check yourselves first," I said.
>
> "What?" Maeve said, a snarl showing up on her perfect nose.
>
> "Tilly's my friend. I won't let you say stuff that's rude about her," I said. I wished my voice was louder and stronger, and my face wasn't burning. But I was glad I was speaking up. I forced my eyes up from the rug to look them in the eyes. They both looked shocked. Liz was leaning all the way forward on the bed now, mouth hanging open.

"In this part of the story, maybe I can add a line or two, a memory that calls up something that helps motivate her to act. Like, right after it says, 'I couldn't take it anymore' I could add":

> My mind went back to that time when I was seven, playing on the jungle gym with my friends when the new girl Joanne came over to play. My friends started to make monkey noises and say, "Here comes the monkey." I didn't say anything at all.

"Just a few sentences, but those sentences give the readers another part of Esmerelda's back story. Yes, she's loyal to her friend. Yes, she's ethical. But also, in her past she did something wrong that she wants to make right. Just a line or two of character history, put in the right place, can make the whole story more believable and layered."

Revising for Authentic Dialogue

Tell students that fiction writers craft authentic-sounding dialogue. Suggest that one way to do this is by eavesdropping on real conversations, noticing how people do—and don't—speak.

"Your stories are getting so incredible and real! So much so that I sometimes am not sure if I am reading realistic fiction or personal narrative. I think you are ready to look closely at something most of you really enjoy writing: dialogue. The tip I want to give you today about dialogue is this: fiction writers craft dialogue with an ear toward authenticity. That is, they ask themselves, 'Is this how people really talk? Is this how this character would really talk?'

"One of the best ways to get good at writing dialogue is to eavesdrop a bit on other people's conversations. I like to listen in on conversations on the bus, in restaurants, at parties. I like to pay attention to the words people use—the ways they speak differently. Moms talk differently than teenagers (most of the time!). Doctors speak differently than preschoolers. I also like to notice the way people talk—not in complete sentences all the time, and often with speech tics, like 'um.' And then there's the actual stuff that people talk about, especially what they say and what they leave out. When we talk to each other, we don't tell each other every bit of information that the person we're talking to already knows, because they already know it. Like I don't say, 'Mom, can you grab me a box of my favorite cereal—Wheaty-Os—from Key Food when you go there after work at 5:00?' Because she knows all of those details. So if I were writing this dialogue in my story, I would write, 'Mom, can you pick up my cereal on your way home?' If I felt like the reader needed to know more details, I could include the extra information in my thoughts or summary.

"I'm giving each of you a little reminder of some tips for writing realistic dialogue." I gestured toward a chart I had created and handed them each a copy.

> ### Tips for Writing Realistic Dialogue
>
> - Make sure each character speaks in a way that makes sense for who they are. Moms should sound like moms. Teachers should sound like teachers. Kids should sound like kids.
> - Include only the information characters would really say to each other. Don't pack dialogue with information for the readers. Use character's thinking or summary for that.
> - Feel free to include speech tics when it makes sense to do so. The character might say "like" a lot, or talk using a lot of big words.

SESSION 12 HOMEWORK

WRITING AUTHENTIC DIALOGUE

"For homework, I'd like you to do a little eavesdropping. I would like you to listen to people who are like the characters in your stories—moms, dads, grandparents, little sisters, basketball players, teachers, other kids on your bus ride home. Then I'd like you to reread your draft with the lens of dialogue. See if you can do a bit of revision to make your dialogue sound and feel more authentic. Try saying the dialogue aloud to test it out. Does it sound like a real person? Does it sound like what the character would actually say?"

Session 13

Conducting the Rhythm of Language

Creating Cadence and Meaning through Syntax

ODAY'S MINILESSON will depart from the usual structure, following not a classic demonstration model, but a guided practice model. I chose this structure for this day because the teaching is subtle and can be challenging. Today you will teach students to pay attention to the rhythm—the cadence—of their writing. You will teach them how to use syntax to create sentences whose cadence conveys a particular effect. There's another way in which this minilesson departs from the usual kind; rather than sharing an anecdote that connects to the instruction, I invite students to be active from the moment the lesson begins, to listen to two portions of two very different songs. In this way, I introduce the fact that today is about hearing as much as it is about writing.

What you'll see, as you read on, is that I break down the instruction into smaller steps, first modeling one step using the shared class story, before giving students a chance to try that step on the spot, in their own stories, then modeling the next step, and again, giving students a chance to give it a go. Then I model how to perform both steps, as needed, alternating between the two. In this way, I offer additional scaffolds. You will see that the steps increase in sophistication; first, I show students how to turn a long sentence into several short ones, to speed up the action. Next, I show them how to add description or clauses to a sentence in a section of the story where my goal is to slow the action down—to get the reader to linger, noticing more detail. Finally, I show students how to do this work not on a sentence level, but on an entire section of text, alternating between short, medium, and long sentences, basing their decisions on both the cadence and meaning they intend to convey.

Of course, you could teach this minilesson differently. If your students are old pros at writing varied sentences, if they have a felt sense of how to alter syntax to create particular effects, you may instead want to teach the first two steps in a traditional demonstration before having them give this a quick try and then sending them off to write. Whatever you decide, make sure to offer additional support to any students who struggle to grasp this teaching—as some surely will.

IN THIS SESSION, you'll teach students that writers pay attention to the pacing and rhythm of their writing as another way to bring out meaning while they revise or draft. In particular, they pay close attention to the ways sentences are stitched together, in terms of length and type.

GETTING READY

- ✔ The instrumental versions of the songs "The Fox," by Ylvis, and "At Last," by Etta James, or two similarly disparate pieces of music of your choice (see Connection)

- ✔ Students' writer's notebooks, drafts, and pens (see Teaching and Active Engagement)

- ✔ Draft of shared class story (see Teaching and Active Engagement)

- ✔ Chart paper and markers (see Teaching and Active Engagement and Mid-Workshop Teaching)

- ✔ "How to Write Compelling Fiction" anchor chart (see Share)

COMMON CORE STATE STANDARDS: W.7.3, W.7.4, W.7.5, RL.7.4, RL.7.5, SL.7.1, L.7.1b, L.7.2, L.7.3

Conducting the Rhythm of Language

Creating Cadence and Meaning through Syntax

CONNECTION

Play two short instrumental sections of two songs with distinctly different rhythms—one fast and one slow—and ask students to notice and name the differences, as well as the effects each song has on them.

"Writers, I'm going to play a couple of short segments of two different songs. As you listen, I want you to pay attention to the rhythm. Here's the first one." I pulled out my iPad and played the instrumental beginning of "The Fox" by Ylvis.

"Now listen to this one." This time, I played the instrumental start of Etta James' "At Last."

"Turn and tell a person near you what you noticed. What was different between these two songs? Focus on what sort of rhythm each one has and how that affected you."

Share what students noticed and explain that musicians use rhythm to create mood.

After thirty seconds, I said, "I heard most of you say that the first song was sort of punchy—with fast beats—and that the second song was slower—that it sounded like more of a swoon.

"Almost all of you felt excited by the first song. I saw some of you kind of grooving to the beat. Some of you said it made you want to dance, or get up and do something—it energized you. Some of you said the second song sounded sort of romantic and corny—like something you might slow dance to. Other of you felt a little sad listening to it, or just kind of pensive.

"Musicians use different beats and instruments to create one rhythm or another—or often, many different kinds of rhythms within one song. They do this, in part, to create a certain mood."

❖ **Name the teaching point.**

"Today I'm going to teach you that sentences are the instruments of writing. Different types of sentences create different kinds of sounds and bring in different kinds of meaning. Writers can affect the rhythm and meaning of their stories by crafting sentences of different lengths and types."

This is an unusual way to begin a minilesson, I know, but it serves me well. Playing music for students does two things: it grabs students' attention and it gives them a clear introduction to today's teaching—which is subtle and sophisticated. So often, we ask students to use their eyes—to watch, read, write. Here, we ask them to use their ears—to listen. Being able to hear the rhythm of these two very different pieces of music will serve them well when they turn next to the task of noticing and experimenting with the rhythm of their writing. You'll also notice I do not play the lyrics. This is because I want the students to focus on the rhythm, and quite frankly, even though these songs may be familiar to many students, the lyrics could create distraction. If you feel that these songs aren't a good match for your students, as always, choose an option that works best for them.

TEACHING AND ACTIVE ENGAGEMENT

Explain the connections between sentence length and rhythm and meaning.

"Just like when you were listening to music a minute ago, and you noticed the different effects each rhythm had on you and how the speed of the beats and the tone of each song affected your mood, writing can do that, too, on the sentence level. I know you've noticed before now—in sixth grade, certainly, and probably even before—that sentences are made up of different lengths. There are short sentences and medium ones, as well as long sentences, and even very, very long ones. What you might *not* have noticed, though, is that sentences do more than just share information, or parts of a story. They also play a role in the sound—or cadence—of a piece, and in conveying an effect—a mood or a meaning.

"Usually, when a sentence is short, it reads very quickly. When there are a bunch of short sentences stacked together in a paragraph, they move the piece along at a faster pace. Sometimes, short, choppy sentences are used to build suspense or create tension. If a sentence is longer, it is often read more slowly, so writers often use longer sentences to give more information to the reader—complex descriptions, thoughts, that sort of thing. Or they might use longer sentences to slow down the action."

Set students up to do some experimenting with their own sentences.

"When you are crafting sentences in your pieces, you might want to play a bit with the sentence length to both alter the rhythm—or way—your readers read your writing and to see if you can make the movement of the story match the movement of your sentences. So let's give this a try together. Let's try some drafting and revision work on the sentence level. Do you all have your writer's notebook and draft handy? We're going to do this a little differently, so you'll need to be ready. First, I'll model a bit of work, and then I'll give you a chance to do it yourselves." I gave students a second to gather their materials.

"As we go through this activity, I'm going to ask you to locate sentences from your draft to experiment with. You'll try these out in your notebook. First, I'll model."

Begin by modeling how to turn a sentence full of information into three short sentences that speed up the action.

"I'm going to go to the beginning of the story, where Esmerelda is watching some of the cool kids at the party try some dangerous stunts. There's the part where the kids are climbing up on a step stool balanced on the dining room table to reach the chandelier and they try to swing on it. Let me just lift a single sentence from that section," I said, and copied this sentence onto chart paper:

> James climbed up onto the table and started to make his way to the step stool.

"There's a lot of information here in this sentence, which is good, but because it's a longer sentence, it slows down the action. Hear that?" I read it again, for effect. "Also, I want it to be clear to the reader that in one quick motion, James climbed—without thinking. If I break this one sentence into a few shorter sentences, I bet I can get things to speed up,

Rather than simply telling students that sentence length affects the rhythm and meaning of a piece, I offer concrete and transferable strategies for when and why a writer might choose longer or shorter sentences—and then of course I share examples of what this looks like.

and readers will see how impulsive this kid James is." I picked up my pen and wrote the following under the original sentence:

> James clambered onto the table. He jumped onto the stool. It wobbled. He shimmied. Then he went for it. He reached for the chandelier.

"Ooh—I like that. The action moves much more quickly now, and the reader gets the idea that James's movements are as fast and jerky as the sentences. Notice how I replaced *climbed* with *clambered*, which gets at James's jerky, clumsy action here. Everything's moving unsteadily and quickly—James, the stool."

Though my focus is on sentence structure, I do not hesitate to tuck in a bit of teaching on word choice. Because I do it quickly, and because it connects with my teaching since word choice, like sentence structure, affects the meaning of the piece, I am confident that the move won't distract from the lesson at hand. Furthermore, it sends the message that as writers set out with one task in mind, other issues often get addressed as well, and I want students to move comfortably among all the issues and opportunities they must attend to in a piece.

✻ We told her it was going to be okay. It wasn't. ~~No one gets higher then a~~

✻ Boy was it hard.

✻ We got through first. second. Third. ~~point~~

✻ We put our arms around her and told her it was going to be okay when we all know it wasn't, no one gets above a 89 on Ms. Gulch's tests. when we ~~all~~ got to the corner of the block, we ~~all~~ went our diferent ways all thinking, "what can we do to help?" Later that after noon, after being greeted at home by two younger twin sisters fighting over a Bitty Baby ™, a mom who was still at

---

We had already told Rose (Ruby's mom) of our plan so we tiptoed up to Ruby's room where apparently she had been sitting since she got home. we barged into Ruby's room and she gasped "What are you doing?" I have to admitt, we may have been a strange sight ✻ me wearing all yellow and having cut-out paper neutrons and electrons taped all over me ; Irma in all red with different elements taped all over her; and May in all blue on one half and all orange on the other, comparing ionic and covaylent bonds. Then, as she realized what we were and why we were here, after all of the explinations had been made she was so happy, she shone like the sun. We helped her study for three hours, and ✻ boy was it hard

---

✻ We got through first, second and third period, lunch, talking science the whole period, and fith. Then around rolled sixth period. Ms. Gulch held her pencil like it was an axe as she told us all the 1,000,000,000 ways we could loose points. Then the test began, I didn't falter or a single question, teaching people really teaches you too! Even the bonus question was easy, I hope Ruby felt so too. At the end of the period we all groupped at the end of the hallway as usual and regroupped. "It wasn't that bad!" Ruby cried and we all had a cheesy group hug.

✻ One week later ✻
Have you ever seen a shiny sticker? Because I have. The one that rested on the top right hand corner of Ruby's test in the hallway signifying she had gotten the highest grade anyone had ever gotten on Ms. Gulch's test, a 96!

FIG. 13–1   Since Miriam tended to write longer sentences, she decided to try short sentences for a new effect.

Ask students to do what you just modeled with a sentence in their own drafts.

"Your turn to give this a go. Find a place in your draft where you want the action to move a little faster, or for it to be a little jerkier, for whatever reason. Once you find that place, lift a sentence and write a shorter version of it, or break it down into a few shorter sentences in your notebook."

I circulated as students worked.

Model taking a different sentence, from a different part of the class story, and extending it for craft and meaning purposes.

"So now that we've created shorter sentences out of a long one, you're probably already thinking about where in the Esmerelda story we might want to craft some longer sentences. Generally, authors use longer sentences for descriptive passages, passages with a lot of information, or else in parts where they want the reader to slow down. This might be a part that provides important information that the reader needs to pay attention to, or it could be a beautiful part that invites readers to linger. Or it could just be a part where timing in the story has slowed down—like slow motion in a movie. Or sometimes a writer will create sentences that are uncomfortably long to show a character's or a situation's discomfort.

Again, I name transferable strategies for students that include when and why a writer might use a particular technique, so students can make purposeful decisions about craft and technique as they write.

"When I think about all of this, I think of the scene we were working on the other day—the one where Esmerelda was sitting in the bedroom at the party with the popular girls, Liz and Maeve. It's a big change from all the wildness out in the living room. So it makes sense to slow the pace down a bit. Also, there's the room itself. Maeve's room is very fancy. It merits being described in some detail. Here's part of the original draft":

> I looked around the room. It had a bed and a dresser. There was a bean bag chair in the corner.
> "Have a seat," Maeve said. Liz was spread out on the bed.

"It's fine. It describes a bit. But not in great detail, and not in a way that distinguishes this room as fancy. And the rhythm is not significantly different than that of the first scene. Let me try to revise, this time working to make some of the sentences longer by adding phrases, clauses, that sort of thing."

> I looked around the room, trying not to stare too long at any one thing. It was decorated exactly the way you might expect a girl like Maeve's room would be decorated. It had a huge white bed, covered in tons of pillows of different shapes and sizes, and there was a tall, ornately carved dresser, that looked like it might have been an antique.

"Notice the difference? I feel like I'm being drawn into Maeve's room—the clauses help me to picture it, and they slow things down, which gets me to linger. I'm also feeling a bit uncomfortable, as I imagine Esmerelda herself feels—out of place, almost."

Ask students to try making a longer sentence from a different section of their draft. Publicly compliment the work you see, so that students will hear what their peers are doing.

"Writers, can you give this a try? Find a place in your draft that would benefit from some slowing down of the rhythm—a place where you want to slow the action down and include more information. You can add phrases and clauses inside the commas to include additional information, like I did. You could also add conjunctions and create compound sentences."

As students worked, I circulated again, voicing over a few additional tips and comments to support those who needed more support with their sentence creations.

"Nice move, combining a couple of shorter sentences together!"

"Oh—is that a semicolon? That's a great piece of punctuation to link clauses, isn't it?"

"I'm seeing a lot of you looking at our example or your mentor text to get ideas for how to craft your sentences. That's a good use of tools."

"Really nice work, writers! I love watching your sentences grow longer and more complex—and feeling the time slow down."

Choose a larger section of text, perhaps a paragraph, from the class story, and model choosing how to revise each sentence in the section to effect rhythm and meaning.

"Ready for the last step? We're going to move from individual sentences to a longer swath of text. We'll take what we just practiced and consider all the sentences in a whole section, deciding which ones could be shortened, which could be lengthened, and which can stay the same. This is the part right after Esmerelda enters the room." I turned the page on my chart pad to an old excerpt.

> "So, Esmé," Maeve interrupted. She was looking at me, calling me a much cooler version of my name than I was used to.
>
> I couldn't help myself, I smiled. She had given me a cool nickname. It was almost like we were friends. My eyes left the spot on the carpet I had been staring at and looked at Maeve. "Yeah?" I said, in what I hoped was my coolest voice.

"Looking at the first sentence, I think it's pretty good. That line of dialogue moves the story along—and it grabs our attention. In the second sentence, I feel like Esmerelda would reflect just a bit more. There's a big shift here. By calling her 'Esmé,' Maeve has in a sense invited her into her inner circle. So here, I think we should slow things down a bit, maybe tuck in more reflection.

Notice that the suggestions I make here also set students up to do language work that the Common Core Standards expect of seventh-graders.

She was looking at me—Maeve, **the most popular girl in school, the one who I had wanted to be friends with for a long time,** calling me a much cooler version of my name than I was used to.

"Now, the next sentence feels like it needs to be shorter to break up the rhythm. Also, I think Esmerelda is a little shocked by how she's feeling, and shock is a fast feeling. This calls for a fast sentence. Let me try breaking up the next sentence":

I couldn't help myself. I smiled.

"Looking over the rest of the sentences, I feel like they really work. It's as if we're drumming out a rhythm here. Medium, s-l-o-w, quick, quick, medium, medium, s-l-o-w, medium. Hear that?" I reread the section again, emphasizing each sentence's speed—fast, medium, or slow—so that students would hear the rhythm.

Ask students to apply the work they just did on a sentence level to a larger section of their text, preferably one rich with either meaning, description, action, or all three.

"One last try for you before you move back to your seat. Look for a paragraph you'd like to study, and revise to support the rhythm and meaning of that section. Read through each sentence and ask yourself, 'Is this sentence the right length? Does it say enough? Does it say too much? How does it sound?' Then do the work that each sentence you've identified needs done."

Once again I circulated around the classroom, mostly murmuring encouragement and taking note of students who appeared to be struggling with sentence writing in general, and with syntax revision in particular. I made a mental note to myself to meet with them later on in a conference or as a small group.

LINK

Remind students that they can pay attention to rhythm and experiment with sentence length and pacing anytime they write fiction.

"Writers, you might have just crafted some new sentences you want to include in your piece, and hopefully you picked up a few tricks you want to try in your writing. But if you decide you don't like any of the things you just experimented with in your notebook, that's okay. The important thing is that you hold on to what you learned today going forward, knowing that you can use it down the line. Anytime you write fiction, whether during this unit or in the future, you can always take this new way of looking at sentences—and of *hearing* the rhythm they make—to craft your own, to play around with length and pacing."

I ask students to do sophisticated work in this lesson, which is not only about varying sentence length, but about figuring out where and why they might do so. By looking first at individual sentences and then at a larger swath of text, I gradually scaffold students' thinking.

Constantly, I informally assess my students as writers. The active engagement of a minilesson provides a perfect opportunity to notice who might benefit from additional support during independent writing.

Always, I emphasize for students how writers make purposeful choices. Sometimes, the purposeful choice is to practice a new technique, in which case one might work inside the writers' notebook, perhaps composing one isolated bit of writing after another. Other times, the purposeful choice is to pop out the meaning of a piece, in which case one is more likely work inside a draft, moving between and relying on different techniques, depending on which best serves the goal.

Studying the Cadence in Dialogue

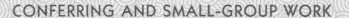

AS YOU WORK WITH YOUR STUDENTS TODAY, plan to follow up right away with any kids who struggle with the basic work of sentence construction. For example, if you see students who are struggling with simple sentence structure, you'll want to support them in that. Additionally, it is not uncommon for students first gesturing toward more sophisticated syntax to create a lot of run-on sentences. Be aware that this is a developmental pitfall, and plan to come up with a toolkit of ways to deal with sentence complexity that does not only teach how to cut up longer sentences into shorter ones. Teaching conjunctions, dashes, semicolons, and other ways to join sentences will go a long way toward helping students. And, of course, there may be other work related to revision that has no relation to syntax, which you will want to address right away. For example, many students at this stage of the game might grapple with

clarity. They think their story is clear, but it is confusing. Or, alternatively, some students' stories could benefit from an additional layer of conflict or tension.

If, however, you want to do work more related to the minilesson topic, or you have time to do both, you might decide to gather a small group of students together who seem to understand the whole sentence length-rhythm-meaning connection, and take them on another exploration of syntax—this time with the cadence of dialogue.

It was my friend and colleague, Kate Roberts, who is also a playwright, who first taught me that when writing dialogue, any dialogue, one thing a writer should keep in mind is that each speaker has a different way of talking, a different rhythm. Some

---

MID-WORKSHOP TEACHING Placing Phrases and Clauses within Sentences

"I'd like to get everyone's attention for just a minute," I said. "Quite a few of you are working on lengthening your sentences by adding more information, so I want to be sure you know some concrete ways to do this. One technique writers use is to write compound sentences—you know, two sentences linked together by a conjunction like *and* or *because*.

"Here's another way to add more information to your sentences. You can also add phrases and clauses to your sentences, like I did with one of the sentences in the scene in Maeve's room, in our Esmerelda story. You can take a simple sentence and use commas to add a phrase or clause. So, for example, here's a simple sentence from our story." I pointed to a piece of chart paper on which I'd written:

I sighed.

"There's definitely room here to give readers information about *how* Esmerelda sighed or about what she was doing while sighing. We can do this by adding a phrase showing this." Underneath the first sentence, I wrote:

I sighed, tucking my hair behind my ear.

"Or I could use a clause, either dependent or independent, to add more information. I could add some action right at the front of the sentence."

As she looked at me, expecting me to say something about Tilly, I sighed.

"I know many of you are already adding phrases and clauses to your sentences, but for those of you who haven't yet given this a go, this is now something you can add to your drafting and revision repertoire."

---

people speak in an upsweep, ending each sentence as if they are asking a question. Other people speak in a more staccato fashion, which can be punctuated with dashes or periods. Certainly people of different ages, from different walks of life, will have different cadences. You might guide your small group to review the dialogue in their stories. Does each speaker speak in an identifiably different way? Or, at the very least, do adults speak differently than kids? Or if an adult speaks like a kid, or vice versa, is it intentional? Does this reflect something about the character's maturity level or carefreeness?

As is often the case, using a mentor text to model examples of this work is a helpful method, as is modeling with your own writing. Another interesting option would be for students to watch a video clip or listen to an audio clip of natural conversation and study how it sounds, and then think how it might look in writing. Then, the group could notice ways they might revise their own writing to reflect those differences in cadence.

Learning from Peers and from Mentor Texts

Suggest that students share whatever revision strategies they have tried, over the past few days, with a person sitting nearby.

"Writers, I've thrown a lot of revision and crafting techniques your way these past couple days. You also are drawing from ones you've learned in prior years. See if you can figure out what's been working especially well for you, to bring out your story's meaning or to make sections of your story clearer or to more accurately reflect what you imagined happening. Right now, turn and tell someone near you some of the things you've tried out in your writing and their effect. If you hear something new that you think you might try, jot it in your notebook, and when you return to your draft, you'll have something new to give a go."

I gave students a few minutes to do this, then reconvened the class.

Suggest that students put aside their writing for the night, instead doing a close reading of their independent reading books and thinking, about whatever they notice, "Why do I think the author did this?"

"I know some of you will want to work on revising your drafts tonight for homework. But instead, I'd like you to take a break from your draft and instead focus on your independent reading. When someone asked the great poet Robert Frost, 'How can I learn to write?' Frost said, 'Read Anna Karenina, read Anna Karenina, read Anna Karenina.' He could have said, 'Read any well-crafted story, again and again and again.' The point is, to learn how to write well, you need to learn how to read well—to read closely.

"Oh, and before you leave, take another look at our anchor chart. I added the last point that summarizes what you learned today about the rhythm of language and how to use it to strengthen your stories. As you read tonight, you may be thinking about how the author used some of the techniques on our chart."

How to Write Compelling Fiction

- Brainstorm a great story idea (think of small moments, places, events, issues, struggles, stories you wish existed in the world).
- Make your characters come alive (with traits, wants and challenges, self-attitude, relationships).
- Test-drive your character in scenes (envision and write actions, feelings, dialogue, setting, point of view).
- Plot several versions of your story, aiming to intensify the problem (use arcs, timelines, storyboards).
- Draft a 3-D story (story-tell bit by bit, include evidence of your characters' actions, thoughts, feelings).
- Manage space and time.
  - Use summary to quickly move a character across space and time.
  - Use transitional words and phrases to show changes in time or place.
- Become the main character, living through the drama of the story—and then allow your writing to unfold.
- Use paragraphs wisely (to move in place and time, to highlight something, for dramatic impact).
- Revise the lead—and hence the entire story (small action, mood, time and place, foreshadow).
- Research key facts to make the story more believable.
- Get rid of extra stuff that weighs the story down!
- Finish strong—make sure the ending shows what the story is <u>really</u> about, fits the story arc, ties up loose ends.
- As you revise (or draft) your stories, keep in mind these points:
  - Develop or increase conflict (tension, obstacles, trouble—between, among, or within characters).
  - Reflect on deeper meanings/central ideas of your story and consider objects, settings, actions that you can develop as symbols, images, or metaphors.
  - **Listen to the rhythm and pacing of your sentences, then craft sentences of varying lengths and types to create the intended meaning, feeling, mood.**

TAKING A BREAK FROM REVISING TO READ CLOSELY

"Tonight, I'd like you to keep your writer's sensibility with you as you read, and I'd like you to read asking yourself, 'Why do I think the author did this? Why did the author structure the text this way? Why did the author organize the actions this way?' When anything stands out for you as a reader, ask yourself, 'Why did the writer do this?' Then mark those pages with sticky notes with your thoughts jotted down. Tomorrow, you'll have a chance to discuss this with your partner."

Using Mentor Texts to Help Match Authorial Intent with the Page

ear Teachers,

Today, rather than including a minilesson, I've offered a letter suggesting ways to help your students make meaningful reading and writing connections. Namely, helping them study the authorial intentions of professional writers to help them shore up their own writing. As teachers and students who align their work with the Common Core Standards become more familiar with that work, one of the areas they report struggling with is understanding and describing authorial intent in their reading. I have come to believe that if something is tricky to understand in reading, it helps to go to the other side of the desk and see it through a writer's eyes, to see where the seams are, how the stitches are made. In addition to offering powerful skills to students' reading repertoires, this session offers another pathway toward meaning. Our students, just like professional writers, need to be writing with intent and making that intent known to their readers.

I suggest you lead an inquiry session in which together with students you explore the question "How does an author's choices affect the reader's experiences?" What this means is that instead of demonstrating a skill or bit of work during the teaching component of today's minilesson, you will instead invite students to research something with you—to conduct an inquiry.

MINILESSON

This session could go a few different ways. You might decide to break students up into small groups, based on their interests and reading strengths, with each group doing their own inquiry on a different mentor short story. Alternatively, you might opt to have the whole class gather, eyes on the whole-class mentor, in our case, "Thirteen and a Half," by Rachel Vail. Or, if you have the resources and your students have the capability, you might opt to have your students work as partners or individuals to find their own mentor texts to study—perhaps from their independent reading stacks.

COMMON CORE STATE STANDARDS: W.7.3, W.7.7, RL.7.1, RL.7.2, RL.7.3, RL.7.10, SL.7.1, SL.7.4, L.7.1, L.7.2, L.7.3

In any event, once students have a text in front of them, you will want to guide them on an inquiry. First, you will want them to reread the text with a lens toward places where they were affected—they laughed, cried, were angered. Have them mark and record those places, being sure to explain how they were affected. I would also encourage them to consider if how they were affected was what the author intended, and have them name it as such. For example, they might note that one section "made me laugh." Push them past the initial response of "the author wanted to be funny" to something more meaningful and connected to the whole: "The author wanted to lighten the mood because something very serious was about to happen."

Once they have accomplished that, it is time for them to put their analytical muscles to the test. What did the author do to accomplish this effect? Was it in the character development? Perhaps something about the description of the setting or choice of words? Could sentence length or punctuation have played a role? Was it the use of metaphor or symbolism? Feel free to use literary terms and encourage students to do the same to specifically describe the moves writers are making.

Of course, there is going to be more than one correct answer for work that the author is doing in any one section of text. But that is less important than the exercise of students seeing that writers make intentional moves to affect readers, and they can use those same moves, too.

This is a writing workshop, and you won't want students to spend their entire time theorizing about other writers' writing. So, wrap up the session by asking students to keep in mind some of the moves used by their mentor author (or another author they admire) and to try them in their own writing when they want to accomplish similar effects. And, as always, remind them that they have a whole repertoire of revision tools they can turn to while working on their pieces, and their own authorial intent.

If you find it helpful, you might create a class chart or have students design their own to keep track of their inquiry. Here's one such example:

Author's Intent			
Part of the text we were affected by	Author's intent (effect on readers)	How author made this happen	Trying it in our own writing:
The Mallomar scene	• Set up the action to come • Make us laugh • Develop character(s)	• The character's dialogue is realistic. • The narrator's is short sentences. Ashley's are long.	

CONFERRING AND SMALL-GROUP WORK

You might have noticed that throughout the whole of this unit there hasn't been a direct lesson about the most uttered word in the writing teacher's vocabulary: details. This was intentional. For one thing, I am well aware that you have probably been teaching and talking about details since the first day of school. You didn't need this book to remind you to do that. For another thing, I believe strongly that an overemphasis on details can result in overwrought and purple prose, overspiced and with only a thin layer of meaning. And sometimes, too many details can obscure meaning altogether.

In today's small-group work, I encourage you to gather kids together based on the sort of detail work they tend to do. Most students will fall into one of three major camps: too few, too many, and just right. Oddly, despite their presentation of work, the teaching point, while needing to be modeled and approached differently for each camp, will contain the same essential teaching nugget: writers know what the heart of their story is and use very specific details to help pop out that heart for their readers.

For students who have too few details, it's about guiding them to the most important parts of the story, maybe having them highlight those places, and then threading through very concrete and specific details. Instead of the red bike, it would be the red ten-speed bike with the racing seat. For students with too many details, I would also guide them to highlighting the most important parts of their stories and then cleaning up the details that fall outside of those highlighted areas. Then rethink each and every detail within the highlighted areas, asking, "Is this necessary? Does this shine a light on what really matters in my story?" For students who seem to have about the right balance, I am willing to bet they could do a little fine-tuning. I would have them look at each detail to see if they could elevate it somewhat to get at the truth. Is there a concrete detail that would make this feel more true? Would this character eat a doughnut for breakfast? If so, would it have chocolate icing and vanilla cream filling, because this character is soft and sweet? Or if the character is tough and has a mean streak, what might he eat for breakfast?

MID-WORKSHOP TEACHING

Earlier in the session you talked about the power of studying a mentor author and how important it is to read as a reader *and* a writer. Today, ask students to do that with each other's work—their colleagues. Have them trade pieces with a partner. Explain that you don't want them to read it with a lens of looking to fix the piece up, or make suggestions for revisions. Instead, let them know you want them to read it as a reader, jotting on Post-it notes their reactions, ideas, and questions, much like they do when reading a story in reading workshop.

When they're done reading their partner's piece and commenting on Post-its, have them trade back. Ask them to look through the reading trail that their partner left. Did the partner pause in the places where the writer had hoped a reader would pause? Did the partner notice or respond in the ways they were hoping? If not, are there changes the writer might want to make to her piece or another reader she'd like to pilot her story on to see if there's a pattern of reaction (or lack of reaction) she'd like to address?

SHARE

Explain to students that they have been studying mentor authors for a long time. They know to look to their peers, their teachers, and other published writers to get ideas for writing moves and to improve their own writing. Let them know that another thing they can do to improve their writing is to study their own successes, look for their places of personal bests, and try to repeat or exceed those places.

Ask them to reread their pieces, looking for areas in their work that they are most proud of—places where their hard work and skills really shine. Have them mark those places, then spend a few minutes annotating the section, or writing in their notebook about the moves they made as a writer. Did they craft a compelling image? Spin a fancy phrase? Evoke an emotional response? Whatever they did, have them name it, then take a stab at their next bit of revision work, mentoring themselves to their own best work.

Enjoy!
Colleen

Economizing on the Sentence and Word Level

"IN WRITING, you must kill all your darlings." The line has been attributed to authors as varied as Dorothy Parker to William Faulkner, so oft repeated a maxim that it is hard to pin down the source. Many creative writing teachers have repeated it since. These are dreaded words for any fiction writer—myself included—who has ever fallen in love with a particular line or bit of description or scene even. Often, in fact, as we know all too well, it is the parts of our writing we love most that we must "kill." Why? Because often these are more distracting decoration than essential to the story. There's a reason we fall in love with these; they're well-crafted, beautiful sentences, moments that get us teary eyed, poetic turns of phrases that sound just right—until we realize that they are just this way to us, not to the reader. These beautiful sentences and phrases can make our writing overwrought and, as such, are better left out.

Today, then, you will join countless fiction writing teachers worldwide in the effort to help your students "kill" their own little darlings. You'll suggest that while fiction writers may know how to write a gorgeous sentence and craft the perfect scene, so too do they know how to let those little perfections go—especially when these start to act more as clutter than gem.

As students embark on the often painful work of cutting bits of beauty or excitement or humor from their drafts, remind them to hold tight to their bigger purpose. As many have learned in narrative units of the past, writers often ask themselves, "What is this piece, or this part even, *mostly* about?" Anything that distracts from that meaning must (gulp) go—whether it's because the detail just doesn't fit or because there is simply too much detail to focus on the bigger picture. By emphasizing for students that the *real* beauty of fiction is conveying a clear and powerful truth, you will help ease the blow as they kill their little darlings.

IN THIS SESSION, you'll teach students that writers sometimes cut out words and sentences to develop stronger prose.

GETTING READY

✔ An excerpt from your own fiction writing, enlarged for the class to see (see Teaching and Active Engagement)

COMMON CORE STATE STANDARDS: W.7.3.d, W.7.5, RL.7.1, RL.7.3, SL.7.1, L.7.1, L.7.2a, L.7.3, L.7.6

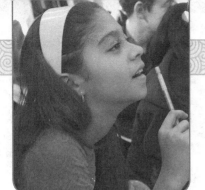

Economizing on the Sentence and Word Level

CONNECTION

◆ COACHING

To set up your teaching point about the importance of picking and choosing during revision, share an anecdote that illustrates what happens when there is too much "trim" on something.

"My family loves birthdays. And what they really love about birthdays is to make sure that you get to do everything you want. All your favorite things. Or at least a few of your favorite things. And one of the things my family knows I love is ice cream. So one year for my birthday they took me to this famous ice cream parlor and I was able to order any ice cream I wanted. I chose something that I thought I would love. It was called 'The Animal' or 'The Monster,' or something like that. It had four flavors of ice cream—chocolate, vanilla, strawberry, and chocolate chip—three flavors of sherbet—orange, cherry, and lime—four toppings—fudge, caramel, butterscotch, and pineapple—as well as whipped cream, cherries, bananas, sprinkles, and peanuts.

"At first I was so excited about it—all these great ice cream and sherbet flavors, the great toppings, everything I loved about ice cream. My whole family grabbed spoons and shared it. It looked impressive, but as we started to eat it, there was just so much going on that no one flavor stood out. Everything mixed together and it was hard to tell what was what. I could only eat a few spoonfuls before I started to get sick. I started wishing for just a simple bowl of vanilla ice cream with just some hot fudge on top."

Name the teaching point.

"Today I want to teach you that writers don't include everything they know how to do just because they like it. Instead, they pick and choose what to use and what not to use so that the story does not get bogged down in extra words, tricks, and craft moves. Writers focus on the words and actions that really matter."

TEACHING

Share with students your own temptation to "decorate" your writing, using all the craft moves you know, and display a piece in which you did this, inviting students to notice what works well and what does not.

"I know that you have all learned so much over the years about writing. I often experience a temptation to include everything I know how to do every time I write. 'Look, I can use onomatopoeia!' I want to say. 'Check out my fancy

I, of course, want to encourage students to take risks and try new techniques in their writing—and to celebrate when they do. But a critical next step in the learning process is learning how to do things with more purpose, which is a concept I return to time and again in any unit of study. Revision is a perfect time to revisit one's writing with an eye on purpose.

foreshadowing' or 'Have you seen all my multisyllable adverbs and adjectives?' And it definitely feels good to know all of these tricks and moves as a writer and to be able to do them. I often think it's a good idea to do them when drafting, just to get them out there. But then in revision, sort through what you've done and take out anything that might be overdone, that might distract from the writing or bog it down.

"Let's take a look at an excerpt from a piece I wrote when I was experimenting with fiction writing a while ago. As I read through this, look to see if you can identify some of the fancy moves I was making, and also what effect you think they have on the piece. Might it be too much in some places? Just right in others?" I indicated the excerpt from my draft that was projected on the board.

> I strolled slowly out onto the giant, green grass soccer field, feeling my cleats dig into the soft mud. It was like I was walking in pudding. I felt my heart hammer quickly in my chest, like a thousand woodpeckers all trying to eat the bugs out of the same tree at the same time. Out of the corner of my chocolate brown eye I saw Sam doing something with the soccer ball. I couldn't tell if he was just feeling the stitches or rubbing something on it. "Oh well," I pondered to myself as I speedily jogged down the field, getting ready to take my position. "I'm sure it is nothing to worry about. Instead I should worry about this championship game."

I nodded knowingly as a few kids covered their mouths to keep from laughing out loud. They weren't being mean; it was just clear to them that the writing was over the top. "So sometimes looking at our old writing can be exciting and make us feel proud because we see what great work we've done. Sometimes looking at our old writing can be exciting (and sort of embarrassing) because we can see how far we've come as writers. Let's just take a quick look at the good things I was trying to do here."

I showed that I was rereading and looking closely, ticking off on my fingers as I spoke. "I see that I'm trying to describe a lot by using adjectives and adverbs like 'slowly' and 'giant green.' I was also trying to use metaphors and similes to describe as well with the 'chocolate brown eye' and the 'thousand woodpeckers.'

"There's a little try at foreshadowing with the other kid, Sam, and the ball," a voice trying to console me called from the back. I nodded. "Yes, and I can see that I was trying to use dialogue, by having the main character talk to himself." I paused to make the turn toward criticism. "But I can also see that the dialogue is problematic because it's not realistic. No one really talks like that, and they definitely don't talk like that to themselves. And it feels like it almost gives too much information. I believe some of you were calling that soap opera dialogue."

"And it sort of feels like you were using big words just to use them," Javi added. "Like *pondered*. It just sort of stands out. It doesn't go with how the rest of it sounds."

In many cases, using an over-the-top example of what not *to do is the best way to drive home a point and give students a clear vision of what to do.*

I model with my own self-assessment the importance of starting with strengths and from there, looking for ways to improve. My conferences follow a similar pattern of complimenting first, then teaching. And when students work with peer writers, I encourage them to focus on what a partner does well before offering suggestions.

"So, if I could go back to my past writing self, I wouldn't want to say, 'Eww! Terrible writing!' Instead, I would want to try to understand what I was trying to do and clear it up. Make it stronger. Just like when it comes to ice cream, with writing, sometimes less is more. For example, instead of using lots of adjectives and adverbs, I can use strong nouns and verbs. Instead of using dialogue to explain what's going on with the character, I can use thoughts and actions. I can replace some of my overdone writing moves with clear, solid, writing."

Fix up your overwrought writing, naming the specific steps you are taking to make it cleaner.

"Let me try that with just the first sentence."

> I strolled slowly out onto the giant, green grass soccer field, feeling my cleats dig into the soft mud.

"If I cut the adjectives and adverbs I don't need and replace them with strong nouns and verbs, I think I can make this writing better." I wrote a new sentence below the excerpt:

> I trudged onto the soccer field, my cleats sinking into the muck.

"Oh, I like that much better. Do you see how it still says the same thing, but I got rid of the things I didn't need, like the description of the soccer field because most people know what soccer fields typically look like? And I strengthened up my verbs, which made it so I didn't need to have all those adjectives and adverbs weighing everything down." I looked back at the piece.

Demonstrate how to know when it's necessary to "kill your darlings" and explain what that means.

"Now, here's something tricky. I actually like the next two similes—the pudding one and the woodpecker one. But the two of them back to back really does feel like too much. Back to that giant ice cream bowl. The reader really can't linger on either one because they're both there, back to back. So I need to do what many famous writers have said to do in the past. I need to 'kill my darlings.' Meaning I need to get rid of something I really love, even though I love it, because it's not making the writing better. So, to decide which one to cut, I'm going to look at the meaning—which one is more significant in the story. How hard it was to walk on the soccer field isn't really that important. How nervous the narrator is, because of the big game, feels important. So, the pudding goes, the woodpecker stays." I crossed out that line.

> I trudged onto the soccer field, my cleats sinking into the muck. ~~It was like I was walking in pudding.~~ I felt my heart hammer quickly in my chest, like a thousand woodpeckers all trying to eat the bugs out of the same tree at the same time.

Powerful demonstration teaching sheds light on the thinking process, not simply the end product, so students can more easily transfer what they see to their own writing—and so they can see that strong writing doesn't emerge with a magic poof, but with a lot of thoughtful work.

Often when I demonstrate repeatedly in a minilesson, it is to highlight a variety of substrategies and considerations within the bigger concept I aim to teach. My overarching point is that writers often cut even their most beloved details. But within that, I have shown students that sometimes writers rewrite a section, sometimes they cut, always they think about a piece's meaning, and often they have to make hard choices about what to let go.

ACTIVE ENGAGEMENT

Invite students to help you tighten your writing.

"Can you guys help me with the rest of the section? Can you look for places I can kill my darlings and tighten my writing? Partner 1s, can you focus on the next two sentences and how we could revise them? Partner 2s, can you focus on the last three sentences? In a minute or two, we'll come together and fix up the rest of this excerpt."

I listened in as the partners talked. I resisted the temptation to go with the fancier fixes, instead helping shore up the simpler, more replicable options. When I had heard a few things I could imagine using, I pulled the class back together.

"Let's take a look at the excerpt again, now with all the changes," I said and projected it onto the board:

> I trudged onto the soccer field, my cleats sinking into the muck. ~~It was like I was walking in pudding.~~ I felt my heart hammer quickly in my chest, like a thousand woodpeckers all trying to eat the bugs out of the same tree at the same time. Out of the corner of my ~~chocolate brown~~ eye I saw Sam doing something with the soccer ball. I couldn't tell if he was just feeling the stitches or rubbing something on it. "Oh well," I ~~pondered~~ thought to myself as I ~~speedily~~ jogged down the field, getting ready to take my position. "I'm sure it is nothing to worry about. Instead I should worry about this big championship game."

LINK

Send students off to write, suggesting that for many of them, today is the final day of revision, and reminding them to draw on the repertoire of revision strategies they know.

"Today when you go off to write, I know many of you are closer to the finish line than the start when it comes to revision. In fact, for most of you today is the last full day of revision work before we move on to editing. I'd like you to consider the idea that cutting words, tightening the language, will help make your writing, along with the effect your writing has on others, exponentially stronger. But I also want you to consider all the other revision and drafting strategies that we've studied together this year. Look over our class charts and take a tour to see if there is anything that might match with your intentions for your piece. You might also consider going back in your memory to think of other revision strategies you've learned in the past."

Emphasize that above all, students should revise by focusing on the meaning, the truth, behind their stories.

"But the key is this: don't get caught up in the revision strategies. Instead, get caught up in the meaning, the truth behind your story. Look to revise in such a way that you are exposing more and more of the truth of what you are trying to say to your readers. That's really the secret to good fiction writing."

When I scaffold student work, I want to stay in the realm of what is realistic for them to do independently. My goal is not to help them make a single piece of writing better, but rather, to help them become stronger writers with an expanding repertoire of tools they can draw upon when I am not there to guide them.

Time and again, I return to the concept of purpose. Whatever the teaching point, at the end of the day, I want my students to ask, "What is this piece really about?" and to use all they're learning to convey that meaning.

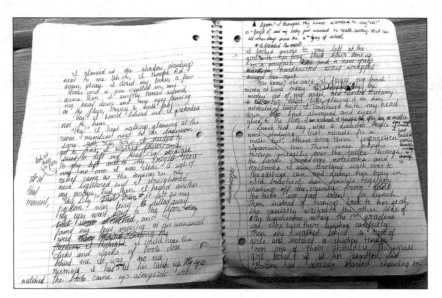

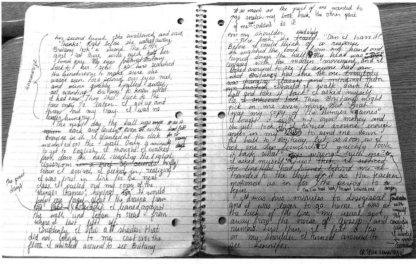

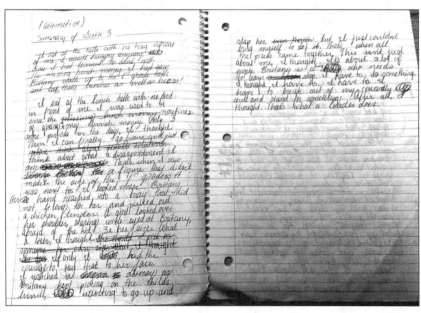

FIG. 15–1   Looking with a sharp eye, Annabelle found many places to cut, extract, and summarize.

Using Commas to Separate Coordinate Adjectives

SOME OF YOUR STUDENTS, who already have a handle on the more basic usage moves for commas, will be ready to start learning about using commas to separate coordinate adjectives. Depending on your students and their facility with conventions, this could be either one-on-one or small-group work.

You might first want to explain to the students what coordinate adjectives are. That is, these are adjectives that are placed together in a sentence to describe the same noun. When writers see them, they want to make sure there is a comma between them. Examples of these are:

It was an ugly, large cockroach.

I found the cockroach on a sunny, beautiful day.

The thing you'll want to make sure they know is that we don't need a comma every time there are two adjectives side by side. That's because those adjectives are not coordinate. One of them, the one right next to the noun, is not coordinate. It goes with the noun like a unit. If you tried to switch them up it would sound odd. You may or may not want to tell your students that those adjectives are cumulative. A couple of examples of these:

(continues)

MID-WORKSHOP TEACHING   *Said* Is Not Dead

"Everyone, can I stop you for a quick minute?" I waited until everyone had looked up. "I hate to bother you, but I wanted to say two quick things. The first is—congratulations! You are so close to the end and you could easily just decide to relax a little, but you are not. You are working hard to make sure these pieces match your intentions all the way through.

"Secondly, I just wanted to note that some of you, while doing a great job economizing language whenever possible, are not doing that work when revising your dialogue tags. As you know, dialogue tags are the words that come before or after a piece of dialogue so that the reader knows who said what. Many of you have many, many fancy words in your dialogue tags. I've seen she muttered, he stated, she queried, he replied, she wondered, she uttered. There's dialogue that looks like this":

"Hi," she stated.

"Hi," he muttered.

"How are you?" she questioned.

"I'm good," he declared.

"Glad to hear it!" she exclaimed.

I can tell from the eyes rolling in this classroom that you can see how those dialogue tags can get very distracting, very quickly. I am going to guess that somewhere along the way in some of your writing careers you picked up the message—maybe even an adult told you, '*Said* is dead.' I'm here to tell you, *said* is *not* dead. *Said* is a very good word that professional writers use *most of the time* to tell a reader who is speaking. Check any good mentor text and you'll see it's true. Readers almost don't read the word. It's like punctuation. We only pay attention to it if we get confused and need to reread. For the most part, try to use *said*. Make exceptions for when a question is asked, or a speaker speaks in a very different way, such as yelling or whispering. Long live *said*!"

I hate those itchy wool pants.

You try to avoid scary circus clowns.

You might want to teach your students that there are two easy ways to know whether you need a comma or not between the adjectives. The first is to try to separate the two adjectives with 'and.' If you are able to and the sentence still makes sense, you need a comma.

It was an ugly and large cockroach.

The other test is to switch up the order of the adjectives. If the sentence still makes sense and sounds right, then you need a comma.

It was a large, ugly cockroach.

If, on the other hand, adding *and* or switching the order doesn't sound right, then they are not coordinating adjectives and they should go without the comma. "You try to avoid circus, scary clowns" just doesn't sound right.

148

Last Chance for Message Sending

Invite students to reflect on the journey they have taken thus far in the unit and to share something essential they've learned that they will hold on to as the unit draws to a close.

"Since the beginning of this unit, we've been working to craft compelling, tension-filled, and meaningful fiction in stories. Stories that share a level of truth more easily conveyed through fiction because we can change any facts we need to order to tell the story that we believe most needs telling. We are at the tail end of that journey.

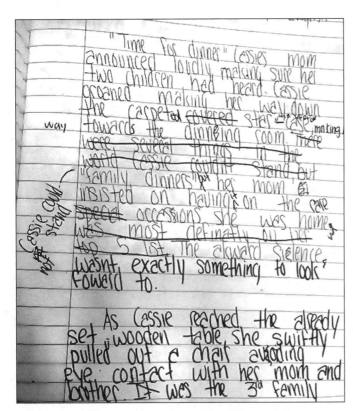

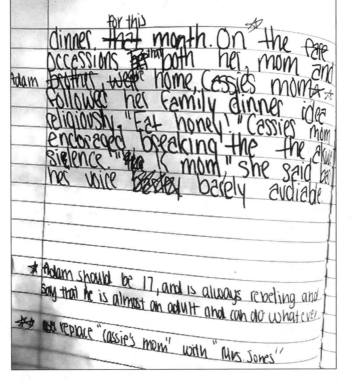

FIG. 15–2 Yasmin economizes as well as elaborates as she revises.

"Right now, will you share with your partner something you've learned during this unit, something that you will remember as we move on to other genres of writing? You may also want to show your partner a spot in your writing where you tried that thing. Tomorrow we will move into editing, as a class."

IDENTIFYING THE MESSAGE IN YOUR WRITING

"Tonight I want you to look through your piece with the lens of your audience one more time. I want you to go, scene by scene, beat by beat, through your story. A famous writing teacher, Donald Graves, used to say that writers need to ask themselves, 'Where does the heart beat in this story?' You might ask, 'What is the message I'm trying to send to the world through my writing, and can I find threads of it throughout the story?' You might ask someone at home or a friend who isn't in this class to read your story and write down what message they are getting from the story. If they or you aren't seeing the message all the way through, then go back and make any changes that you think need to be made for your story to serve the purposes you hope for it."

Editing with Lenses and Independence

I HAVE NEVER HAD THE TALENT for being a social butterfly. In fact, I have always been a classic introvert, much more at home and energized when I am by myself, not talking to anyone. Not even friends and family. For years, I admired people who could talk with others comfortably from an appreciative yet detached stance, much the same way I might fantasize about having moves like Mick Jagger—would be fun, but for someone who has the grace of a rhino, I didn't waste a second thinking it could ever happen. But then I became a staff developer and I needed to be able to talk to lots of people about a lot of things, all the time, and suddenly, the way I watched other people talk has changed. No longer do I just spy. Instead, I find myself trying different lenses as I study people's conversation moves. Perhaps it's the talk about people's kids or a controversial topic or simply a compliment. And then I try to replicate their conversation moves.

After several days of revising and fine-tuning their drafts, your students are nearing the publishing line. But before they cross over, they must tackle the arduous—and all too often disengaging—work of editing. How often do you feel students' passivity rise to the surface when it comes time to check for paragraphs, spelling, end punctuation? For many, editing feels more like the dirty work of cleaning than the rousing work of decorating. Plus, it's *hard*.

In today's lesson, however, you break down the process for students in a way that makes editing more accessible and—dare I say it?—fun. By engaging students in a game much like "I spy," you teach them the power of putting on different lenses each time they read through their draft. Without undermining the serious nature of editing, I encourage you to make the work playful, a scavenger hunt for misspelled words, inconsistent tense, missing commas.

The beauty of editing with a lens is that it really works—which also means that students are much more likely to keep at it. For many, the thrill of uncovering another mistake will fuel their motivation to read on, and then to reread again and again, each time with a new lens. Soon enough, just like I am slowly transforming my ability to talk more easily with people, students will transform their drafts with their final touches.

IN THIS SESSION, you'll teach students that just as fiction writers revise with "lenses," they edit with them as well, rereading their writing several times through different lenses, making edits as they go.

GETTING READY

✔ Students' writer's notebooks and pens (see Connection)

✔ A sample of student's work to edit, enlarged for the class to see (see Teaching)

✔ A second sample of student work to edit, enlarged for the class as well as copied for partnerships to work with (see Active Engagement)

✔ A chart with the definition of "misplaced modifiers" (see Mid-Workshop Teaching)

✔ Grade 7 and 8 Narrative Writing Checklists, copies for each student (see Share)

COMMON CORE STATE STANDARDS: W.7.3, W.7.5, RL.7.10, SL.7.1, L.7.1, L.7.2, L.7.3

Editing with Lenses and Independence

CONNECTION

Ask students to take ten seconds to look around the classroom, and then time them as they record in their notebooks everything they noticed.

"Everyone pull out your notebook and find a fresh page," I said as the students got settled in the meeting area. I saw a few exchanging glances, a bit confused, as if thinking I was going to give a pop quiz. "I'm going to give you ten seconds to look around this classroom, and then I'm going to ask you to do something. Just take in as much information as you can when you look." I started the timer, and when the clock buzzed, I said, "Now, list everything you noticed in the room. Absolutely everything you just saw."

The students wrote long lists in their notebooks, mentioning everything from the light fixtures to my coffee cup.

Ask students to repeat this exercise, this time looking through the lens of literature.

When most of them had started to peter out, I got their attention again. "Now, I'm going to give you a lens to look with. I'd like you to look with the lens of literature. Look around the room for ten seconds, just looking for literature. Then I'll have you list everything you see." Again I waited ten seconds, then called them back, "Go ahead, list every piece of literature you saw in our classroom." I waited for the students to look back at me.

◆ COACHING

SMARTBOARD
CHARTS
RUG
HALLPASS
CLOCK
AGENDA
DOOR
PHONE
WINDOWS
DESKS
PENS
TAPE
STAPLERS
WHIT-OUT
DICTIONARY
BOOKS
PAPER
FOLDERS
LIGHTS
LIGHT SWITCH
CLOSETS
BACKPACK
PENS
TRASH
RECYCLING

WHITEBOARD
MAGNETS
TABLE
MARKERS
COMPUTERS
PRINTER
DOORKNOB
EXIT SIGN

I use the connections of my minilessons to contextualize my teaching, but also to engage students. Whether it's with a personal story or metaphor or fun activity that connects with the work at hand, I try to begin the day's learning with something that will grab students' attention.

FIG. 16–1   A fast listing of the classroom

Repeat the same exercise through two more lenses, then ask students to talk to a partner about each of the four lists.

"Now look through the lens of furniture. Then look through the lens of people."

When students were done with the last lens, I asked them to turn and talk to a partner across all four lists. When they were through I said, "Lenses are powerful things. When we try to look at everything, we inevitably miss something. But when we look with lenses, even many times, each time with a different lens, we can see much more."

❖ **Name the teaching point.**

"Today I want to teach you that writers can use lenses in their writing, to study things for them to work on, such as editing. One way they do that is they pick an area where they will likely need help and sweep through their piece looking for and bettering those places."

TEACHING

Share one student's editing experience, and invite her to walk the class through the particular lens she used to edit.

"Yesterday, I met with Miriam about her piece. She was finished with her revision work and had already moved to editing. She told me that she started with the basics, the capital letters. Then, she moved onto the periods, exclamation points, and question marks. Then, because she was working on a very tension-filled story, she did some work with other kinds of punctuation—like ellipses and dashes, so she knew to check those next. Finally, she moved onto something I know a lot of people find tricky—spelling. She looked through her whole piece to make sure that everything was spelled the way it should be. Here's her piece. (See Figure 16–2.)

"Miriam is going to talk us through how she looked through her writing with the lens of spelling." Miriam pointed to an excerpt of her draft on the document camera. "I actually saved the spelling for a while because I know it's probably going to be the thing I have to do the most work on. What I did was first I started reading, just circling the words I was pretty sure I didn't spell right. And, now, I'm going back and looking at those circles and either asking someone to help me or else looking them up to correct them."

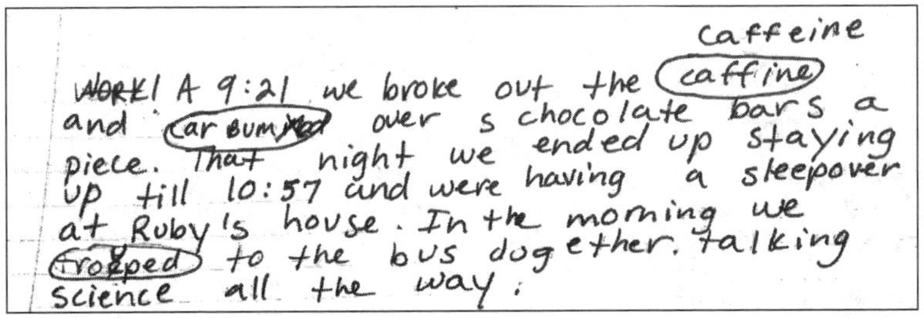

FIG. 16–2   Miriam shows how she edits with a lens for spelling.

When you teach this minilesson, you might display a cumulative chart of all that the class has learned about mechanics and conventions thus far in the year. That chart can contain skills you have taught during word study time as well as the writing workshop, and of course it will be a very different chart for more inexperienced writers than for students who have grown up in a writing workshop.

You could choose to use your own writing to demonstrate this teaching. But especially since students often disengage from editing, highlighting the work of one of their peers could go a long way toward enticing others to commit to similar work.

"Writers," I interjected, "what I'm hearing from Miriam that is making me think of my own writing is that she was aware of places where she would definitely need to do more work—areas that she knew were rough for her. Then, she made sure she set aside some time to look carefully at that area. In this case, it was spelling. But I'm sure when she's done with spelling she'll be ready for something else she knows she needs to work on—such as tense."

ACTIVE ENGAGEMENT

Set students up to follow the model you have given them, editing a paragraph of another writer's story.

"Now it's time for you to become the editors. Working with your partner, could you read a section of Taylor's story?" I passed out copies of just that paragraph. "Read it once, checking for and fixing ending punctuation. Then read it again, checking for and fixing tenses. Then put on your 'check-for-commas' lenses. Look especially for those commas in between adjectives that we've spoken about in the past. If you find something that you're not sure about or that you can't fix immediately, have a go on the side of the page, seeing if you can make things look the way that you think they should look. Remember that you can use resources outside yourselves, such as other writers in our community:"

> When I get home Know one is home but my oldest brother Jason. So when I got home I had my snack did my homework and then watched tv untill my got home. By the time mom got home it was 6:30. So she had made dinner told me to take a shower and By 9:30 it was bedtime and I said okay. 9:30 came I said good night to everyone and I set my alarm and I Fell alseep.

FIG. 16–3 Taylor's piece is ready to edit.

"Writers, as I talked to some of you about your editing work on this section, I heard many of you say that you had found places where you could fix missing words, tenses, and a few missing commas. You'll not be surprised to know those were places that Taylor fixed yesterday when he was working on his piece."

LINK

Remind students what they have learned and send them off to edit their own work.

"As you work on editing your stories, I want you to remember that all of us, as writers, take editing very seriously. We generally reread our writing once, twice, three times, and often we make a decision, saying, 'This time I will read with this lens,' or 'This time I will reread with that lens.' I have emphasized rereading for punctuation and tenses, but you may know that you need to reread and think about spelling or about being sure your draft makes sense. Some writers might even decide to make a personal editing checklist for themselves and use that as a reminder of what they want to read on the lookout for. No matter what you look for, or how you look for it, I want you to remember that you are in control of your own writing, and the real goal is to make sure that every word, every dot, is the best that it can be."

When students overlook mistakes in their writing, the first thing to consider is whether they have a grasp on the convention at hand. I cannot hold them accountable for fixing something they do not know how to do in the first place.

Central to today's lesson is the act of rereading. Think how often students read through a draft once and claim, "Done." When I teach students to edit, much of my coaching involves simply encouraging them to read yet again. For students who continue to miss mistakes, even when they understand how to do the convention correctly, I might specify the lens for them, saying something like, "Read it again with an eye on end punctuation." Or even, "Read it again and find at least four spelling errors."

Just as I teach students to edit their own work by rereading with different lenses, so too can they approach peer editing.

Working with Students Whose Grammar and Conventions Are Significantly below Seventh-Grade Level

IF YOU ARE ANYTHING LIKE ME, there is a part of you that is aware, perhaps overly so, of when students are struggling mightily with grammar. Sometimes you might even wonder, "How did this student get to seventh grade not knowing how to write a complete sentence?" There are many possible reasons this may be true. The student might be an English language learner or was new to the language when the grade he was in was learning some of those grammar basics. It could be that the student has an issue with memory. It could also be that the student is not developmentally ready to tackle some of those ins and outs of grammar that are more abstract. As frustrating as it may be, we might never get to the bottom of that question. Instead, as with many things we teach our students, we need to meet them where they are.

(continues)

MID-WORKSHOP TEACHING **Recognizing and Replacing Misplaced Modifiers**

"I just want to grab your attention for a minute," I said as I headed over to where my chart was posted. "There are some great editing moves going on all over the place. People working on paragraphing. People torturing themselves with all the punctuation that goes inside of quotation marks. I thought it would be fun to add one more option for you to consider—one that could be really funny if you make the mistake. That is, we're going to talk for a bit about misplaced modifiers."

I paused and pointed to a chart that contained the definition and read it aloud, "A misplaced modifier is a modifier (a word or phrase that changes or modifies something else) that is placed in a spot or has punctuation that makes the modifier mean something different than the writer intended.

"I personally, almost don't want to tell you about these, because these can end up being some of the funniest grammar mistakes. They can change the whole meaning of a sentence. Here's an example."

Painted green, I admired the walls in Liz's room.

"Now, what this sentence literally says is that Esmerelda is painted green! Which is ridiculous and kind of funny. We all know the modifier is supposed to be describing the walls. The modifier, 'painted green' got placed in the wrong spot. So to make it right, I need to switch things around a bit."

I admired the walls in Liz's room which were painted green.

"Let me show you another one."

On my way out of the room I saw a purple girl's scarf.

The students started to chuckle. "I see that you're getting this! The way this sentence is written makes it that there's a purple girl that Esmerelda sees and the purple girl has a scarf. This one is actually a bit easier to fix."

On my way out of the room I saw a girl's purple scarf.

"Misplaced modifiers are a great lens to add to your repertoire—not just for today. They happen all the time in your writing life. Definitely be on the lookout!"

Lucy Calkins has said that roughly 20% or our writing instruction should deal with conventions and grammar. Hopefully that has been the case for you. Research tells us that struggling writers get more comments on their conventions and grammar than their content. The irony, of course, is that to have a good handle on grammar and conventions, writers need to have a strong grasp on their content. I urge you to take copious conference and small-group notes to ensure that all students, struggling or not, are getting roughly 20% of their instructional time in grammar and convention. Not much more. And not much less.

I would also suggest that you spend some time poring over your students' on-demand pieces and their notebook entries—pieces that you know for sure they wrote on their own, without anyone intervening. Those independently written pieces will give you the best window into their mastery and struggles with grammar and conventions. You may want to create a grid with different topics to help track issues that students are struggling with. Then you might plop kids' names into that grid to help form small groups and plan for conferences.

Class 702	End points	Paragraphs	Capital letters	Commas with phrases and clauses
Almost there	Jada Gobin	Taylor Harriet Jada		Harriet
Tries sometimes	Joey			
Little or no evidence		Joey		

From there you could decide, is this topic a one-off session where you can pull one small group or have one conference, maybe with a quick follow-up and they'll be fine? Or is this a bigger topic or issue that requires repeated sessions? If so, you could design a quick cycle of two to five sessions where you would almost be creating a mini-unit on this topic, one session building on the other, making this work transparent to the students. You could then create a schedule for that work.

Week	Monday	Tuesday	Wednesday	Thursday	Friday
One	Joey—paragraphs: explicit			Small group: end points (Jada, Gobin)—mentor	
Two	Joey—paragraphs: inquiry		Small group: paragraphs (Taylor, Harriet, Jada)—inquiry		
Three	Joey—paragraphs: mentor				

This is a practice I feel is important to do all year long, but especially at the beginning of the year when you want to develop routines and state your values and expectations. You want students to know that grammar and conventions count in your classroom—all the time. By creating a system where you are monitoring their progress and offering teaching to students who need it, your purposes are clear. For additional ideas on grammar curriculum and instructional methods, see *The Power of Grammar* (2005) by Mary Ehrenworth and Vicki Vinton.

Using the Student Checklist for Double-Checks and Final Touches

Remind students that their finished stories are due tomorrow. Ask them to review their pieces against the Grade 7 Narrative Writing Checklist, asking, "Did I do ___, and did I do it well?", perhaps stretching themselves to look to the next level, too.

I made a point of plopping into my chair comically, dramatically. "I am exhausted! You?" A few students laughed. Others nodded. "We are very close to the finish line. As many of you know from looking at our calendar, our celebration is right around the corner. Your finished pieces are due tomorrow. So that means that tonight is the last night for you to make any final tweaks to your piece before it is shared at the celebration.

"I know for many of you, if you are anything like me, that can be intimidating. How will I know what to look for without my colleagues, my teacher, or even the class charts? That's where I want to remind you that you have a lot of tools at your disposal. You have your notes from lessons in your notebook. You have your mentor texts. You have your own best writing. You have your notes from your colleagues. You have our charts that are hung around the room. And, you have your checklists. I want to encourage you to look at your checklists right now with a very sharp eye. Check each item more than once. Ask yourself, 'Did I truly do this thing—and did I do it well?' If not, go ahead and work on that piece. If yes, then maybe you want to take a peek at the next level up on the checklist, to see if there are ways in which you are already approaching that next level, or could be if you did a few things."

Narrative Writing Checklist

	Grade 7	NOT YET	STARTING TO	YES!	**Grade 8**	NOT YET	STARTING TO	YES!
	Structure				**Structure**			
Overall	I created a narrative that has realistic characters, tension, and change; and that not only conveys, but also develops an idea, lesson, or theme.	☐	☐	☐	I not only created a narrative with well-developed characters who change, I used the story to comment on a social issue, teach a lesson, and/or develop a point of view.	☐	☐	☐
Lead	I wrote a beginning that not only sets the story in motion, it also grounds it in a place or situation. It included details that will later be important to the story. These details might point to the central issue or conflict, show how story elements connect, or hint at key character traits.	☐	☐	☐	In establishing the situation and place, I hinted at a bigger context for the story (revealing issues that have been brewing, showing how the setting affects the character, contextualizing a time in history, and/or developing one out of many points of view).	☐	☐	☐
Transitions	I used transitional phrases and clauses to connect what happened to why it happened (*If he hadn't … he might not have, because of, although, little did she know that*).	☐	☐	☐	I used transitional phrases and clauses, grammatical structures (for example, paragraphing, descriptive phrases, and clauses) and text structures (such as chapter divisions and extended italics) to alert my reader to changes in the setting, the mood, the point of view, or the time in the story.	☐	☐	☐
Ending	I gave the reader a sense of closure by showing clearly how the character or place has changed or the problem has been resolved. If there wasn't resolution, I gave details to leave the reader thinking about a central idea or theme.	☐	☐	☐	I gave the reader a sense of closure by revealing character change(s) that followed from events in the story, or perhaps a resolution. If there wasn't resolution, I wrote to convey how the events of the story affected the characters, and to circle back to a central idea, issue, or theme.	☐	☐	☐
Organization	I used a traditional—or slightly modified—story structure (rising action, conflict, falling action) to best bring out the meaning of my story and reach my audience.	☐	☐	☐	I modified a traditional story structure, dealing with time in purposeful ways, to best suit my genre, bring out the meaning of my story, and reach my audience.	☐	☐	☐

CHOOSING SELECT HIGHER-LEVEL REVISIONS

"Tonight, as you prepare your pieces for the celebration, I do want to caution you about that higher-level work. Tonight is not the night to dismantle all your current work simply to try to work at the next level up from the one you've been working at for a majority of this unit. It's only a good idea to stretch yourself for an item or two—not the whole checklist. After all, your pieces are due tomorrow!"

Session 17

Publishing Anthologies
A Celebration

 ear Teachers,

Today is a big day for you and your students—a day to celebrate writing! To help mark the day with appropriate fanfare, instead of a minilesson, I offer you another letter with suggestions and ideas for your end of unit celebration. This session should be personalized to meet the needs of your students, and you should feel free to opt in or out of any of the suggestions, knowing that what is most important is that you make this celebration work for your students. Depending on the number of classes and the number of students you will teach this unit to, it might make sense to do this same celebration multiple times or to figure out a way to combine classes, perhaps teaming up for a period with other teachers who have your students at the same time.

As you likely know, when a novelist or short-story writer's book is released, it is common practice to have a book party. Often the author does a reading of an excerpt of the book. The copies of the book are made available, and the author is available to autograph them. Friends, family, even press come to the party. It is a way to celebrate the author's huge accomplishment, as well as to generate energy and interest for the book now that it's out in the world.

Today you'll want to give your adolescent authors a taste of what it feels like to be an author at his book party. The guests this time could be any group of people that makes sense for your class—another class, family members, younger students visiting from the elementary school. The stories that will be shared will likely be longer than most of the pieces the students are used to sharing at school celebrations, yet it will probably be important for students to share their whole stories. This means, that instead of convening the entire group to hear a few shared texts before dispersing into smaller reading circles, you may want to start the small circles from the start, and you may have more of these circles than usual, each containing fewer readers to keep the pace brisk.

Writers, no matter what their age, always long to hear a response to their writing. One writer once said that writing can feel like dropping rose petals into a well and waiting to

COMMON CORE STATE STANDARDS: W.7.3, RL.7.10, SL.7.1, SL.7.6, L.7.1, L.7.2, L.7.3

hear the splash. The stories your students have written for this unit, which focus heavily on meaning and audience, will make the audience reception doubly important. To make sure each writer gets that feedback, be sure each student has a page titled "Critics Agree" (just like the back of many books with positive reviews to trumpet), and be sure you create time for students to write on each other's "Critic's Agree" pages.

And finally, keep in mind that although teens want responses from their peers and their families, probably, for many students, you will be the reader who matters most. You will want to let every kid know you have thought carefully about her work. I urge you, if you possibly can, to print out a poem, a story, or even an image that you believe represents the story this student has written. If possible, try to inscribe a message for each student. Clearly these messages don't need to be long if you intend to write one for everyone. Instead, aim for a specific detail to compliment or a piece of universal wisdom about writing.

> Dear Taylor, When I read this poem _____, I thought of you and your passion for justice. Cherish this passion of yours because it makes you a passionate writer and human.

> Or

> Dear Miriam, I've chosen this quote about friendship because I think it reflects the meaning of your story. Your story will inspire readers to think about their own friendships.

Sometime very soon, you and your students will begin your next unit on writing about reading. It cannot be overstated how important it will be for them to leave this first publication of the year, particularly one in the fiction genre, filled with confidence and a desire to write more. You will want them to view this celebration not only as a culmination of one project, but a launch into their next one.

BEFORE THE CELEBRATION

Before the festivities begin, you will want the room to be dressed up for the special event. Students can work together to create carefully planned anthologies of stories, whether whole class or grouped in a special way, and to practice reading aloud, as well as prepare for signing their all-important autographs. On the day of the event, students should help you set up the tables, decorating, maybe covering desks with butcher paper, and laying out the snacks if you plan to have them.

Ask your young authors to perform different roles in today's celebration. Two can welcome visitors at the door. Others can escort visitors to their assigned reading circles, a couple can be emcees and explain how the day's festivities will progress. There are endless ways to plan, prepare, and carry out this celebration. You will no doubt want to make sure every student has a role, if not onstage, then off, that feels important.

When our actual appointed time arrived, I assumed my post, and the students assumed theirs. Two were at the door saying, "Welcome to our realistic fiction celebration." Others showed visitors to their seats, based on preplanned rosters for each group. Still, other authors waited in the small groups, stories in hand, ready to welcome any newcomers.

THE CELEBRATION

To begin the celebration, you may want to bring out a large box filled with students' anthologies, and set it on a table—with a dramatic flourish. I did this with my class, and even though they all knew what was inside, they craned their necks to see the final published pieces. Reaching ever so gingerly into the box, I produced a stack of published anthologies—one for each writer and each visitor.

I delivered the books to each small group, and one student after another read his story aloud. If you decide to give your writers the gift of a story or poem, at the end of the period, as kids leave, you'll want to pass these out. Be sure also to send a letter home to families if they were not at the celebration, asking them to read over their student's story in the anthology, and ask them to give very specific, detailed responses.

AFTER THE CELEBRATION

You'll want to decide how to make the party a happy one for your teen writers. Do you want it to be a prelude to a special outdoor activity? A field trip to the local coffee shop to sip hot cocoa? Perhaps make arrangements in advance to visit the local bookstore to see their stories displayed in the windows? Or maybe a walk downstairs to visit their pieces now housed in a case set up in the school lobby? Do you want to gather the class for some reflection about how the unit went for them and what they learned? There are endless possibilities!

Enjoy!
Colleen

Helping Ruby
By Miriam

Ruby has been my best friend since we were in diapers, as my mom would say. She is the most tenderhearted person you could ever know, and is scared of many things: spiders, disappointing anyone in any way shape or form, and Ms. Gulch.

Ms. Gulch was our science teacher. Even her name was terrible. Ms. Gulch has eyes like a vulture waiting for someone to give the wrong answer, fingers like a eagle, waiting to give out detention slips, and feet the size of snowshoes, ready to crush anyone who does or even implies they did something wrong.

"Come on. Get in. I don't have all day!" she snapped at me.

"Could you get any slower?" she yelled at Ruby.

"Why are you staring at my forehead?!" she bellowed at our two closest, but not best, friends.

What a kind person.

She yelled at the whole class for dropping stuff, going slowly and even looking in the wrong direction. She even scares our principal. She's taller than him too!

Once we had checked the agenda board, we knew we were done for; we had a test the next day! I think the clock broke during that period, seconds turned into days, minutes turned into centuries, and 45 minutes turned into a millennium.

But right before the bell rang Ms. Gulch called out "Ruby, after class, five minutes!" We all exchanged nervous glances, when Ms. Gulch called you after school she meant business. Then the bell rang, and Luna, and me, May, dutifully waited at the end of the hallway for Ruby.

When she finally came out the room the tears were spilling out of her eyes already. "What happened?" we all said in unison.

"Ms. Gulch told me that if I don't get above a ninety-five on the test, my average will stay below a 65 and this is the last time I can raise my grade before the end of the semester," she cried out in a sad, choked, miserable voice.

We put our arms around her. We told her it was going to be okay. It wasn't. No one gets above a 89 on Ms. Gulch's tests. When we got to the corner of the block we went our different ways all thinking, "What can we do to help?"

Later that afternoon, after being greeted at home by two younger twin sisters fighting over a Bitty Baby®, a mom who was still at work and a dad who was cleaning his glasses with lemon juice like it was a normal thing to do. I

Helping Ruby

By Miriam

Ruby has been my best friend since were in diapers, as my mom would say. She is the most tenderhearted person you could ever know, and is scared of many things: spiders, disappointing anyone in any way shape or form, and Ms. Gulch.

Ms. Gulch was our science teacher. Even her name was terrible. Ms. Gulch has eyes like a vulture waiting for someone to give the wrong answer, fingers like a eagle, waiting to give out detention slips, and feet the size of snowshoes, ready to crush anyone who does or even implies they did something wrong.

"Come on. Get in. I don't have all day!" she snapped at me.

"Could you get any slower?" she yelled at Ruby.

"Why are you starting at my forehead?!" she bellowed at our two closest, but not best, friends.

What a kind person.

She yelled at the whole class for dropping stuff, going slowly and even looking in the wrong direction. She even scares out principal. She's taller than him too!

Once we had checked the agenda board, we knew we were done for; we had a test the next day! I think the clock broke during that period, seconds turned into days, minutes turned into centuries, and 45 minutes turned into a millennium.

But right before the bell rang Ms. Gulch called out "Ruby, after class, five minutes!" We all exchanged nervous glances, when Ms. Gulch called you after school

FIG. 17–1   Miriam's final piece

felt so bad for Ruby, I mean, she tries so hard, works her butt off in every subject, and is such a kid person. So I sat there and did my favorite thing to do, make a list

How to Help Ruby
- Fail the test, so she doesn't feel bad
- Help her cheat on the test
- Help her study

The last one was definitely the one I was going to do, so I called Luna and May. We devised our plan and met outside Ruby's house at 6:43pm sharp.

We has already told Rose (Ruby's mom) of our plan so we tiptoed up to Ruby's room where apparently she had been sitting since she got home. We barged into Ruby's room and she gasped, "What are you doing?"

I have to admit we may have been a strange sight. I was wearing all yellow with cutout paper neutrons and electrons taped all over me. "I am neutrons and electrons," I said.

Luna was wearing all red with different elements taped all over her. "I am all of the elements of the periodic table," Luna said.

May was in all blue on one half and all orange on the other. "I am showing the differences between ionic and covalent bonds," May said.

Then, as she realized what we were and why we were here, after all of the explanations had been made she was so happy. She shone like the sun. We helped her study for three hours. Boy was it hard.

At 9:21, we broke out the caffeine and consumed over 3 chocolate bars a piece. That night we ended up staying up till 10:57 and then having a sleepover at Ruby's house. In the morning we trouped to the bus together, talking science all the way.

We got through first. Second. Third. Lunch. We talked science all the way through fifth period. Then around rolled sixth period. Ms. Gulch held her pencil like it was an axe as she told us all the 1,000,000,000 ways we could lose points. Then the test began, I didn't falter on a single question, teaching people really teaches you too! Even the bonus question was easy, I hope Ruby felt so too. At the end of the period we all grouped at the end of the hallway as usual and re-grouped. "It wasn't that bad!" Ruby cried out and we all had a cheesy group hug.

One Week Later

Have you ever seen a shiny sticker? Because I have. The one that rested on the top right hand corner of Ruby's test in the hallway, signifying she had gotten the highest grade anyone had ever gotten on Ms. Gulch's test, a 96!

Realistic Fiction Story
By Annabelle

I glanced at the shadow standing next to me. Uh oh, I thought. Not again, please. I shut my eyes tight, hoping it was all a dream. But when I opened them, the shadow was still there. I closed my locker, a few books and a pen cradled in my arms. Then I swiftly turned around, trying to walk fast with my head down and eyes focused on the floor.

"Hey!" I heard behind me. I pretended I wasn't paying attention. I kept walking past all the shoes on the hallway floor. I lost her, I thought, daring to look up straight. To my left and to my right there was no one. Clear. A sigh of relief washed over me as the tension in my neck lightened, and I straightened my posture. Just then I heard another,

"Hey, Lily!" Suddenly my freedom was being pulled away. I tried, but couldn't do anything about it. Without my control, my eyes went down to the floor, and I found my legs moving at unusual speed. Behind me, the steady and confident rhythm of clicks and clacks from boots were amplified in the silent end of the hallway. My eyes watched in dismay as the boots came up alongside me and stopped. My heart sank. It was no use running. I stopped too and looked up.

"Hey . . . Brittany," I said in a quavering voice. "What's up?"

"You know," she replied coldly. Yes, I did know. I reached my shaking hand into my pocket and wrapped my fingers around two folded dollar bills, pulling them out slowly, and placing them carefully in Brittany's outstretched hand. She pulled her hand away quickly, so I couldn't take the money back, and then turned swiftly down the hall. I turned in the opposite direction, and once again focusing my eyes on the floor. Only this time, it was in shame.

For another day, the hall was dim, taking in the dark light from the overcast sky. I walked through it silently, my shoulder brushing the wall. My eyes wandered from bulletin board to bulletin board, the papers and papers filled with writing. Then my eyes caught at the neon yellow poster that stood out from all the rest. "Lily for student council," it read. That was followed by,

- I will encourage more afterschool activities
- I will motivate kids to show good character

And

- I will take a stand against bullying.

That last point made me swallow. I am Lily, I thought. My name is on this poster, and what I believe is on this poster. But was that last idea really honest? I asked myself.

I glanced at the shadow standing next to me. Uh oh, I thought. Not again, please. I shut my eyes tight, hoping it was all a dream. But when I opened them, the shadow was still there. I closed my locker, a few books and a pen cradled in my arms. Then I swiftly turned around, trying to walk fast with my head down and eyes focusing on the floor.

"Hey!" I heard behind me. I pretended I wasn't paying attention. I kept walking, past all the shoes on the hallway floor. I lost her, I thought, daring to look up straight. To my left and to my right there was no one. Clear. A sigh of relief washed over me as the tension in my neck lightened, and I straightened my posture. Just then I heard another,

"Hey, Lily!" Suddenly my freedom was being pulled away. I tried, but couldn't do anything about it. Without my control, my eyes went down to the floor, and I found my legs moving at an unusual speed. Behind me, the steady and confident rhythm of clicks and clacks from boots were amplified in the silent end of the hallway. My eyes watched in dismay as the boots came up alongside me and stopped. My heart sank. It was no use running. I stopped too and looked up.

"Hey...Brittany," I said in a quavering voice. "What's up?"

"You know," she replied coldly. Yes, I did know. I reached my shaking hand into my pocket and wrapped my fingers around two folded dollar bills, pulling them out slowly, and placing them carefully in Brittany's outstretched hand. She pulled her hand away quickly, so I couldn't take the money back, and then turned swiftly down the hall. I turned in the opposite direction, and once again focusing my eyes on the floor. Only this time, it was in shame.

For another day, the hall was dim, taking in the dark light from the overcast sky. I walked through it silently, my shoulder brushing the wall. My eyes wandered from bulletin board to bulletin board, the papers and papers filled with writing. Then my eyes caught at the

FIG. 17–2   Annabelle's published story

My mind flashed back to the day three weeks ago when the announcement had come over the loud speaker announcing the student council representatives. When my name was called, a smile lit up my face. At the time, I didn't know what was to come.

Obviously people believed in me, I thought. My peers voted for me because they believed I would benefit the school. Would I? I questioned myself. Would I? Or was I just making promises I could never fulfill? How could I prevent bullying if I was too scared to stand up to it myself?

My head was mixed up with all these questions, all these thoughts, crying for a break. I glanced around me to see if anyone was looking, and in frustration, viciously tore the poster off the wall, digging my fingernails into the top of the hard paper.

"It needed to come down anyway," I mumbled. Just then, my best friend Jennifer pulled up alongside me, her backpack thrown lazily over one shoulder. Immediately, my grip on the poster loosened and it fell to the ground. I hurriedly bent over, and pick it up, embarrassed.

"Hey," Jen said.

"Hey," I replied.

"What's up with the poster?" She asked. "You don't have to take it down for another two days. Besides, it add some color to the hallway."

"It's alright," I said trying to smile. "I better take it down before I forget." Jennifer looked at me skeptically, confidently placing her hands on her hips before continuing.

"Makes sense. Well I have Spanish now so I'll see you later."

"Sure thing," I said, saluting her. She saluted back and turned down the hallway. I continued walking in the opposite direction, and clutched the paper as the jumbled up thoughts seeped into my head once more.

Later that day, I sat at the lunch table with no food in front of me. Only three more periods in the day, I thought. Then I could finally go home and just think about what a disappointment I was.

That's when I saw the figure that did not match the size of the first graders it stood next to. I looked closer . . . Brittany. Her hand reached into a tray that belonged to a child and pulled out a chicken tender. A fretted first grader looked over her shoulder, staring wide eyed at the giant standing over her. What a heartless person, I thought. If only I had the courage to say that to Brittany's face. Do something! I thought. Stop being a bystander! But I couldn't bring myself to move. I was glued to my seat. I watched in dismay as Brittany kept picking on the child's lunch.

Brittany started to walk away from the first grade table, her steady and confident stride turning into a rushed walk as she passed the eighth grade table. That's when all the pieces came together. This isn't just about me, I thought. Brittany is a bully, to many people, who needs to be stopped. I have to do something, I thought. I have to. I have to break out of my cowardly shell and stand up for something. After all, I thought, that's what a leader does.

A period later, the hallway was once again dark and lonely, even with everyone in it. I was determined to do something about Brittany. I had to . . . otherwise I was no more than a liar . . . a failure. I stood outside the English classroom, reading my watch. Four minutes early, I thought. I pulled out my copy of "The Hunger Games," hoping it would help me forget about all the drama that had been going on lately. I learned against the wall, and began to read.

Suddenly, I felt a tingling sensation up my spine. I was not alone. I whirled around to see Brittany over my shoulder. This is my chance, I thought. Say something, now! I opened my mouth to say something-anything, but no words came out. Instead, Brittany took the opportunity.

"Nice book." Before I could respond, Brittany snatched the book from my hand and turned down the hall.

My head was confused with the sudden movement. As soon as it cleared, I looked around to see if anyone had seen what Brittany had done. No one. Should I walk down the hall and take it back? I asked myself. No, then Brittany would pick on me even more. I looked behind me, spotting Brittany at the other end of the hall. She was waiting in line for her next class. Her arms were crossed, and she seemed to be avoiding any social interactions. She tried to squeeze herself into the wall, as a group of eighth graders walked by, pushing her to the side, refusing to share the hallway. She seemed like a nobody. Maybe bullying me is her source of power, I thought.

But that was my book that I had bought with my own money, I thought. I clenched my fists by my sides, enough anger in my head to send me down the hall to Brittany, but as soon as I took one step forward, I quickly took it back. What was wrong with me? As much as the part of me wanted to snatch the book back, the other part of me just couldn't do it. Why couldn't I do anything right? My cowardly self! As I dwelled on these thoughts, I traveled to the back of the line that had formed behind me just as the science teacher motioned us in for the period to begin.

It was two minutes to dismissal and I was eager to go home. I was at the back of the line, my usual spot, away from the noise of gossip and rumors. Just then, I felt a tap on my shoulder. I turned around to see Jennifer.

"Hey," she said. "What's up?"

"Nothin' much."

"Did you lose a book, by any chance? "The Hunger Games" maybe?" How did Jen know?

"Yeah," I replied surprised. "Have you seen it?" Jennifer pulled the book out of her book bag. "In math class, Brittany was reading it. The teacher took it from her and found your name on the inside cover. I promised I'd return it to you." Jennifer handed me the book.

"Thanks!" I exclaimed appreciatively.

"Sure. Did you lend it to her or something?" My excitement and relief faded into nervousness and doubt. Should I tell her the truth? I asked myself. Should I tell Jennifer that Brittany stole it from me? No, it's my problem, so I should deal with it, right? But I knew I'd never muster up enough courage to deal with it.

Meanwhile, this pause was making Jen curious. Her eyes narrowed. Could I lie to her? I asked myself once again? After all, she just wanted to help.

"Brittany took it from me," I said, slowly and softly, hoping she was no longer paying attention. But Jennifer was paying full attention. She frowned in response.

"Did you tell anyone?" I shook my head.

"No."

"I was scared," I said, in a voice gentler than the last. Jen looked at me, confused. She couldn't understand. I looked at the situation from Jennifer's point of view. If she was getting bullied, she wouldn't be afraid to stop it. She wasn't a coward like me.

"Do you want to tell a teacher, maybe?"

"No, don't tell anyone, okay?" I said quickly.

"Are you sure? I can talk to Brittany if you'd like."

"I'm sure I can handle it." That last statement was a lie.

"Okay," Jen said, placing her hands on her hips, not sure if she should take my word. "But let's practice. I'm Brittany headed for class. What are you going to say?" I sighed, but figured I'd play along. I could see Jen was concerned. She was just trying to be a good friend.

"Brittany, I am sick of your nonsense. Leave me alone." A gentle smile slowly spread across Jen's face.

"Perfect."

The next morning came too quickly. For the first time in a while, the hall was filled with sunshine. The beams of bright light spilled through the windows. The hall was buzzing with noise, everybody talking about their weekend plans. But I talked to no one. I had too much on my mind. My heart pounded. Would I really be able to walk over to Brittany and say something? What was I thinking? I couldn't do it! But I promised, I thought, sighing with regret. Then a thought occurred to me . . . Why was I doing this for Jen? I should be doing this for myself, because this is what I had wanted. I should be doing this as a leader, because that's what leaders do. My heart beat faster, faster, faster. My eyes spotted Brittany, by her locker, gathering her books. I took one step forward, and held it there, refusing to take it back. Then I planted my other foot. I knew that I looked like some weird robot, but I didn't care. My heart was pounding now, vibrating like a coo coo clock constantly going off inside my chest. My bones were bending backwards, trying to force me to turn around but I wouldn't listen to them. What will I say? I'll say what I practiced yesterday. Wait, what did I practice yesterday? I was too nervous to worry about it anymore. I took the remaining steps across the unfriendly gray to Brittany's locker, standing next to her. Brittany saw me out of the corner of her eye, and looked at me confused. I had never confronted her. This was my chance, and this time, I was determined to take advantage of it.

But once again, Brittany beat me to it.

"I forgot my lunch money again." She reached out her hand, expecting me to place in it the two dollar bills as the usual routine was. I didn't know what to do except roll my eyes. Smart move Lily, I thought.

"Come on!" Brittany said impatiently. "Stop wasting time!" I panicked, not knowing what to say. I reached my now shaking hand into my pocket, feeling the two folded dollar bills. I bent my fingers around them, ready to pull them out. If I just give her the money now, I thought, this can all be over. I wasn't controlling my fingers anymore, and I felt them slowly pulling the money out of my pocket. By now I knew Brittany could see the top of the bills. NO! My mind screamed. I managed to gain control of my and force the money back into my pocket. Brittany's eyes were wide open, surprised at this action.

"Stop it with this nonsense Lily!" Brittany shouted at me. Frustration sprung tears to my eyes, and my throat burned. But I made myself swallow and calm down.

"Just leave me alone, okay? I'm so sick of putting up with your nonsense by now, so just quit it! You're just a bully, not more. You pick on little kids. What kind of person are you?"

Brittany rolled her eyes, trying to surpress her hurt. Had I gone too far? No, this is what I wanted, right? I needed to tell Brittany to stop, and isn't that what I did? Was this how things were supposed to be? Was I supposed to hurt Brittany's feelings? She would stop now, wouldn't she?

I looked at Brittany, the depressed look still stuck to her face, which also had a sense of coldness to it. She might as well have said "Leave."

I reached my hand into my pocket and gave the money to Brittany.

"I'm sorry," I said. I wasn't sure if it was the right thing to do, but I knew it would help. Both Brittany and I knew if she took this as a sign of weakness, she was wrong. Brittany had seen I was capable of confronting her. Still, I had to use the money to try to make peace between us.

That moment felt like the weight of the world was lifted from my shoulders. I was not longer a failure, a liar, a disappointment, a coward. I had tried my best to fulfill my promise. I had taken my first step to becoming a leader. Satisfied with where I was at, I turned down the hall. As I walked, I moved away from the walls, though not yet ready to walk through the middle. I walked away, into the comforting sunshine of the hallway that seemed to guide my way.

One Friend to Another

By Samee

"Hey Jimmy, want to play tag?"

"Sure why not?" I replied, forgetting that I always play cat's cradle with Carter every recess. I joined a group of kids getting ready to play, not spotting Carter anywhere. Today the air felt different as well. I felt as inflammable as ever knowing that I probably wouldn't have to play cat's cradle. I still really hoped that Carter wouldn't walk outside and demand me to play cat's cradle even though he is my best friend. I'm sure he wouldn't mind me playing with a couple of other friends especially during the small amount of time scheduled for recess. Suddenly, I spotted Carter. "Hey Carter."

"Hey Jimmy, want to play some cat's cradle?" he asked holding up the worn string we always played with whenever we played cat's cradle together. "Sorry, I'm playing tag with a couple of my other friends."

"Oh okay." He responded with his head dropped. He walked along and with every step, making me feel a little guilty about what I had just said. If only I had said okay to playing with him he would be okay right now and I wouldn't feel so guilty, bored, but not guilty. I wanted to go talk to him to see if he was okay, but I knew it would make matters worse.

He took out the string and wrapped around his fists. He looked like he was about to break the string that has through many years of twisting and turning. A small boy walked up to him. He dropped the string on the ground and stood upright. He said "Hey Carter, want to jump some rope? I'm sure it'll be -"

"No! I don't want to jump some rope with you! Now leave me alone!" he screamed. I stumbled backwards a few steps. What was that about? Was he going to be okay? I had a million questions in my head that I didn't have an answer to. Carter picked the string back up and stuffed it deep down into his back pocket.

This seemed unusual. As Carter's best friend I know that he never puts anything in his back pocket because he feels like he'll lose whatever falls out. That string is so important to both of us. I stood still trying to soak in what had happened. I hoped he was going to be okay and wasn't going to lose that string. That string holds years of cat's cradle. But, it doesn't only hold years of cat's cradle. It holds years of smiles, laughter, fun and the things that make you feel happy in life. Carter had obviously forgotten that considering what had just broke down. If only he hadn't felt what he is feeling right now which I don't know what he is actually feeling. I want to make him feel better and explain why that worn out string shouldn't go in his back pocket which he fears he'll lose things which means he doesn't want the string. I want to help that string move from his back pocket to his front pocket or even his shirt pocket where he can keep a sharp eye on it. I really hoped

Samee

English

<u>One Friend to Another</u>

"Hey Jimmy, want to play tag?"

"Sure why not?" I replied, forgetting that I always play cat's cradle with Carter every recess. I joined a group of kids getting ready to play, not spotting Carter anywhere. Today the air felt different as well. I felt as inflammable as ever knowing that I probably wouldn't have to play cat's cradle. I still really hoped that Carter wouldn't walk outside and demand me to play cat's cradle even though he is my best friend. I'm sure he wouldn't mind me playing with a couple of other friends especially during the small amount of time scheduled for recess. Suddenly, I spotted Carter. "Hey Carter."

"Hey Jimmy, want to play some cat's cradle?" he asked holding up the worn string we always played with whenever we played cat's cradle together. "Sorry, I'm playing tag with a couple of my other friends."

"Oh okay." He responded with his head dropped. He walked along and with every step, making me feel a little guilty about what I had just said. If only I had said okay to playing with him he would be okay right now and I wouldn't feel so guilty, bored, but not guilty. I wanted to go talk to him to see if he was okay, but I knew it would make matters worse.

FIG. 17–3 Samee's finished piece

that he got that into his head as soon as possible before he loses the string or at least before he thinks he loses the string so no one would know for sure. I would need to know.

I slammed my locker shut and walked along down the hallway when . . . . . . ch-clang! A locker from the bottom row swung wide open and crashed straight into my knee. I held my left knee tight to my chest. I heard a voice laughing fruitfully at me. "Hahahaha!" Adrian snorted. I certainly am not Adrian's friend but I choose to think as him as my "arch nemesis." "Why can't you just leave me alone man?"

"Why can you just leave me alone man?" he mimicked in an annoying high pitched voice.

"Because he feels like it, got a problem with that?" I looked up to see who spoke such words. My eyes widened and my eyes dropped. I swallowed hard.

"Carter?" I asked trembling.

"What do you want?" I opened my mouth knowing he knew what I was about to ask. He interrupted me. "I'm doing this because of the day you ditched me to go play with your other friends during recess. Best friends don't ditch each other and since you did that to me, I went ahead and found other friends like Adrian here. What a coincidence that he doesn't like you. All of a sudden, Adrian's expression changed from happy to a bit concerned. Carter reached down into his back pocket and dangled a worn out string in front of my face. "This didn't mean anything to you did it?" I stared at the string almost wanting to scream out under all of this pressure. "But-" I froze in the middle of my sentence as the bell rang. They both walked away and headed to class.

Adrian walked up to me slowly looking a bit regretful. "Jimmy, I'm sorry about what happened with Carter. He was kind of harsh. Here, I got you a piece of the string. He kind of got mad and broke it. I thought it would be nice to give a piece to you." I looked at the string. That string that we always played cat's cradle with represented our friendship. Since it's broken, we no longer have a friendship. This struck me with fury and hatred. This hurt a lot. I appreciate that Adrian gave this to me, but why would he? He used to bully me but now he wants to be friends? That doesn't make any sense at all to me. "Adrian, why did you give this to me? I thought you didn't like me?"

"I guess I-" he froze. He looked at me amiably and walked away from me in the opposite direction and headed to class. "Adrian!" I called out to him. I looked at the string held in my hand. I couldn't keep this with me. I hated the new feel of the string. It felt of hatred and anger. The string that was once smooth and for playing is now rough with no use for anything. I walked over to a nearby trash can and held the string over the can and looked at it dangle above. I was helpless as I had the power to control it. I scrunched the string in my hand instead of throwing it away. If I threw it away, I would never have a friendship with Carter again. Adrian gave me this for a reason and that's another reason why I wouldn't throw it away. I had this hunch I would regret doing that single motion of just letting go where I would never see it again. If I held on to this single strand, there was a chance, a small chance, that everything would be okay between me and Carter or maybe even that everything would be okay in general.

I started to walk up to Adrian as soon as he came out of math class. Sudddenly, I was bumped into by Carter, purposefully. There was a long awkward pause. "Get out of the way I'm trying to get to my friend." I glared back at him and he winced. He stood upright and threw his arms out repeatedly. I kept moving inch by inch backwards when finally, I fell flat on my bottom. I was entirely mortified by this, and even more because he was pointing his finger at me, making me stand out as much as possible and I just wanted to disappear. All f of a sudden my mood went from embarrassed to half shocked as I spotted out of the corner of my eye Adrian looking at Carter not in a mood of happiness or excitement, but of disgust. This was one of the most shocking things I've ever seen. The day when he offered me the piece of string, it was meant to show me a sign of respect and friendship. I thought he just felt bad for me. He didn't just feel bad for me, but he also wanted to show me a sign of friendship and respect. I don't mean that shock was the wrong thing to feel. But it definitely was true. Adrian paced slowly towards Carter. "Carter come on man, let's leave Jimmy alone and go somewhere else." "I'm having too much fun right now."

"Leave him alone!" he screamed. Carter took his eyes off of me and turned his attention to Adrian. "Look, not now!"

"No, you look! You're an-"

"A what?!"

"An obnoxious snob who has no friends, and a matter of fact, no feelings!"

Carter shrunk back as people started to stare at him, also adopting the look of disgust Adrian had on his face. People started to aid me and help me up as I just continued to look at Adrian. What would happen after this? Would Carter blame his now former friendship on me? I went after Adrian as soon as I got back on my feet. I stopped and turned around looking at Carter who stared at me with a blank expression. I saw Adrian fade out of my sight as a crowd formed bigger and bigger up to the point where it became colossal. I wanted to thank him for what he did; I guess I feel better that I didn't do it right away. I would have to sooner or later but I didn't feel alone since the first time Carter and I weren't friends.

After school was dismissed, I started to walk home steadily, pondering about what I had caused and when I would find the perfect moment to sincerely thank Adrian and maybe even apologize to him for being the cause of him doing such a thing to his friend despite the fact I don't like his friend any longer. "Jimmy?" I turned to look who'd called me, I raised an eyebrow, "Yeah?"

"I'm sorry about what happened today. I can't believe Adrian turned on me like that. But now since I'm not his friend anymore we can get back at him for what he did." He held the piece of string out to me. "I accept your apology Carter but you can't do what you did to me to Adrian. I know that he's been pretty cruel to me in the past but he made up for that today." I pulled out the broken piece of string and held it out to him. His mood changed from desperate to angry. He probably didn't know that I had the string with me after he broke the piece off and tried tricking me into thinking that the piece was a whole. Carter frowned and stomped away from me, dropping the string as he walked along. A firm hand tapped my shoulder. I spun around swiftly. "I saw that man, you made the right decision. I'm sorry for all the times I bullied you too. I realized Carter was just using me to bully you and I realized that."

"It's totally okay, after what you did today, you made up for it and I'm glad that you did realize. I was hoping to have both of you as a friend."

"Well you have me as a friend." He winked and walked away. I watched him walk knowing that he was a true friend unlike Carter and wouldn't get mad over small things and bully me if he got mad at me. He stopped at the end of the block and waved me a friendly wave. I waved back and reached deep down into my pocket. I pulled out the string that represented our friendship. I walked along holding it and finally let go and dropped it.

* * * *

"Ring, ring riiiiight" my phone shrieked, disturbing my sleep. I reached over to my nightstand, catching the time. 4:36 a.m, the green clock read. I groaned, wondering who would be calling me at this time.

"Rosenthal Hospital," the words appeared on my cell phone screen.

Why would the hospital be calling me? I thought.

"Mom would have called me from her cell phone if she had to work overtime at the hospital," I started to reason.

"Is Adam ok? I swear, if he got into another fight . . ." I stop myself from thinking about what my brother could have done.

Dad . . . . . . oh my god . . . . is dad okay?

"Hello." I answer the phone worriedly. As I drew the phone to my ear, I flinched at the wailing and screaming in the background startling me. "CassieCassieCassieitsyourdad" a voice that sounded somewhat like my mom sobbed.

"What!?" I choked out, refusing to believe what I had just heard.

"Mom? Is that you? What's wrong!?" I asked, already knowing the answer.

"You dad," she breathed. "He's gone."

"To do list:

Plan sweet 16

Study for drivers test

Study for upcoming Regents test," I read aloud to myself.

Yasmin   English

"Ring ring riiiiight" my phone shrieked, disturbing my sleep. I reached over to my nightstand, catching the time. 4:36 a.m, the green clock read. I groaned, wondering who would be calling me at this time.

"Rosenthal Hospital," the words appeared on my cell phone screen.

Why would the hospital be calling me? I thought.

"Mom would have called me from her cell phone if she had to work overtime at the hospital," I started to reason.

"Is Adam ok? I swear, if he got into another fight..." I stop myself from thinking about what my brother could have done.

Dad......oh my god..... is dad okay?

"Hello." I answer the phone worriedly. As I drew the phone to my ear, I flinched at the wailing and screaming in the background starling me. "CassieCassieCassieitsyourdad" a voice that sounded somewhat like my mom sobbed.

"What!?" I choked out, refusing to believe what I had just heard.

"Mom? is that you? what's wrong!?" I asked, already knowing the answer.

"Your dad," she breathed. "He's gone."

FIG. 17–4   Yasmin's completed story

Why are you planning a sweet 16 Cassie? My inner voice questioned. It isn't like you have any friends.

"How about you shut up," I retorted, earning myself strange glances from the pedestrians near by. I ignored them and stormed down the block. I opened my house door and slammed it behind me, muttering "Stupid people, stupid brain, stupid everything . . ."

I threw my keys on the table, which made a barely audible clang in the noise of the closing front door. "Hello" I shouted out to see if anyone was home. My voice echoed off the wall proving no one was home. "Of course no ones home" I thought bitterly.

"Time for dinner" mom announced loudly making sure Adam and I heard. I groaned walking down the carpeted staircase making my way toward the dining room. I absolutely loathed family dinners, the awkward silence wasn't exactly something to look forward to. But mom insisted on having them on the rare occasions she was at home.

I arrived to the dining room to find the table set. I swiftly pulled out a chair avoiding eye contact with mom and Adam. This was the third family dinner for that month—so the third time mom and Adam were both home. Even though mom was rarely home, she followed her 'family dinner' idea religiously whenever she could.

"Eat honey" mom encouraged breaking the awkward silence.

"Im not hungry" I mumbled bitterly, picking up my plate and leaving the room before she had time to reply.

I look up at the trees taking the sweet scent of nature. "Where was I, I don't remember this park."

"You're having a dream Sherlock" my inner voice mocked. Ignoring it, I placed my hands on either sides of my thighs and slowly push myself off on the bench I was seated at. I look around taking in my surroundings to notice a lonesome looking man sitting on the grass. Noticing I was staring at him, he slowly gets up from the ground lightly brushing of his pants. His hands were in his pockets, and he was walking towards me slowly, not once breaking eye contact with me.

"Hold on" I froze his face suddenly becoming recognizable with every step he took, "Dad" I breathed disbelief evident in my voice.

"Cassie" he smiles calmly.

"Dad what are you doing here? What's going on? Where are we?" I questioned.

"I love you. I always have and I always will, whether I'm with you or not I need you to know I love you. Never forget it." He said his voice fading with every word. It wasn't until he had completely faded away that I suddenly took notice of the cold winter air that engulfed me making me aware of the warm tears on my cheek.

I woke up shaken by my dreams, brushing it off. I forced myself to get up. I slowly lifted up my duvet I wanted to savor the warmth of my sheets. I stood up slowly shuffling towards my dresser. Reaching out to the far corner of the wooden dresser, I lifted up the snowglobe my father had given to me when I was 6. Turning the round object upside down, I reached into it the broken rubber base pulling out my silver key. I walked back to my bed crouching down to my floor and stretching my arm out and moving my hand around the jagged edged wooden box that came into my grasp. I lifted the box inserting the key inside the small metal keyhold and twisting it. I sighed reaching into the small box pulling out the locket. As soon as the picture of my dad came into view, tears clouded my eyes. Wiping them away, I secured the metal chain around my neck.

"Class we have a new student in our class" Mr. Slot, my english teacher started, "I expect you all to make her feel welcome and treat her with respect" he continued the standard 'new student speech' rolling my eyes I bury my face back into my tattered copy of 'Bad Girls Don't Die' "Erin sit . . ." He started his eyes scanning the room. I peered around the classroom making sure there was more than one empty chair beside the chair adjacent to me to only be let down.

"Crap," I muttered shifting uncontrollably as Mr. Slot eyes landed on me.

"Next to Cassie" he finished. The whole class turn their heads for the far back corner of the room staring straight at me. I slid back down in my chair wanting to avoid the inevitable of being noticed.

"Hey Cassie, I'm Erin" the girl sat next to me.

"Hey" I mumbled, curtly showing no interest of having a conversation.

* * * *

"Class you're dismissed," Mr. Slot announced. I quickly gathered my things and scurried towards the door. "Hold on Cassie" Mr. Slot stopped me.

Oh now what did I do, I started to fret.

"Cassie I was wondering if you could show Erin around the school," he interrupted my thoughts. Noticing my skeptical expression he quickly reasoned with me, "It'll count as extra credit," I nodded immediately knowing I need all the extra points I could get.

"I'll do it," I sighed.

"Thank you" he said curtly signaling me to leave.

"CASSIE!!!!!!" a voice shouted through the crowded hallway. I stood still mortified by the attention that was brought upon me. I slowly turned around as a small hand rested its hand on my shoulder. Looking up I meet eyes with Erin.

"Hey ummm Mr. Slot said you would show me around the school me being the new student an all . . ." she babbled nervously.

"Yea," I stated blankly.

"Well um do know where Mr. Young's room is" she questioned not even noticing my hostility. I started walking to Mr. Young's room leaving Erin standing in the hallway. "Tsk, tsk, tsk" my inner voice scolded. "Your dad would be horrified if he saw how you were acting" clutching my locket, I abrubtly turned around before any tears escapted "Are you coming or what?" I sassed Erin who was still standing in the same place I left her, her mouth ajar.

"Come on, you don't wanna be late on your first day" I said softer clutching onto the metal chain tighter.

"Yea" she whisper still shocked by my hostile behavior.

We stood outside Ms. Youngs room. "Hey umm I was wondering if you wanted to hang out after school," I asked awkwardly trying to make up for my horrendous behavior.

"Yea, that would be cool" she said smiled turning on her heel and walking into her class.

* * * *

Forever Strong
By Gabriel

Part 1

I felt sick. My stomach was in a countless amount of knots. I abruptly pause my actions to ponder on the thought that, "Today . . . my grandfather's heart stopped." For a moment, I shed a tear and then reluctantly resumed my chores. Suddenly, my phone glowed alive. I staggered towards it bracing for the worst. "Hello?" I said in a shaky voice. My uncle answered. "He's at the hospital and the doctors say that while reviving him . . . an eerie silence fell over me. "He went into a coma." At that moment it seems as if the world froze. My eyes shot a barrage of tears. Flashes of thoughts passed by me. My parents are dead. All I have is my grandfather. Will he be able to make it out alive? If not, where will I go? Will I have to go to a foster home? These overwhelming thoughts surged in my heard. As if my uncle could hear my thoughts, he said in a calming voice, "You can stay with me if you want to." I hesitated for a moment and said, "I guess so." Without a moment to waste, he quickly uttered, "OK. I'll pick you up tonight." I hung up and let out a sigh. Then I ran upstairs to my bed, shut the door closed and cried myself to sleep.

Later on that night, I heard a loud honk outside. My uncle was waiting for me. I ran outside with my personal belongings, a picture of my parents, a pillow and my stuffed bear. The car ride was silent. Not a sound could be heard, except the soft humming of the engine. "Listen Johnny, I know this is hard for you. It's hard for me too, but you have to stay strong, no matter what." he finally said breaking the silence. "All we can do is hope. Hope that he can make it out of this." he continued. I listened to him as he spoke, nodding my head. As he is speaking I suddenly realize that I have never been able to hope for something and whatever I have hoped for doesn't happen. For the rest of the long ride I ignored his unconvincing words and continued staring blankly at the rain outside.

Gabriel

Realistic Fiction

Forever Strong

❖ Part 1

I felt sick. My stomach was in a countless amount of knots. I abruptly pause my actions to ponder on the thought that, "Today… my grandfather's heart stopped". For a moment, I shed a tear and then reluctantly resumed my chores. Suddenly, my phone glowed alive. I staggered towards it bracing for the worst. "Hello?" I said in a shaky voice. My uncle answered. "He's at the hospital and the doctors say that while reviving him…" an eerie silence fell over me. "He went into a coma." At that moment it seemed as if the world froze. My eyes shot a barrage of tears. Flashes of thoughts passed by me. My parents are dead. All I have is my grandfather. Will he be able to make it out alive? If not, where will I go? Will I have to go to a foster home? These overwhelming thoughts surged in my head. As if my uncle could hear my thoughts, he said in a calming voice, "You can stay with me if you want to". I hesitated for a moment and said. "I guess so." Without a moment to waste, he quickly uttered, "OK. I'll pick you up tonight." I hung up and let out a sigh. Then I ran upstairs to my bed, shut the door closed and cried myself to sleep.

Later on that night, I heard a loud honk outside. My uncle was waiting for me. I ran outside with my personal belongings, a picture of my parents, a pillow and my stuffed bear. The car ride was silent. Not a sound could be heard, except the soft humming of the engine. "Listen Johnny, I know this is hard for you. It's hard for me too, but you have to stay strong, no matter what." he finally said breaking the silence. "All we can do is hope. Hope that he can make it

FIG. 17–5   Gabriel's published short story

Part 2

We were driving in the Downtown area, until we came across his apartment. I wasn't impressed: it was a simple and small apartment building on the outside. Each apartment looked the same as the one before it, keeping this pattern until a mile or so down the road. We walk in and I put down my stuff. "You'll sleep on the couch tonight" he said while walking to another room. Tired from the long car ride, I went to sleep. When I woke up, about to get ready for school, I noticed a note taped to the fridge door. It said, "Had to go in to work early. You're gonna have to walk to school today." I was worried, not about the walking, because now I am actually closer to the school so I didn't have to rely on someone giving me a ride to school or having to take the long bus ride to school. What I was mostly worried about was the school itself. I hated everything about it, and so my mind was elsewhere. I needed to act normal. As I entered through the school entrance, almost instantaneously I noticed people walking past me and saying "Freak" or "Weirdo." It was a regular school day for me, something that I was always used to, people not wanting to talk, see, or even think of me. As I walked past people in the hallway, they looked at me like I was some sort of alien from a far away galaxy. I found my way to my first period class. Math. Ms. Jackson was a very bitter teacher who wasn't afraid of embarrassing students like me. "You are late again, Johnny!" she said harshly. I sat in the back of the classroom where it is easy to ignore her. I dozed off for a few minutes and before I know it, she's right over me telling me that I now have detention. I shrug my shoulders, as if I don't care. However not wanting to get yelled at again and draw everyone's attention to me, I decide to sit up and act like I am paying attention to the words on the board. Then, as music to my ears, I hear the sound of the bell and I quickly prepare to leave the Algbraic torture I was enduring. That feeling of relief quickly changes, when I remember that I have seven more periods to go. I slowly walk down the hall once again toward my next class, only to be greeted by another wave of insults.

Part 3

The rest of the day was a blur. I hid in the shadows during classes ignoring everyone around me. When I was dismissed, I casually walked back to the apartment. Across the street a little girl with a smile so bright-like the sun. She was playing hop-scotch, with her parents happily cheering her on. I wish I had a moment like that. I quietly muttered to myself as I threw on my hoodie and walked at a faster pace trying to run away from my problems. When I entered the apartment I immediately noticed my uncle poised in a slouching position over a chair with arms crossed and a frown directly facing me. Bewildered, I asked him, "Why are you home early?" He said, "Your teachers wanted to speak to me immediately about your behavior. They say that if you keep on acting like how you did today you will flunk and have to go to summer school, and fail the grade. What do you have to say about this, Johnny?" I stood there motionless thinking, "What do I think?" Then my uncle carried on saying, "Your parents would not be proud." The words hung in the air like a disgusting stench repelling anything living. Not being to take anymore of it, I said "Shut up." under my breath, with tears filling up my eyes and hoping my uncle didn't hear me. "What!?" my uncle said sternly. I couldn't help it and almost with no control of what comes of my mouth, I roared "Shut up!" again, only this time with an antagonized facial expression that only read the words fury. The whole apartment was shaking. "Don't ever talk about my parents and what they think!" My uncle was speechless. He left and I was alone in the living room with nothing but my overwhelming anger and depression.

Part 4

As I sat on the couch staring at the darkness of the wall, my uncle sat on the cushion next to me. "I'm sorry I talked about your parents Johnny. I didn't realize how much you miss them." I teared up a little remembering my parents or at least as much as I remembered about them. It's been a long time since. Then I remembered the sweetest memories of my grandfather, when he went to my award ceremony and the proudness on his face. This made me feel a little at ease. "I just didn't know what terrible things you were going through," he said. I simply nodded in agreement. "Tell me if there's anything I could do to make this easier, please tell me what exactly is making this hard." I responded by saying, " My parents—not being here. the thought of losing the only person I really care about—my grandfather, and how my entire school is bullying me." My uncle started crying and unexpectedly said "I am such a bad uncle. I didn't know . . . I just want to let you know, Johnny, that despite not being around in the past for you, I do love you." He was sobbing like a three year old. He grabbed his keys and said, "Let's go see grand-dad." Five minutes into the car ride, I asked "Why are we going to see grand-dad?" It took him a few seconds to register the question. "Johnny, you probably don't know this but I am going through something similar to you. I really need to see him, thinking about him had been effecting everything I do. To think he may be gone forever is a nightmare for me. I just want to see him one more time. I'm sure you understand. "I do," I said. I never thought of how my uncle might feel about grand-dad. This is maybe the first time I have felt a connection with my uncle. I was left with this thought in my mind for the rest of the ride.

Part 5

"Beep!" the automatic doors alerted everyone around as we entered. A lady patiently waiting at the front desk knew who we were coming to see. I was trying to be strong, bracing myself for the misery on my poor grandfather's face. Dazed by the thought, the lady suddenly pointed to the door across the hall and said in a soft mellow voice, "He's in there." The nurse was opening the door that led to my grandfather. When I was walking towards him, I felt a warm feeling, like the sun suddenly beaming on me after a long and treacherous walk along the beach on a cold winter day. As I walked closer I noticed his eyes were closed, he looked peaceful, and I focused my attention to his face that he had an unusual happy smile. The room felt like a calming sanctuary. nothing I had expected. Then I hear my uncle beside me crying and sobbing wildly. "It's okay." I tell him while softly rubbing his back. Then I sad "He's probably thinking about us." This appeared to calm him down. He looked up at me, smiled and said, "You are probably right." Ten minutes later we decided to leave. Before leaving, I lean forward and kiss him on the forehead. Then without giving it a second thought I took hold of one of this buttons from his soft sweater, yanked it off and slipped it into my pocket without anyone even noticing. I felt like my soul was stitched back together bit by bit coming closer to form a better, more happier self. "Oh, no!", the nurse yelled as she ran towards us. "He's gone!" she said. I was in shock. Feeling vulnerable and feeling as if I couldn't deal with it alone, I quickly grabbed my uncle and hugged him. That hug seemed to last forever. I felt that it not only made me feel better, but my uncle needed it just as much as me. "Let's leave. we said our good-byes to grand-dad. while he was alive." I said.

The thought of seeing him dead was just too much for us to deal with. We returned home. The apartment was silent. We knew we needed time for ourselves to mourn, but knew we had each other. So we respected our space and parted ways. He went into his room and I laid down on the couch. I then went to bed with a hopeful smile on my face—for the first time I felt hopeful that things would work out. The resemblance of a smile on my face was obvious. "You're at a better place." I said.

Part 6

The next day I entered the school cautiously like I was entering a blazing and wild fire, preparing for the sting and burn of insults. The first to come was from a girl who passed by me. "Get out of my way, stupid!" she yelled at me. The words echoed, but something amazing happened . . . It was as if I had a fireproof suit on. I was immune to the fire, the insults didn't hurt me. The reassuring voice of my uncle was going through my head. "You have to be strong!" I continued walking casually down the hall to Math class. I took a seat in the front of the class. "Pop quiz" she immediately says with an evil grin. As she hands everyone a paper, I could hear the whispers of "Oh, no! I'm going to fail." and the groaning from the students around me. As the teacher hands me the quiz, she asked me, "Do you think you're ready?" "Yes, Miss Jackson." I confidently reply. I take one look at the quiz and almost immediately I start answering those questions. I realize that I know the answers, and that I knew them all along.

By the end of the class, Miss Jackson was able to grade them, and give them back to us. On the top of the quiz I saw, 100%. "I did it!" I said so happily. I walked back home with a big grin on my face. When I arrived home I set down my book bag and took a glance at my possessions, a picture of my parents, my stuffed bear which my parents had given me, and my new prized possessions—my grandfather's button and the pop quiz, which I am going to frame.